THE LAND OF EVERLASTING SKY

THE LAND OF EVERLASTING SKY

A Memoir of Loss and Legacy
on Lake of the Woods

Jill D. Swenson

SHE WRITES PRESS

Published in 2026 by
She Writes Press, an imprint of The Stable Book Group

1569 Solano Ave #546
Berkeley, CA 94707
https://shewritespress.com
Library of Congress Control Number: 2026904414
ISBN: 979-8-89636-318-7
eISBN: 979-8-89636-319-4

Interior Designer: Kiran Spees
Map and family trees courtesy of Erin Greb Cartography

Printed in the United States
Names and identifying characteristics have been changed to protect the privacy of certain individuals.

THE LAND OF EVERLASTING SKY

A Memoir of Loss and Legacy on Lake of the Woods

Jill D. Swenson

SHE WRITES PRESS

Published in 2026 by
She Writes Press, an imprint of The Stable Book Group

1569 Solano Ave #546
Berkeley, CA 94707
https://shewritespress.com
Library of Congress Control Number: 2026904414
ISBN: 979-8-89636-318-7
eISBN: 979-8-89636-319-4

Interior Designer: Kiran Spees
Map and family trees courtesy of Erin Greb Cartography

Printed in the United States
Names and identifying characteristics have been changed to protect the privacy of certain individuals.

For my sister, Barb

Where you come from is gone, where you thought you were going to never was there, and where you are is no good unless you can get away from it.

—Flannery O'Connor, *Wise Blood*, 1952

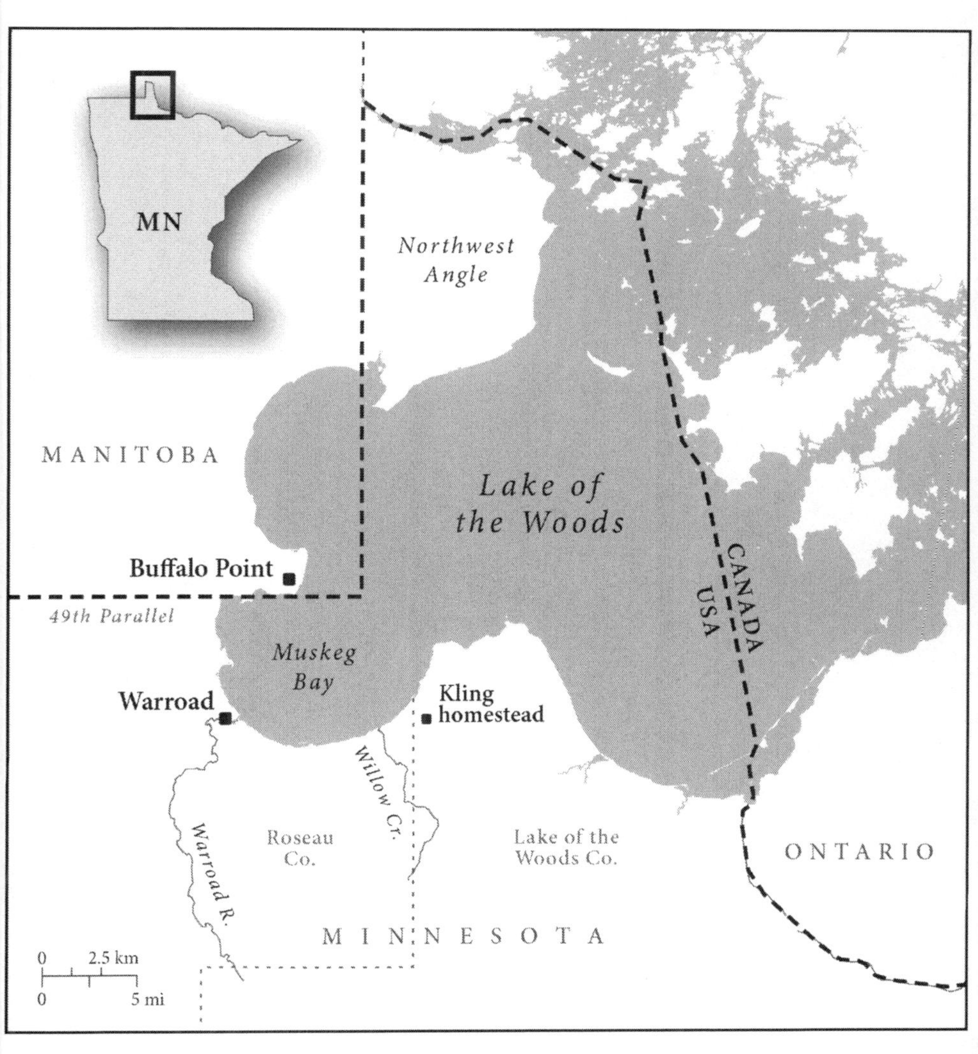
MN
Northwest Angle
MANITOBA
Lake of the Woods
Buffalo Point
49th Parallel
CANADA
USA
Muskeg Bay
Warroad
Kling homestead
Willow Cr.
Warroad R.
Roseau Co.
Lake of the Woods Co.
ONTARIO
MINNESOTA
0 2.5 km
0 5 mi

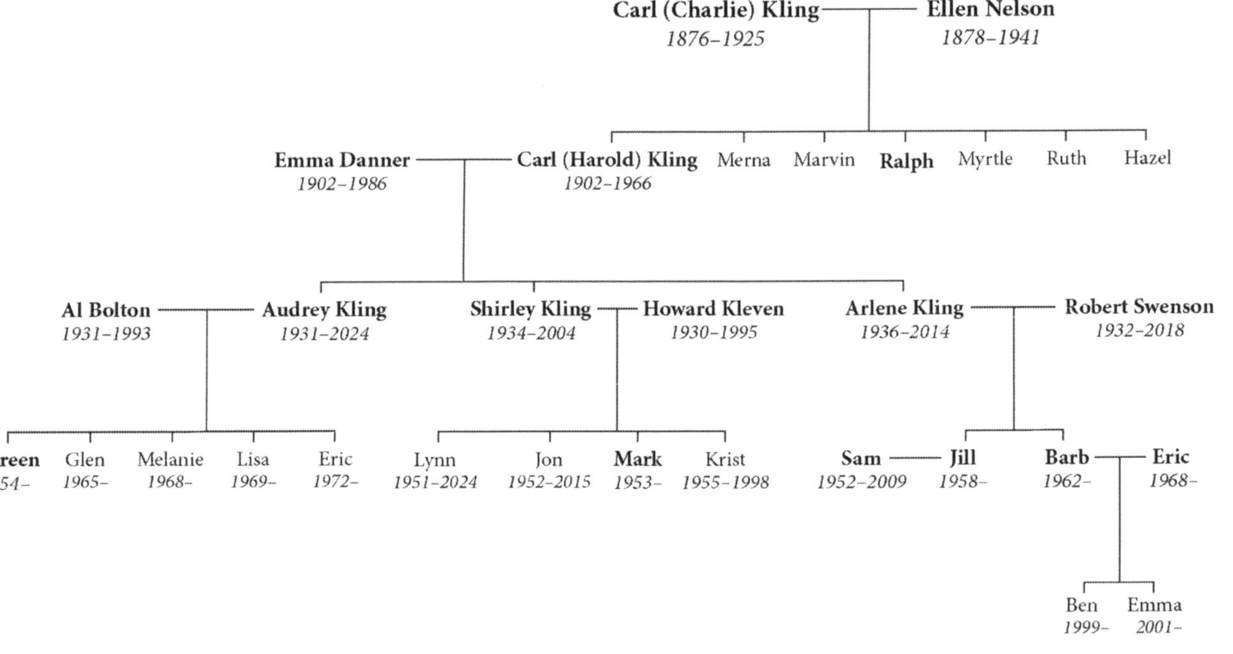
Carl (Charlie) Kling
1876–1925
Ellen Nelson
1878–1941
Emma Danner
1902–1986
Carl (Harold) Kling
1902–1966
Merna
Marvin
Ralph
Myrtle
Ruth
Hazel
Al Bolton
1931–1993
Audrey Kling
1931–2024
Shirley Kling
1934–2004
Howard Kleven
1930–1995
Arlene Kling
1936–2014
Robert Swenson
1932–2018
Shireen
1954–
Glen
1965–
Melanie
1968–
Lisa
1969–
Eric
1972–
Lynn
1951–2024
Jon
1952–2015
Mark
1953–
Krist
1955–1998
Sam
1952–2009
Jill
1958–
Barb
1962–
Eric
1968–
Ben
1999–
Emma
2001–

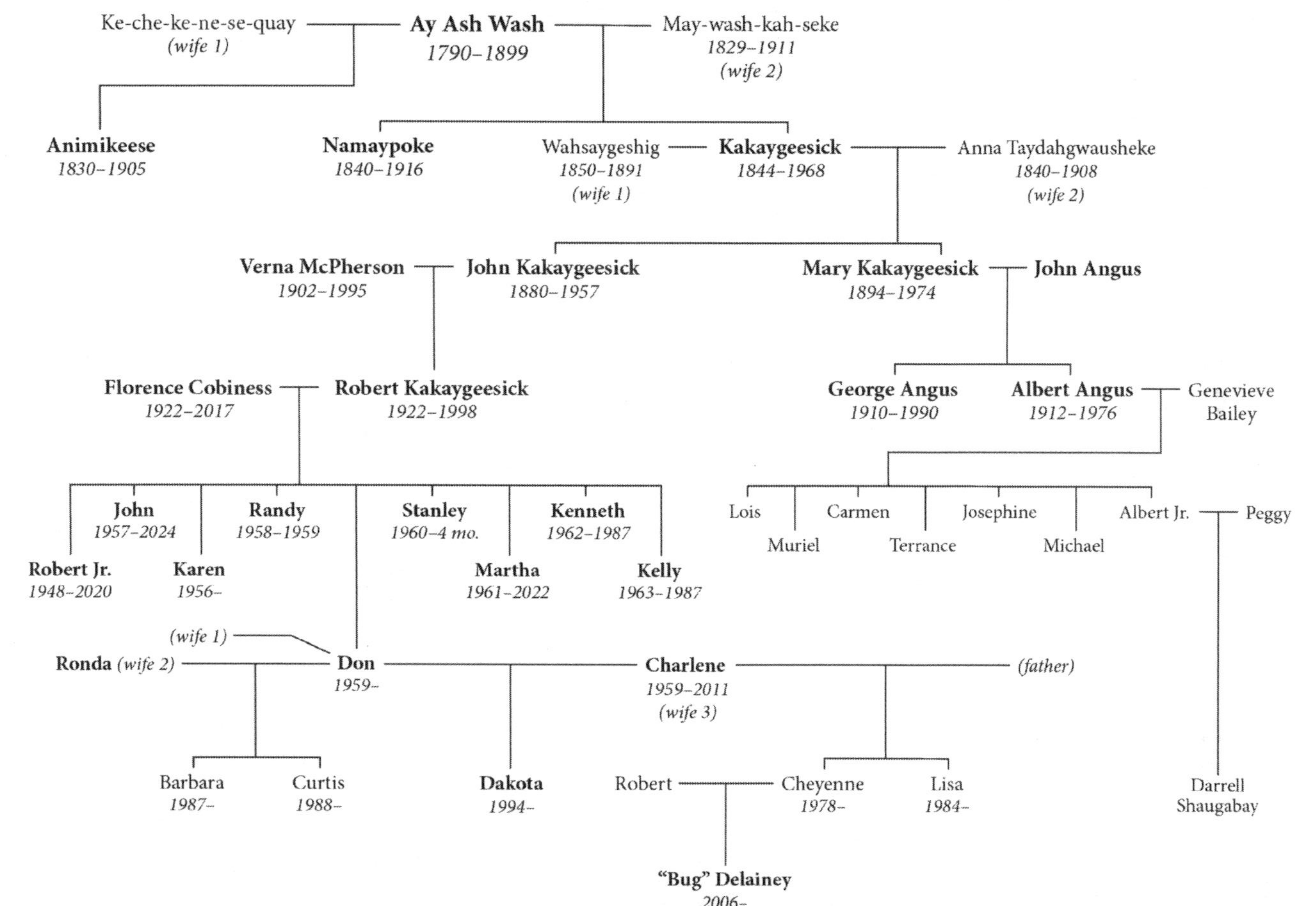

Ke-che-ke-ne-se-quay
(wife 1)
Ay Ash Wash
1790–1899
May-wash-kah-seke
1829–1911
(wife 2)
Animikeese
1830–1905
Namaypoke
1840–1916
Wahsaygeshig
1850–1891
(wife 1)
Kakaygeesick
1844–1968
Anna Taydahgwausheke
1840–1908
(wife 2)
Verna McPherson
1902–1995
John Kakaygeesick
1880–1957
Mary Kakaygeesick
1894–1974
John Angus
Florence Cobiness
1922–2017
Robert Kakaygeesick
1922–1998
George Angus
1910–1990
Albert Angus
1912–1976
Genevieve
Bailey
John
1957–2024
Randy
1958–1959
Stanley
1960–4 mo.
Kenneth
1962–1987
Robert Jr.
1948–2020
Karen
1956–
Martha
1961–2022
Kelly
1963–1987
Lois
Muriel
Carmen
Terrance
Josephine
Michael
Albert Jr.
Peggy
(wife 1)
Ronda (wife 2)
Don
1959–
Charlene
1959–2011
(wife 3)
(father)
Barbara
1987–
Curtis
1988–
Dakota
1994–
Robert
Cheyenne
1978–
Lisa
1984–
Darrell
Shaugabay
"Bug" Delainey
2006–

NOTE ON TERMINOLOGY

The words used to identify people by race, culture, and ethnicity have changed over the course of my lifetime. These changes reflect ongoing struggles to reckon with our colonialist history. During the first decade of my life I watched the spelling of "Chippewa" be replaced with "Ojibway," and that spelling has now largely been replaced with "Ojibwe" in publishing style guides. The origin of this term for the tribe comes from what English speakers heard their enemies call them: the people who wear puckered moccasins. Their enemies were known as the Sioux, the term given by French traders who heard the Chippewa call them snakes. Dakota replaced the French term "Sioux," but today they are known as Oceti Sakowin. The English words and their spellings may change, but they can't erase what happened in the past.

I am a descendant of Northern European immigrants and make no claim to Indigenous lineage. I do not speak, read, or write the Ojibway language. I used the terms and spellings preferred by members of the Kakaygeesick family and those used most prevalently in the vernacular language in the Warroad community.

The term "Indian" has largely been replaced with "Native American" or "Indigenous." The word "Indian" traces its origins back to early colonial history, when millions of people—who lived on the land colonists claimed—were lumped together into a single political category: enemy. United to stop westward expansion and encroachment on their lands, the Pan-Indian Movement ultimately allied with the British against the US government in the War of 1812. So, as much as "Indian" is a colonialist term, it also has a long history as a term of allied resistance. When I was growing up, the American Indian Movement reclaimed the power of the word "Indian." My choice to use it reflects its vernacular usage and a conscious awareness of its many connotations.

Variations in terminology and spelling appear when printed source materials are directly quoted. I have otherwise tried to follow the principles and advice found in Gregory Youngling's *Elements of Indigenous Style: A Guide for Writing by and About Indigenous People.*

CHAPTER 1

I stood there waiting in the gravel driveway, kicking dirt into dust clouds, surrounded by flat open fields six miles south of the Canadian border. Summer vacation with Mom's side of the family felt like an escape from the heat and tension at home at the end of June 1968.

Grandma Kling came out Aunt Audrey's back door with both hands full, carrying a tray of sweet rolls. She elbowed the front seat of her Buick forward and leaned into the back, where she slid the tray onto the rear window ledge. After we piled in her car, she looked over the seat and backed out onto Highway 313. Grandma tuned in KRWB-AM and pushed the lighter on the dashboard. Out of her purse she pulled a tube of primrose pink and her pack of Salems—same brand Mom smoked. Grandma applied a fresh coat of lipstick while glancing in the rearview mirror. She hummed along, tapping the beat on the steering wheel, and then lit a cigarette from the glowing red-hot coil. She turned left onto Highway 11 past the Marvin Windows factory.

On the side of the road, I saw the sign: WELCOME TO WARROAD. WORLD CAPITAL OF WALLEYE, WINDOWS, AND HOCKEY. POPULATION 1,173.

Grandma turned left on Lake Street and drove through downtown. She pulled in and parked at the Warroad Memorial Hospital and Nursing Home. A solid gray bulk of a building, one of the few two-stories in town, it was where they sent the old, sick, and dying. I blanketed myself in the scent of cinnamon rolls in case it stunk of sickness and death in there.

We left the bright sunlight behind and slipped into the quiet and cool lobby. Dressed in matching seersucker shorts and tops Mom had sewn for us, my little sister and I held hands. Cousin Shireen held the door for Grandma Kling with her tray of sweets. We stood behind Grandma in front of the elevator doors.

When the doors opened, a wheelchair rolled out with an old man in it. I stared at the deep leathery wrinkles in his tan skin. He stared back.

Mumbling and grunting, the old man used his hands to direct the nurse who stood behind him to roll his chair forward through the gaggle of us three girls with our granny. The nurse situated him near the front door so he could look out the window. He muttered some more.

Shireen walked over to him. I followed, dragging Barb by the hand.

"You're not getting any of my fresh-baked buns, Kakaygeesick," Grandma clucked to our backs. Then she put her hand on her hip. Even though Grandpa, Harold Kling, had died, Emma Kling continued to do what she knew best: bake sweet rolls, take to heart the daily message of the Lutheran Hour on the radio, and tend to sick and dying friends and relatives. "Come on, kids." She said it like she didn't mean it.

The three of us stood in front of his wheelchair. He looked old—really old.

"These are my cousins, Jill and Barb," Shireen said loudly, introducing us as if he were hard of hearing. Kakaygeesick looked at us.

Shireen, age fourteen, the tallest with her carrot-red hair, me with mine straight brown, and Barbara Dawn, a six-year-old blonde.

He looked at me. Me in the middle. I felt no fear—pulled toward him by the magnetic force of his presence. He scrunched up his face and made even more wrinkles across his wide forehead. He caught my brown eyes in his gaze and held them. He leaned forward, picked up his large hands, and reached for my head. His smooth palms covered my ears. *Be-boom, be-boom*, beat my heart. *Be-boom.* He spoke low and slow. I didn't understand a word, but felt his spirit enter me. His hands were warm and soft, and the heat flushed my head, neck, and shoulders, and moved down to my gut where I felt both his urgency and his sorrow.

I put my hands on top of his big gnarly fingers, and he pulled his hands back and folded them in his lap. He kept nodding at me, intoning his secret lament, as though I understood. My breathing slowed as I listened with curiosity.

"Come on, let's go," Grandma said. "I want to deliver these before they get cold." The three of us skedaddled into the elevator. Barb got to push the button. Number two. Going up.

"Who *was* that?" I asked Grandma as soon as the doors closed. I could hear Shireen gulp as the floor began to lift.

"That's Kakaygeesick. He's sick," Shireen volunteered.

"What's he sick with, Grandma?" I asked.

"Old age," she replied. The doors to the elevator opened, and in the lobby on the second floor there was a large oil portrait on the wall.

"Look!" Shireen pointed to the painting. "See? That's him. 'Kakaygeesick' means Everlasting Sky."

And there he was in full headdress, in silhouette, and without so many lines on his face. A headdress with black crow feathers and the downy tufts of the white partridge. Across his forehead, he wore a leather band with beadwork. The portrait didn't really look much like the old man wearing a plaid shirt and navy-blue pants in the wheelchair downstairs. I read the small plaque on the bottom of the wooden frame: KAKAYGEESICK. BORN 1844 ALONG THE SHORES OF LAKE OF THE WOODS. TRAPPER, MEDICINE MAN, AND TRIBAL LEADER OF THE OJIBWAY.

I had to do the math, subtract 1844 from 1968. *That makes him one hundred and twenty-four years old.* I didn't know what he had said to me, but I felt his story caught between my ears.

"Don't fall asleep," Shireen whispered. She turned off the light and crawled into the double bed with me. We could hear our parents talking and laughing in the living room. Mom and Audrey sounded so much alike we couldn't tell who was saying what.

"Watch the sky in my mirror," Shireen said. She pointed to the foot of the bed, where a large looking glass hung above the built-in set of drawers and said, softly, "When you can see colored lights reflected, it's time for the show." She lay down and pulled the sheet up to her chin.

My eyes adjusted slowly to the darkness. Above our heads was a window as wide as the bed. Lying on my back I could see the mirror just over the tips of my toes. It was a long time before I saw something glow in the mirror.

I sat up in bed, turned around, and knelt before an altar of the night sky. As I pressed against the window screen, the hatch marks disappeared from view. I knelt on the pillows and rested my elbows on the windowsill. Staring at the horizon of pine trees along the hedgerow, hues began to dance. Streaks of green, blues, and lemon yellow jumped the horizon. Flashes of reds and oranges, lime streaks against a purple haze. The North Star and the outline of the Big Dipper popped out against the black moonless sky.

Shireen sat up, turned around, and knelt with me—elbow to elbow—silently staring out the window. Watching the earth's undulating energy, I felt goose bumps on my skin. On a small swatch of land between the highway and the train tracks, I witnessed the mystical aurora borealis.

Shortly after dawn, my head popped up, and I opened the window where the northern lights had danced the night before. In the paddock stood Shireen's mare, a red quarter horse. Beebe stomped her feet but did not move. She flicked her tail, shooing the big black deerflies. I watched the cat disappear down a row of beans in the garden. Only then did I notice my tall, lanky uncle squatting in the garden, down deep on his haunches. Chest and thighs touching, his butt rested on the back of his black leather boots. Still and centered, he pulled weeds.

On CBS Nightly News I'd seen people squat like that in rice paddies somewhere in Vietnam. Down so low to the ground you hardly saw them. They wore big round hats to keep the sun from their eyes. Helicopters and machine guns provided the soundtrack. People in their straw hats gunned down and killed. Uncle Al served in the Army during the Korean War, Mom had told me. Then she'd said not to ask him about that.

I watched while Uncle Al worked silently down the row. He had a pan he pulled along with him. He grabbed weeds by the roots, gently pulled, and laid them down to die. From the pan his fingertips slipped something into the ground where he'd pulled the weeds out. He had been out on the lake already and fileted his catch in the garage. I knelt at the window and watched him bury the guts in the bean patch. The cat kept trying to lick the pan, and he stroked its tail instead of pushing it away.

As if he sensed someone watching, Uncle Al turned around and looked in my direction. When he saw me in the window, he gestured for me to come out to the garden. I quickly dressed in jeans and a T-shirt. As I headed out the back door, Aunt Audrey handed me two empty one-gallon plastic ice cream buckets. She had already put the coffee on the stove to percolate. Mom and Dad were still asleep on the hide-a-bed in the living room. I quietly let myself out the back door and walked out to the garden in my flip-flops.

"Do you know how to pick peas, Jill?" Uncle Al didn't expect me to answer even though I was almost ten years old. He showed me with his hands. He pushed before he pulled the pea pod loose from the vine. Then he dropped the pod into one of the ice cream buckets. He showed me again, tenderly grasping the plant first with one hand. Then with the other, he took hold of a pod and pushed it toward the plant before gently pulling it back and free.

I pushed the pod toward where it attached itself to the vine and then tugged. It popped off into my hand. I looked at Uncle Al's hands. Long fingers, tender pink palms, and weathered knuckles. I watched how he touched them. He cupped his fingers around the pod to see whether it was full or flat. Sometimes he released his grasp because it wasn't ready. He saw me watching and stopped to inspect what I had put in my pail. He opened a pod to show me the size of the peas. Running his thumbnail along the seam, Uncle Al split the shell open and shoved the peas into his mouth. He smiled. Then he popped open a pod for me.

Better than a Pez dispenser. Sweetness and green. He smiled

back at my happy face and showed me again without saying a word. Then we walked back to the house. I already knew he had to go be postmaster in town. He'd be back for the lunch hour—if not to eat, perhaps to mow the lawn.

Shireen had prepared bowls of shredded wheat with strawberries from yesterday's pickings. I poured fresh milk over mine, sprinkling a tablespoon of sugar on top. When we'd slurped the last drop of sweet pink milk from the bottom of our bowls, Shireen washed the breakfast dishes while I wiped them. Then we went out to tend to her horse. She brought the strawberry scraps and some carrots along.

"Don't touch the electric fence. It's on," Shireen said, as I ran ahead of her walking across the lawn toward the horse pasture. "Let me shut it off."

She switched it off, then slipped between the two strands of wire fencing. I followed after her, and we made our way to the shed; it wasn't really big enough to call a barn.

"You can be my shadow, Jill," Shireen said. She gave Beebe the berry scraps and gave me the carrots to hand-feed her while Shireen used a curry brush on the horse's sides. When Beebe finished chomping down the carrots, Shireen handed me the brush. "Give it a try."

Copying Shireen, I took the brush in my right hand and made small circles on Beebe's girth. My left hand rested behind her shoulder, where I felt her breathe. The horse leaned her weight ever so lightly against my right hand stroking her side.

Shireen grabbed a halter off a nail on the wall and put it over Beebe's head and nose, then attached a long lead. While we walked her around the paddock, Shireen let me hold the lead. She filled the grain bin and filled the trough with water from the garden hose.

"I like you sharing chores with me," she said, looking down at me with a smile. "Makes things easier around here."

I learned how to use a pitchfork cleaning out the manure from the stall. I hoped maybe she'd let me ride her horse sometime soon.

The rest of that morning we spent picking the eight rows of peas and talking about horses.

"Good job, girls!" Mom was thrilled to see our full pea buckets when we came in for lunch. She ushered us to chairs at the dining room table as though we were special guests. Even offered us dessert after we ate our grilled cheese sandwiches and tomato soup.

While Aunt Audrey and Mom lingered over coffee and strawberry-rhubarb pie, Shireen and I shelled peas at the table the rest of the afternoon. The pods went in one bowl, the peas in the other. Barb played with her Skipper doll. Dad slipped away to the trading post in town for more postcards, some souvenirs, and then to the Main Street Bar & Grill, where he'd meet Al after work for a beer with his buddies. Hamm's on tap.

Waiting for the men to come home from town, Mom, Aunt Audrey, and us girls noticed a dark figure approaching the house across the three acres of lawn. We got up and looked out the picture window in the dining room.

It wasn't a horse, I realized quickly. It was much bigger. *A moose!*

He walked right up the concrete steps to the front door and pushed his nose on the doorbell. Ding-dong. Nobody ever used the front door except the Avon Lady. The moose leaned his big head and antlers against the picture window of the dining room. For a moment, I feared he'd bust it. Blackie barked. Then the moose tipped his head down and looked right at the dog jumping at the lower ledge of the window. Blackie turned tail and hid under the dining room table. The moose backed down and headed around the side of the house. Shireen and I ran to her bedroom window and watched it tromp through the garden and take out most of what was left of the pea plants.

Beebe didn't pay it any attention until she smelled the crushed pods. Then her head bobbed up.

We heard the car pull into the driveway, and the moose trotted off through the hedgerow. Uncle Al and Dad came in the back door.

"Dad, Dad!" I shouted. "Did you see it?"

After pan-fried walleye filets, boiled potatoes, fresh-baked bread, and steamed sweet peas smothered in butter, Shireen and I did the dinner dishes and got into our pajamas early in hopes of seeing the northern lights again. We each had a dish of ice cream sprinkled with Nesquik chocolate milk powder before bed.

Darkness enveloped me like plush black velvet. Clouds obscured the stars from view. Night crept inside and brought a deep stillness. A streak of chain lightning flashed with a simultaneous rumble. The patter of rain kept a steady beat. My breath slowed, and the lids of my eyes lowered.

The map of North America on the wall to the right of the mirror seemed to glow. In my dream, I was swept up in a storm, with lightning and thunder, swimming and flying with fishes and birds, the currents pulling me along. I had seen the outline of what the Ojibway creation story calls this continent: Turtle Island. The right back leg was Florida, with six toes of islands. The left hind leg was Mexico, with Panama for a foot. The round shell covered the land, and its fluttering right claw, Canada's Baffin Island, reached out into the

North Atlantic. Turtle's left front flipper rose up out of the Rockies and reached past the Yukon of Alaska. Its head bobbed in and out of the Arctic Ocean, and its nose pointed toward Greenland. The currents and tides swirled around thousands of isles in the Canadian North Country. The beating of my heart became one with the patter of raindrops.

Half-awake, I heard Shireen sleep soundly next to me while the map swayed like a hallucination on the wall. Her breathing slowed down my racing heart. I retracted my head down into my shoulders and stretched the cool white sheet over my head.

Snap! Snap! We rubbed stones across the dots on the red tape of the cap rolls to make them pop and smoke. We had the ammo, but no toy cap guns. Dad had promised us sparklers. If we were good.

"Good" meant washing the lunch dishes, taking out the garbage to the burn barrel, hanging wet laundry on the clothesline, picking beans from the garden. "Good" meant waiting without whining. And no sass.

Grandma had spent much of the day sitting on Aunt Audrey's hide-a-bed crocheting squares in rainbow colors framed in black acrylic yarn. She worked a pattern more intricate than the God's Eyes we'd made at Bible camp from two sticks crossed and wrapped in scraps of yarn.

"Do you think you'd have time to perm my hair next Wednesday?" Grandma asked Aunt Audrey.

I looked at Grandma. Her dark brown hair looked speckled salt-and-pepper at the roots.

"Sure, Mom. I'll pick up a perm and color rinse at the pharmacy," said Aunt Audrey.

"They're probably closed today," Mom said. "But let's go into town now and go to the beach for a swim, eh?"

I heard that. In a flash I was down the hall and into my suitcase, from which I pulled out my swimsuit. Shireen was right behind me. She closed the door and peeled off her T-shirt. She pulled open her bureau drawer and yanked out her tank suit. I stripped and put mine on, too. We wore our shorts and shirts over our swimsuits, grabbed bath towels, and presented ourselves quickly as ready.

We waited impatiently as Mom helped Barb change into her two-piece bikini. Then we all piled into one car and drove into town.

There had been an Independence Day parade earlier, and Lake Street was littered with tissue-paper scraps from cheerleader pom-poms.

Downtown consisted of three blocks running east to west along the Warroad River. A drug store with a soda fountain on the north side of Lake Street, the two-story Wing's Department Store on the south, the Fox movie theater to the left, the American Legion and the bank on the right. On the side streets, there were a couple of grocery stores—Red Owl and Milo's—plus a Ben Franklin five-and-dime, a hair salon, and several bars.

Aunt Audrey drove straight down to the end of Lake Street to the public beach. We jumped out to play on the teeter-totter and swings, and then walked along the shore. The white pelicans flew only so close to us. I couldn't see anything but water across the eastern horizon.

Shireen noticed me staring at the water. "Lake of the Woods is almost seventy miles long and seventy miles wide," she informed me. She knew I liked maps and geography. "There's about fifteen thousand islands."

She pulled off her shorts, shirt, and sneakers, leaving them in the sand, as I stood there looking across the enormous expanse of the lake.

To me, it looked as big as the Atlantic Ocean. My parents had taken us on a road trip to the New York City World's Fair in 1964, and somewhere in Connecticut, there's a beach where home movies were taken of me chasing and being chased by waves. Like the ocean, Lake of the Woods had a shoreline that extended farther than I could see in either direction, and when I looked across the lake, the distant shore was invisible to me. The surface of the water was still and flat.

During the long ride up north in my parents' car, I loved studying our road map of Minnesota. I knew Lake of the Woods had an irregular shape and was the sixth-largest freshwater lake in North America. The border with Canada ran across the water. If the lake were my handprint, the southern round end would be the heel of my hand, and the palm would divide into a million wiggling fingers as you head north. The northern end bent toward the west, where it drained into the Winnipeg River and then into Lake Winnipeg. From there, the water flowed north into the Hudson Bay.

Shireen walked out into the lake and made it almost waist-high before she turned around with her teeth chattering from the cold. There were places miles out in the middle where Lake of the Woods went hundreds of feet deep, but the water was shallow along the shores, sometimes for several hundred yards.

"Come on, Jill," she called out. "I'll beat you to the dock." She dropped her shoulders and started swimming.

I accepted her challenge, pumped my arms, and flutter-kicked. The smooth surface of the water hid the weedy, mossy bottom. Muskeg Bay, the large southwestern edge of this enormous lake, got its name from the peat bog formed after the last glacial retreat of Lake Agassiz. There was no bedrock bottom if you put your feet down; only moss into which you sank. I didn't stop kicking until I touched the side of the floating dock where Shireen stood looking down at me.

"I'll beat you back!" I challenged her.

"No you won't!" Shireen dove off and raced me to shore.

Back on land, we hiked along the pier and let the sun dry our swimsuits. Shireen pointed to islands on Lake of the Woods in an endless horizon where the blue of the water met the blue of sky.

Once we were dry, we walked to the trading post, an old log cabin at the north end of the beach. The screen door slammed behind us. Canoes were overhead; bins of paddles, racks of waders, and stands of fishing poles and nets filled the floor, and they had live bait in big coolers. Two short aisles were stocked with canned goods and dry ingredients: pancake mix, potted venison, flour, coffee. I walked to the magnificent glass case with Indian artifacts—arrowheads, earthenware bowls, dolls dressed in beaded outfits, bolo neckties with turtle amulets, silver jewelry, agates and other precious stones.

I picked out six postcards from the circular wire rack and walked over to the young woman sitting behind the cash register. I put the cards on the counter and a dollar bill from my pocket plus the nickel for tax. Without saying a word, she slipped my postcards into a glassine bag and handed it to me. I planned to keep the picture postcard of Kakaygeesick in his headdress for myself.

After supper, Uncle Al lit the sparklers. Shireen and I danced in the yard like fireflies. The clear sky didn't darken until after 10 p.m.

When we finally went to bed, I kept watch in the mirror for

colors in the window over the headboard of Shireen's bed. I heard voices in the distance. A small group of people talking far off in the woods behind the pasture, along the tracks. I couldn't make out what they were saying.

"Who *is* that?" I asked Shireen.

She was lying next to me, trying to fall asleep.

"Trampers," she muttered.

"Who?"

"Tramps. Bums. Indians. Draft dodgers. Catching the train tonight." She sighed.

I could see the faint glow of bonfires back behind the hedgerow, along the unpaved road I had heard Uncle Al call Loonshit Lane. It sounded more and more like a party. A guitar strumming and a woman's voice. "Who?"

"They're waiting for the train to pull out of Marvin's factory and head up into Winnipeg. If they can jump it, they get into Canada without getting stopped at the border." Shireen seemed embarrassed I'd asked.

"Instead of going to *Vietnam*?" I had to ask.

Shireen snapped her head in my direction and turned her full attention to me.

"Yes. Dad doesn't want them on our property. Draft dodgers. Some of the Indians cook up chicken and charge them for a meal. They just better stay away from the house and barn. They're not doing nothing now. Beebe would cause a stir if they were. She's not. So be quiet."

The train whistle blew. I swallowed my curiosity and went to sleep hungry to hear more.

CHAPTER 2

My cell phone rang at 5 a.m., waking me from a deep sleep.

"Are you on your way?" Barb asked.

"Yes," I said groggily.

"Well, hurry. Or it may be too late."

Barb had phoned me the previous afternoon at home near Ithaca, New York, to tell me that if I wanted to come home before Mom died, I'd better "get on the road now."

I dropped everything, threw a few things in a suitcase, and let adrenaline fuel my drive. I got as far as Madison before I had to pull over at 3 a.m. Two hours of sleep in the guest bedroom at my friend Amy's house before Barb called; five more hours of driving ahead. Even though you think you might be ready when your mother has lived on oxygen tanks for almost twenty years, you're never ready.

Driving across New York, Pennsylvania, Ohio, and Indiana had given me lots of time to think about Mom. How she took me and Barb tobogganing when we were kids, squealing with joy herself. How she made our clothes and hers, the excitement of trips to the fabric store, the hum of her sewing machine late into the night. How petite and professional she looked every morning ready for work. How she cried when Dad hurt her feelings. How she made homemade lefse, belonged to a bowling league, played golf, and attended church faithfully. How she hummed without realizing she was doing it. How she'd gotten in the car with Dad to make this same trip in the opposite direction five years earlier, driving through the night to be by my side when I'd called her to say Sam, the love of my life, had died.

I arrived at Lakeview Hospital. Standing out in the hallway, I looked through the small window into her room. Propped up with pillows, Mom lay in a bed attached to machines that spit out her heart rate, oxygen levels, temperature, and blood pressure on screens behind her. Tubes in her nose, IV line in her arm, catheter connected to a bag attached to the leg of the bed. A cup of ice chips on the tray across her lap. All the color had disappeared from her skin and hair; she was a ghost in gray. I could see death inside her. My diaphragm constricted involuntarily, sucking air into my lungs with an inward wheeze. It took me a minute to regain my composure and not burst into tears.

When I walked into the room, she opened her eyes.

"Hi, Mom," I greeted her. "You get to go home today."

Dad sat at the foot of her bed, holding her feet in his hands, his body in the shape of a question mark. Behind him a nurse stood gently massaging his shoulders; he leaned over and whispered in his ear, "Your other daughter is here, Bob."

Dad nodded, but he kept his eyes on Mom.

Barb arrived right behind me and gave me a hug. Tears welled up as we exchanged a glance, acknowledging the imminence of Mom's death.

Barb blew her nose. "The ambulance is ready to take you home, Mom." My sister had already gone ahead and made space in our parents' townhouse to set up a hospital bed in the sunroom where Mom could watch the hummingbirds at the feeders.

The morphine drops alleviated her pain. The pastor came to pray with us, and the last words Mom spoke were those of the Lord's Prayer. Late in the afternoon as the sun began to set behind her shoulders, she reached up as though God were picking her up in his arms.

Arlene Janice Kling Swenson died the same day she came home from the hospital. June 11, 2014.

She had been born a deer baby—at home on the farm during the first day of hunting season in 1936. Grandma Kling was home alone with her two young daughters when she gave birth while Grandpa was out in the woods. The youngest of Harold and Emma Kling's three children, Arlene grew up near Willow Creek in the Swedish settlement east of Warroad, on Lake of the Woods, in northern Minnesota only a few miles south of the Canadian border.

Planning a date for Mom's funeral, we found the folder from the mortuary where she had planned her prepaid funeral. Dad, Barb, and I sat around the dining room table and went through the documents. I picked up a pamphlet, *Your Story*, and inside I found Mom had written answers to questions about her life. Her voice came across the page in her familiar left-handed cursive penmanship. She described looking out her childhood bedroom window to a field of blue flax as vast as an ocean under an endless open sky. While she couldn't wait as a teenager to escape the empty landscape for the Twin Cities, I yearned to return to where she left her childhood behind.

After the funeral, I felt lost in a vast flood of memories and sadness. Dad sat in his chair with the television on but nodding off. He jolted awake and looked at the screen. I had been lying on the couch with the newspaper.

"Hand me the remote, would you?" Dad snapped at me. "I don't want to watch this."

I don't even know what was on the television set. I wasn't watching it. I was looking for Mom's obituary. I sat up. I looked at him. The remote was closer to him than it was to me. All he had to do was lean over and grab it. He wanted me to wait on him the way Mom had. I couldn't do that. Barb could, and did—yet instead of being grateful, Dad complained to me that my sister didn't need to watch over him like she was his mother. No matter what I did, it wouldn't be right.

I made no move toward the remote. *Go ahead and disown me again.*

He needed some time to himself.

I needed time too.

Shireen had suggested at Mom's funeral that I come for a visit. "You know my mom lost her sister, too, and is going to miss her terribly."

She thought it would be good for me to spend some time again up north.

I thought she might be right.

CHAPTER 3

A few weeks after Mom died, I drove up to Lake of the Woods. Aunt Audrey now lived west of Warroad on the pine ridge with the house set back in the woods from Highway 11. Before Uncle Al died, they'd sold their land on Highway 313 to Marvin Windows, which wanted to build another factory. With highways to the west and south and train tracks to the east, there was only one direction to expand, and that was to the north: on their land. When they sold, Audrey and Al moved their house four miles west. Warroad had long been a one-company town: most people either worked at Marvin Windows or worked for a Marvin. Or they commuted twenty miles to Roseau and worked for Polaris in the factory making snowmobiles.

Warroad is a full day's drive north from the Twin Cities. You aren't in northern Minnesota until the interstate ends and you cross over the largest bog in the lower forty-eight states. It's a lonely stretch of highway.

Driving due north through Red Lake Reservation, I saw no one, and there was almost no vehicular traffic. I glimpsed to my right and saw the miles-long boardwalk extend out into an otherwise inaccessible landscape. It looked like the shooting location for a postnuclear Armageddon movie: stark, bleak, and largely uninhabited.

What I didn't know then driving through Red Lake Reservation was how many endangered or threatened native plants grew there, many with medicinal properties. Not did I know about the reclamation of the bog, which had been a barrier to European settlers who had all but drained it.

I lost cell phone reception. I couldn't help but notice the road signs marking this as reservation land had been riddled with bullet holes. I only saw unpaved side roads that seemed to be swallowed up by the forest. Those who lived on the reservation were invisible to me. There were few residences along the highway and no billboards. Miles after miles of wide open wilderness without any signs of human interference.

On the last leg from Baudette to Warroad, the highway runs parallel to the train tracks. The same feeling of eager anticipation from childhood family road trips along this stretch washed over me as I felt my chest tighten and tears flood my eyes. Bittersweet without Mom.

Where the speed limit sign at the eastern edge of Warroad was posted, a billboard announced a new Seven Clans Casino opening in September. After driving through Red Lake Reservation, it wasn't obvious to me how proceeds from gambling had improved the quality of life. I associated gambling with prostitution, narcotics, guns, and money laundering. The mob. A big new casino seemed to me like the last thing Warroad needed.

I drove to the lakefront, where I walked the shoreline as years collapsed between my childhood memories and my mother's death.

Lake of the Woods, exactly as I remembered. The water stretched across the horizon. Blue against blue.

Looking south, I noticed the currents of the Warroad River running into Lake of the Woods, a dark swath churning in the water. Across the reedy shore of Muskeg Bay, I saw construction cranes working on the new casino's big hotel. Like a Monopoly game piece, the big-box building didn't look real. I had to look away. Then I noticed the old trading post had been replaced with a replica. New log construction with a sitting porch faced the lakeshore. A tornado had wiped out the old one several years ago. Now it was a tavern and pizza joint. Instead of bait and postcards, they sold New York–style pizza by the slice.

Driving through town I saw little had changed, except the population. Warroad had gained about eight hundred residents in the past forty years. I would later learn newcomers included Laotian refugees, Red Lake tribal members, and those who came from other states for jobs at Marvin Windows.

It was still a company town; Marvin Windows remained the primary employer. The company had grown, with manufacturing plants in Tennessee and North Dakota and twenty locations coast to coast. The old hospital and nursing home were gone, but there sat a pretty city park with a gazebo and playground. There was an outpatient health clinic near the water tower and a swanky new senior living center on the west end of town. The old Fox movie theater had been divided into apartments. Memorial Arena, the old ice rink on the corner of Main and MacKenzie, had been torn down long ago, and there was a new world-class hockey arena next to the high school. Otherwise, the town looked pretty much the same.

I headed west to the pine ridge to see Aunt Audrey.

Walking in the door and up three steps into her kitchen felt like stepping through time.

Aunt Aundrey looked and sounded so much like Mom. The short curly hair framing her face, the sighs in between her sentences, the way she asked right away if I wanted a cup of coffee. It felt good to wrap my arms around her and give her a hug. I kept staring at her, seeing so much of Mom in her, alive.

"You better call your sister so she knows you made it here okay," Audrey suggested. Just as Mom would have.

When I turned out the lights in Shireen's old bedroom that night, crickets chirped outside the window. I couldn't recall any nights this hot in Warroad before. Instead, I remembered many summer days needing a jacket because the temperature didn't get above seventy. I heard the long low whistle of the train headed for the border.

The dreamscape of my childhood summers had followed me well into adulthood. The mirror on the wall across from the end of the bed beckoned to me as a portal into my past. I lay there and wondered: Whatever had happened to Kakaygeesick? What had he said to me when he held my head in his hands? Why had I always known he was trying to tell me something about the future, about what would happen when he was gone?

That first night back in Warroad, I slept deeply and got up with the sun. I didn't want to wake Aunt Audrey, so I slipped out the door quietly and headed to town for Caribou Coffee at Doug's Supermarket. From the parking lot where I sat sipping my coffee, I saw a building in the prairie style of architecture that housed the Warroad Heritage Center and Public Library.

That building hadn't been there when I was a kid. After I finished my coffee, I headed over to check it out.

When I entered the air-conditioned foyer, I saw to my left the local history museum behind closed doors and a wall of glass. Through the windows, I could see a birchbark wigwam in the center of the room. Bent poles made from tree saplings created the frame of the domed hut, and long strips of bark were lashed to the poles. Paintings by local Indigenous artists hung on a display wall. If I wanted to find out what happened to the Kakaygeesick family, I was in the right place to start.

The museum opened at 1 p.m., so I had the morning to see what books on local history I could find. The library doors straight ahead stood open. A wooden pew lined the hallway to its entrance. Inside, sturdy wooden bookshelves stood back to back in orderly rows under a high ceiling. On the south wall was a fireplace and a plaque with an acknowledgment to the Margaret W. Marvin Fund of the Minnesota Foundation for financing construction of the building. On the coffee table in front of the upholstered chairs circling the hearth were current issues of local and regional newspapers. I walked to the back of the stacks, pulled up a chair in front of a desk looking out the window, and plugged in my computer for access to free Wi-Fi.

Libraries have always felt like sanctuaries to me. From an early age, what I found in libraries that I didn't find at home or school or church were answers to questions I had. The answers I found in books at the library were always more satisfying than the excuses most adults offered, with incomplete or inaccurate information.

When I found the local history section of the library, I settled in at a big seminar table. It didn't take long to find references to my Kling family.

It wasn't until 1903 that my mother's grandfather, Carl Peter—Charlie—Kling arrived at Lake of the Woods. As an infant, he had come to Minnesota with his unmarried mother and her aunt and uncle from Göteborg, Sweden, in 1876. They settled near Marine on Saint Croix, the site of a commercial sawmill, which had attracted Swedish settlers to the area since the 1830s. His mother married John Palm, and Charlie grew up with younger stepsiblings. He married Ellen Nelson in 1901.

In a letter from his brother-in-law Albert Hessler, Charlie Kling read of the fine timber on Lake of the Woods and was convinced to try his luck there. He and Albert had both married Nelson sisters. The sisters' mother and their brother, Walter Nelson, moved with Charlie, his wife, and Charlie's bachelor brother, John. They traveled north three hundred and fifty miles from Marine on Saint Croix to the Swedish settlement about twenty miles east of Warroad near Willow Creek. The men cleared acres of timber, then farmed with a plow and oxen on acreage adjacent to the homestead of Charlie's brother-in-law Albert Hessler. They grew wheat and flax, and they helped build Mt. Carmel Lutheran Church and a one-room schoolhouse. The Homestead Act allowed them to claim the land, and like so many white European immigrants, they made the land their home.

Twelve years before my great-grandparents arrived on Lake of the Woods, a rumor had spread that Indians near Warroad planned to go on the warpath. Many of the white settlers fled their homes and farmsteads in January 1891, leaving their livestock behind without food or water. The previous month, on December 29, 1890, fears of an Indian uprising on the Pine Ridge Indian Reservation in the state of South Dakota had led to the Wounded Knee Massacre. Indians had amassed at Pine Ridge awaiting provisions long promised by the US government. They faced starvation without them. An estimated three hundred Lakota died there when the Seventh Calvary indiscriminately opened fire.

The Kah-bay-kah-nong band of Chippewa Indians who lived along the shores of Lake of the Woods had given the European settlers in their village no cause to worry about an attack. They had not been forced to relocate to reservation land nor did they have reason to anticipate government rations. Warroad had been named for the many battles waged between the Sioux (Dakota) and Chippewa (Ojibway). Since the Dakota lost and the whites had not waged war against the Ojibway, the band along the shores of Lake of the Woods had no reason to provoke conflict.

Thoroughly absorbed by the accounts of local history, I discovered it was John Torfin in Roseau, twenty-two miles to the west of Warroad, who first spread talk of an Indian uprising early in January 1891. His family business, Roseau Milling Company, advertised their white flour ground from local wheat in some of the first editions of the *Roseau Times*. John Torfin spoke to others about the Indians readying for an attack on settlers.

John Westerson, the recorder for the county of Roseau, sent a telegram to Governor Merriam in Saint Paul to sound the alarm. He wasn't the only one who sent the governor telegrams. Sheriff Oscar Youngren on January 26 requested three hundred rifles to be sent for Roseau County residents. T. J. Wikstrom sent a telegram warning authorities of wild Indian dances. Ed H. Love, mayor of Hallock, sent one, too.

A scout "trusted because of his Swede father's name" was sent to Warroad to investigate the supposed Indian uprising "before the first sap in the maple trees began to run." The scout found the town empty and no signs of war along his path. Instead, he discovered Kakaygeesick had trekked to the abandoned homesteads in deep snow and tended the settlers' animals with food and fresh water in the sheds and barns until the families returned a few weeks later.

This I read in one of the many dozens of pamphlets put together by the Warroad and Roseau County Historical Societies on the library *shelves*.

Hours flew by. Glad I'd left a note for Aunt Audrey that I'd be back in time for supper, I kept reading.

When the Warroad Heritage Center opened at 1 p.m., I signed my name into the visitor's book and relished the air-conditioned chill in this room of old treasures. To my right stood the wigwam replica of Kakaygeesick's home on Muskeg Bay. Above my head on a ledge that ran around the room, there were jingle dresses and willow baskets attributed to Florence and Verna Kakaygeesick on exhibit. Inside a tall glass case were beaded moccasins, vests, belts, leggings, breast panels, cradle boards, and bandolier bags. I sank to the floor, humbled by the artistry, and began writing field notes in my composition book. For the first time since Mom died—honestly, since Sam died—I found something more compelling than my grief.

The director walked out of her office and found me sprawled and enthralled. I scrambled to my feet; my backpack, notebook, pens, and phone scattered across the floor.

"Hi," I said, a bit flustered. "I'm Jill Swenson. My mother was a Kling."

"I'm Heidi, the museum director. Glad to meet you," she said with a smile. "Are you related to Ralph Kling, who managed the old ice arena?"

"Great-Uncle Ralph," I confirmed. "His brother, Harold, was my grandpa. I'm here to see if I can learn more about what happened to the Kakaygeesick family." I didn't know until I said it out loud that I couldn't let this go.

"I've got somebody who can help you find anything we've got in our files," Heidi said. "Follow me."

She led me toward the back and into a glorified closet, where a woman older than Mom sat slumped at a table covered in newspaper clippings. Next to her were manila folders piled high and behind her, a wall of shelves full of pamphlets and mono-colored clothbound volumes. Filing cabinets lined another wall, their drawers pulled partially open.

"Jill, this is Beth Marvin," Heidi said, and then she told Beth I was interested in information about the Kakaygeesicks.

Beth's face lit up. "Please, sit down! Tell me what you're looking for."

"I'll leave you to it, then." Heidi ducked out of the small cluttered space and back to her office.

I wanted to know Beth's story first and whether she had known Kakaygeesick or any of his family. "First, tell me about yourself."

"I've lived in Warroad since 1940, when I arrived as a new teacher," she began. Then, smiling, she told me she'd caused a bit of a local scandal her first year. "I took my pupils outdoors for Nature Studies and Physical Education."

Miss Williams, as her students called her then, met Calvin Marvin at a dance. Cal's father owned Marvin Lumber and Cedar Company. The business began in 1912, and in 1939 they began to build window frames, which kept men working during the winter season. It was two years after Beth first met Cal that they married. They ran Cal's Resort and Fishing Lodge together for more than fifty years.

Beth said she'd known the Kakaygeesick family since those early days in Warroad. The old man's trapline had run right in front of her and Cal's shoreline property. Cal had hired Kakaygeesick's son, John, as a professional guide and fisherman. Beth remembered John Kakaygeesick from her teaching years, when she lived in a boarding house. Her kind landlady left the door unlocked for him in the winter because it was almost two miles to walk back to his allotment from town. One morning on her way out to get to school early, Beth stumbled over John, sleeping in the hallway. She could smell that he was drunk.

"But he wasn't a mean drunk," she added quickly. "Understand: *everybody* drank back then. John could cut fish. Filet walleye like nobody else."

She handed me several file folders to look through. Inside the first folder, I saw Kakaygeesick's obituary from the front page of the *St. Paul Pioneer and Dispatch* in December 1968. His remarkable age of 124 years made him headline news. There is also a small clipping with the death notice of his son John. He had died the year before I was born, in 1957, in Grand Forks, at the age of seventy-seven.

Beth had current news clippings on her desk in a pile; she pushed them in my direction. "Glad to know somebody's interested in their story," she said. "Damn shame what happened."

"What do you mean? What happened?" I had come to Warroad looking for memories about spending my summers here as Arlene Kling's daughter, but now I felt drawn to follow my curiosity about Kakaygeesick.

Beth showed me the news articles. A new Seven Clans Casino would open in less than six weeks. The Kakaygeesick family had been forced off their property by Red Lake Nation.

Heidi stuck her head in the door. "Five o'clock. Closing time."

Five already? The time had flown. I thanked Beth for her time and promised to come back soon. On the way out, I stopped at the front desk and purchased ten picture postcards of Kakaygeesick, identical to the one I had kept all these years, still hanging on my fridge.

Back in my car, I drove east out of Warroad on the state highway and turned north toward the lake onto the county road so I could drive by where Mom had grown up, on the old Kling farm. The flat open stretch of road made the sky seem so much higher than high. Flax bloomed bright blue in the fields on either side for as far as I could see.

I wept for the plain beauty of it.

I sobbed because Mom couldn't see it.

CHAPTER 4

Dad fit the clean muslin bag over my left hand. He pulled the drawstrings and tied it loosely around my five-year-old wrist for a dusting rag. He handed me a spray bottle filled with Guardsman polish. I squirted with my right and polished with my left, massaging every wooden surface including the banisters on the grand staircase. Strokes always with the grain of the wood, the way Dad taught me.

When I wasn't in kindergarten, I was at the furniture store learning the family business. One I assumed I would inherit with my sister one day. Pearson & Swenson Furniture had been in north Minneapolis since the beginning of the twentieth century. Fine-quality merchandise filled the two-story building. Living and dining room furniture on the first floor, bedroom suites and mattresses on the second floor, and in the basement, kitchen sets and home appliances like washers and dryers and televisions. Grandpa Swenson bought out old Mr. Pearson after I was born. Dad started working there before I went to kindergarten.

Dusting started with the pieces at the back of the showroom floor, and I made my way toward the front entrance, where a grandfather clock stood sentry between two enormous storefront windows facing West Broadway, each decorated with elegant home furnishings. I'd seen Bob Barker draw back stage curtains to reveal similar settings for contestants to guess the retail price on *The Price*

Is Right. When polishing the pieces in the front windows with street pedestrians as my audience, I imagined myself on stage performing like Barker's beautiful blonde assistants.

When I finished dusting the first-floor furniture, I headed toward the backroom, where I found Grandpa. A master tinkerer, he kept his work bench clean and organized. His hands fascinated me as he worked with his tiny wood drills, nails of every shape and size, hammers and clamps, oil cans, rags, tags with strings. In a corner stood a black-and-white television set I could watch. Mom never missed *As the World Turns* during her lunch hour.

"We have to go," Mom said in a low voice, grabbing my hand.

I was six and attending my first white elephant sale in the basement of my grandparents' church with my parents. We'd just eaten a smorgasbord dinner that October evening, and I was strolling past the display tables with used items for sale: Lincoln logs, a hobbyhorse, ice skates. *Why do we have to go?* I'd barely gotten to look at anything.

I scowled at her and pulled back my hand, shaking my head no.

"Now," she said.

I looked past her and saw a commotion in the church kitchen. Grandma stood near the telephone, and ladies circled around her as her back heaved with sobs. Dad rushed to her side.

Before I could ask any questions, Mom took my hand, picked up my little sister, and hurried us both out to the car. She started the ignition and sighed deeply. "When we get home, I need you girls to get into your pajamas."

I could feel her fear, her urge to protect me from seeing reality, from speaking up, to keep me small, safe.

Grandpa had dropped dead of a heart attack at age sixty-three.

We were as sad as the previous November when President Kennedy had been killed.

It became a weekly ritual for Dad to take his mother, Mom, me, and my younger sister, Barb, to visit his father's grave.

On Sunday we went over to Grandma Swenson's after church for roast beef, mashed potatoes, and gravy. Then we all drove over to Crystal Lake Cemetery, where Barb and I wandered through the plots, enchanted by the pretty plastic flowers and little flags, looking for angel statues.

Afterward, Grandma put the coffee on, and we played rummy. A nickel a hand. A dime for the kitty.

"Bob, are you sure the kids should be playing cards?" Mom asked, tucking her chin.

"Teaches the girls how to count," Grandma said, without lifting her eyes from the deck of cards in her hands.

"Not like it's gambling," Dad added.

"This will help me in school with math," I told Mom. But it was really winning I wanted to learn.

Grandma kept score, and she won the kitty. She pulled out fresh-baked lemon squares, freshened up the coffee cups, and asked who wanted to play another game.

"I do," I said.

"Not tonight," Dad said. "You have school tomorrow morning."

We each had one of Grandma's lemon squares before leaving.

On the way home in the dark that evening, we listened to WCCO on the car radio. My parents sat in complete silence as we drove home; I stayed quiet too, staring out the window from the back seat.

Only a half century later could I understand what they hadn't discussed in front of me. Instead of receiving a weekly salary from his father, Dad at the age of thirty-two was now responsible for the business and supporting his widowed mother. Mom, meanwhile, missed her own family, far away in a small town in the northernmost part of Minnesota.

Several years after Mom died, Dad confided in me that Grandpa's ghost had haunted the furniture store. Every morning he heard his father come in from the back alley. Behind the store there had been a loading dock. His father's feet made a specific shuffling sound as he arrived and climbed the concrete steps up to the back door. When the keys turned in the lock and the ghost of Grandpa let himself in the back door, Dad knew he had better get to work.

He did business the way his father had. He extended credit to everyone who walked in the door and offered layaway accounts. His word was his father's honor. Dad couldn't carry a tune, but I often heard him whistle my favorite Sunday school song while he puttered at Grandpa's workbench. "Jesus loves the little children, all the children of the world. Red and yellow, black and white, they are precious in his sight."

Almost two years later—on October 19, 1966, the night of my parents' ninth wedding anniversary—the phone rang shortly after 9 p.m.

Mom picked up the receiver in the kitchen. "Hello?"

Barb and I were already in bed and supposed to be asleep. Nobody phoned this late.

"Bob! It's the fire department!" Mom screamed. I heard Dad scramble to his feet out of his recliner in the den. "Bob, the store is on fire!" She handed him the phone and rushed into our bedroom.

"Get dressed girls, hurry!" Mom turned on the bedroom light and helped Barb out of her pajamas and put her socks on her feet. All of us scrambled to get in the car, and Dad raced down West Broadway. He told Mom to stay with us, lock the doors, and not get out. He ran across the street toward the fire.

"I have to go to the bathroom," I complained. "Badly."

"No," Mom shouted at me, angry. Then she started crying.

Across the street, the building stood engulfed in flames. From the roof, the fire roared up into the night sky. Two fire trucks with multiple hoses sprayed water at the front door. The storefront windows burst; dark smoke rolled out into the street. Then a whooshing sound, more flames ignited inside, visible through the front showcase window frames. Sirens and flashing lights everywhere, police cars blocked off traffic.

My thighs started shaking. I wet myself. A pool of urine on the floor in the back seat. Humiliated and afraid. I didn't mean to do anything wrong. It wasn't my fault the store was on fire. None of it was my fault. I knew that, but I felt like bad things happened because I was a bad girl.

Fire investigators determined it wasn't arson. They discovered it started near the center of the showroom floor where there had stood an ashtray, bigger than a dinner plate, set on a brass stand. An ashtray overflowing with cigarette butts. Dad smoked close to three packs a day.

The newspaper reported the two-alarm fire at 609 West Broadway had an estimated hundred thousand dollars in damages. The building wasn't a total loss. The insurance paid the claim, and Dad rented a small office space across the street. It was next door to Mickey's Diner, where he bought me a twenty-nine-cent hamburger for lunch, which made me feel special. I can't imagine how stressed my parents were at the time because I only recall their eager anticipation for the "grand reopening," as though it were going to be a big party.

For months, Dad went to work every day as always, except he went to the office across the street from the furniture store and took inventory, organized the renovations, met with contractors, and made plans to reopen. Mom took a job a few blocks down West Broadway as a receptionist for Iten Chevrolet, working afternoons and evenings.

Late one night I lay in bed awake and heard Mom in the basement. I listened to her sewing machine—her foot heavy on the pedal, racing the motor in an angry rush to stitch a seam—while Dad sat in the den watching *The Tonight Show* with the volume low. Maybe it was their fear I felt. I prayed I wouldn't say or do anything to upset either one of them and tried to be good.

"Girls, go wake up your father. It's time to get ready for church."

I tried to wake Dad up. I grabbed one arm and raised it up and let go. It dropped with a thud, like he was a corpse. Barb tried tickling his armpit. But he wouldn't laugh.

We went to church without him.

After Sunday school, my teacher asked to speak with my mother. Alone. I'd brought my offering in a pretty purple velvet bag with a gold cord drawstring. The colors of advent at our Lutheran church had seemed so fitting. The teacher wanted to know if there was a problem at home. The Crown Royal bag was not appropriate for a seven-year-old to bring to church.

"How dare you humiliate me in church, young lady," Mom hissed at me as we crossed the parking lot to leave.

I felt confused and then ashamed. I didn't know why I was bad.

My eyes crossed. I didn't do it on purpose. None of it seemed my fault—the furniture store fire, peeing my pants, embarrassing Mom, Grandma crying, Grandpa dying—and still it felt like I was being punished.

Mom took me downtown to see a special eye doctor, Dr. Cooper, who wore a white coat and spoke in a kind voice.

"Glasses won't fix your problem, Jill," Dr. Cooper said. "We are going to operate."

Surgery happened at the start of summer vacation after first grade. I don't remember much about being in the hospital except the moment when Dr. Cooper finally removed the gauze bandages. After months of double vision, the world suddenly appeared before me clearly.

When I returned home, it was to a different house. My family had moved from north Minneapolis to Robbinsdale, three miles west. I didn't ask why, but I knew Black and American Indian families had moved into the city, and white families moved out to the suburbs. I didn't know any of the kids on our block yet, but at least none of them knew me as the cross-eyed girl.

Victory Memorial Parkway divided Minneapolis from the suburbs. My parents allowed me to ride my bike anywhere, except into the city. The elms lined the parkway and created a green tunnel of shade for miles. Who needed friends? I had the freedom of my blue Schwinn.

I looked forward to watching the Torchlight Parade at the start of the annual Aquatennial Festival. I dreamed of twirling my baton, wearing white boots with pom-poms, and being *in* the parade someday. But Mom heard on WCCO radio that the police expected trouble.

"We won't get to see the parade this year," she said. "It's not safe."

I would miss seeing the majorettes, the marching bands, and the drum and bugle corps? Eye surgery, the move, no parade—I was so bored and lonely, and it was so hot and muggy. I crumpled with disappointment.

"We'll make the best of it," Dad promised—and he delivered. He brought home two big watermelons from Joe Reeves's vegetable stand down near the river. One *only* for kids. As for the other—Dad poked a hole into it, inverted an open bottle of vodka into the rind, and let it set for several hours. Meanwhile, he went door to door, inviting everyone over for melon—spiked for the adults.

By the time the neighborhood block party started, I'd forgotten about the parade. We watched the fireworks from folding chairs in the middle of our street. A transistor radio tuned to WDGY played Aretha Franklin, James Brown, and Tina Turner, and we kids raced around with water pistols.

Later that same night—July 19, 1967—after we came inside and Mom turned on the late-night TV news in the den, I watched violence erupt on the streets of north Minneapolis. White uniformed police officers used their clubs to beat Black people in the crowded streets.

"Turn that up," Dad called from the kitchen.

"Come watch this!" Mom called.

Although we weren't near the intersection of West Broadway and Plymouth Avenue in north Minneapolis when the fight broke out along the parade route, I recognized it was only a few blocks from the furniture store. I crossed my arms over my chest and felt my heart beat in my ears.

"The Jewish grocers—Silver's and Knox Food Markets—burning," Dad pointed to the scenes on the screen. Reporters said young Black men broke windows and set fires to businesses. Firefighters refused to respond without police protection. The film footage showed West Broadway with storefronts in flames.

When the newscaster cut to a commercial break, my stomach felt the way it did when the elevator stopped.

"It's past your bedtime," Mom said. She stood up and ushered me and Barb down the hallway into our bedroom, tucked us in, and shut the door. And the next night on the late-night TV news we heard more people in north Minneapolis had broken windows, looted, and tossed firebombs.

No one called it a race riot. No one. Not my parents. Not Grandma. Not the *Minneapolis Star* or *Pioneer Press*. Not WCCO. But I had watched what happened in Watts and Newark on the *CBS Evening News* with Walter Cronkite and I could see clearly that what happened on West Broadway had looked much the same.

A few weeks later, Dad left work at the furniture store out the back entrance and walked to the alley and got in the driver's seat of his

Impala like he usually did. But as soon as he closed the door, someone in the back seat reached over and held a knife under his throat. Dad told me he looked in the rearview mirror and couldn't see anyone. But he heard a man say, "Give me your wallet."

Dad slid his hips forward a bit and reached into his right rear pocket for the brown leather wad. The wallet was snatched from his raised hand. The back door opened, slammed, and running footsteps sounded in the dark. Dad went back inside the store and called the police. When he got home late for supper, Mom cried when she heard he'd been robbed.

It happened again a few weeks later, around the corner from the store. "Broad daylight!" I heard him scream at Mom when he came home with a black eye and emptied wallet. His anger frightened me.

Recently my sister found a newspaper clipping Mom had saved about Dad getting robbed the first time. According to the news article—from November 1966, less than a month after the fire and seven months before violence erupted the night of the Torchlight Parade in July 1967—Dad told police he stopped for a traffic light at Lyndale and West Broadway when two men who had hid in the back seat ordered him to drive through north Minneapolis to an alley where they beat him and robbed him of fourteen dollars.

On Sunday over pot roast dinner, Grandma whispered under her breath to Dad, "You shouldn't be taking the girls down there to the ghetto."

She didn't turn red when she got mad; she turned white, with fear and grief. And when we watched the national news together, her blue eyes pierced the TV screen in the living room. She nodded her head as she watched fire hydrants and dogs unleashed against civil rights protesters, the flesh of her jowls jiggling.

It didn't make sense to me that Grandma said the store was in a ghetto or that someone would rob Dad. I didn't have the vocabulary to name my feelings. I couldn't quite articulate how confusing I found grief and injustice. I knew it was all wrong, and it made me mad and sad.

CHAPTER 5

I checked into the Patch Motel on Highway 11, directly across from the window factory and the railroad tracks. The motel was adjacent to Izzy's Lounge & Grill. Like many of the businesses in Warroad, it was owned by someone in the Marvin Family: Beth and Cal Marvin's son, Izzy.

I sat alone at the bar that night and ordered the walleye for supper. I'd decided to get a motel room to avoid becoming a burdensome houseguest to Aunt Audrey. And to have the privacy to cry.

I went back to my hotel room and found myself searching the internet for information about the new casino and the Kakaygeesick family. Out the window of my hotel room, I saw a row of ice fishing houses sitting on blocks in the lawn. If I hadn't known better, I might have mistaken them for a small village of garden sheds. An odd-looking off-road utility vehicle stood at the end of the row. About the size of a small bus or large van, it had skis instead of tires in front. The chassis sat on bulldozer tracks. Painted bright neon yellow with all black trim, I had never seen anything like it before.

Googling, I learned it was called a Bombardier and was used by people in northern remote communities for ice fishing and transportation across Canada and Alaska. Ice fishing had been little more than a punchline to jokes and not a part of my personal experience. But Uncle Al had gone ice fishing when I was a kid. I knew most families who lived near Lake of the Woods had one or more members who contributed fresh fish to their family's diet. I hadn't then understood its origins in Ojibway culture or the history of the local commercial fishing industry. But it began to dawn on me the extent to which ice fishing today provided a winter tourism industry on Lake of the Woods.

A year later, in the National Museum of the American Indian in Washington, DC, I would see an old Bombardier in the center of a historical diorama on ice fishing. That one looked like a World War I relic. Seeing it there made it seem as though this way of life were a thing of the past. Yet, Izzy Marvin had one to rent during ice fishing season.

Once again, I was reminded: the past is present.

Waiting at the front doors of the Warroad Heritage Center as soon as it opened the next afternoon, I stopped again to admire the beadwork in the glass case. I noticed a three-ring binder next to it filled with genealogical records of Warroad's three original families, going back to 1790. Furiously taking notes and creating a kinship tree, I spent two hours in silent concentration.

Kakaygeesick's father was Chief Ay Ash Wash (1790–1891). Kakaygeesick had two children, John and Mary. His daughter, Mary, married John Angus and had two sons. His son, John, married Verna, and they'd had one son, Robert. Robert married Florence, and they'd had nine children.

When I stood up to stretch, I noticed Beth Marvin in the back office. I knocked on the open door and asked whether I could pester her again with questions.

"Where have you been?" she asked.

"Out there on the floor." I pointed to the gallery. "I found the three-ring binder."

"C'mon," she said, rising from her seat. "I hope you don't mind, but I've called Don Kakaygeesick, and he's invited us out to interview him. Let's go!"

From copying the family tree, I knew Donald was one of the nine children of Kakaygeesick's grandson Robert. I had noticed his birth date was only eleven months after mine, so I recognized his name.

"Really? Great!" I hadn't anticipated her generous and immediate help in making introductions to the family, and I was thrilled with the opportunity to interview Kakaygeesick's great-grandson. On the other hand, I felt I didn't know enough yet to ask good questions—and having spent decades doing research and conducting interviews as a journalist, I didn't like going in unprepared. I wasn't certain how to phrase the questions I wanted to ask him.

But I wasn't going to pass up this opportunity, either—so I followed Beth to her car.

"Get in," Beth said to me as she swung into the driver's seat.

When I climbed in, I noticed the fine dust on the dashboard. Sand crystals from the prehistoric beaches of Lake Agassiz. On this hot summer afternoon, the dust had settled in the sun. Under glass inside a closed car, it smelled faintly like fish.

I buckled my seat belt and tried to imagine what Don Kakaygeesick would think when we showed up at his home. Who was I, asking him to give an account for Red Lake taking his land?

As I wondered this, Beth sped east on Route 11.

A few miles out of town, we turned right into Brewster's Trailer Park. Beth wasn't sure which one of the eight trailers belonged to Don and his family. She pulled over to a single-wide near the back of the park with a Nissan pickup in front. The hood was up.

The screen door of the trailer opened, and Don Kakaygeesick walked down the front steps and waved at Beth. The door opened again and out came a young girl, dressed in shorts and a tank top. She met my gaze and held it.

I stared back.

She stood with legs spread and her arms across her chest. She didn't smile, and I could almost hear her wondering what I wanted.

"I'm Jill," I said. "What's your name?"

"I'm Delainey." She escorted me up the ramp to the front door of the trailer home. "You can call me Bug. Grandpa does." She kept turning back to look at me as I followed her inside. She walked through the screen door, and I stepped close behind.

Bug took my hand and escorted me to the couch. Beth and I sat down. Don's mother, Florence Kakaygeesick, sat on the loveseat with her daughter, Karen, next to her. Don pulled a kitchen chair over to sit on. Bug stood next to him.

"How old are you, Bug?" I asked her.

She turned her face away from me and looked at Don.

"She's nine," Don said.

Ever since I was her age, I loved sending and receiving postcards. "Will you be my pen pal, Bug?" I asked.

She looked at me suspiciously.

"Do you know what a pen pal is?" Don asked her. She held his gaze silently. "They write each other."

Delainey pushed her head into her grandfather's torso and hid her face from me.

"I'll send you postcards from my travels," I said. "I've come from New York, and I'm going to drive across states where I'll drop you a card in the mail, okay?" I turned to Don. "Would that be okay? Can I have her address?"

"It's a post box number in Red Lake," he said. "I'll email it to you."

With that, he pulled the folding chair closer to the coffee table in front of the couch and began telling me about why they were no longer living on Muskeg Bay.

Bug listened intensely, making herself a silent witness to her grandfather's testimony.

"How did Red Lake get your land?" I asked, my words heavy with indignation.

"That's a good question. We're still trying to figure that out." Don smiled. His granddaughter stood next to him. "Right, Bug?" He wrapped his arm around her shoulder and pulled her close. She hid her face in his armpit.

I pulled out my composition book and pen. Florence Kakaygeesick gave me a sideways glance.

"Do you mind if I make some notes?" I asked her.

She tilted her face toward Don.

"Sure," Don said. "Go ahead. Yeah. Let me show you the land deed President Teddy Roosevelt signed in 1905 for Allotment 3." He went into a back bedroom and returned with a stack of documents and a long wooden case he set on the polished coffee table in front of us.

Bug stood at the end of the sofa, a sentry to the hallway.

Don presented the deed. In cursive penmanship, the document was made out to "Ka-Kee-Ka-Kee-Sick, or Everlasting Sky," described as "an Indian of the Red Lake Reservation." Allotments were held in trust by the US government for twenty-five years, after which they could be converted to a deed with a clear title as long as the Indian resided on the land and lived in accordance with white standards.

"This is Kakaygeesick's will," Don said and passed me several more pages of paper. "September 20, 1968. It has his thumbprint."

I noticed almost immediately the will had been altered. The beneficiary changed from Robert Kakaygeesick Sr., to Mary Angus. Don could tell when I'd seen the strikethrough. I felt him watching me read it to see what I thought. But I didn't know what to think yet.

Don fascinated me with his story as he unpacked the material evidence in front of us.

He leaned over the wooden case on the table and opened it. Inside the box lined in maroon velvet, a medal lay tucked alongside a pipe. I'd never seen a Purple Heart before. Don's father had been awarded one for his valor in service at the Battle of the Bulge in World War II, though it was years before he learned he'd been awarded the medal and even more years of paperwork and bureaucracy before he actually received it in the mail. Don kept the medal inside the case.

"This is great-grandfather's pipe." Don waved his hand over the red and charcoal gray stone pipe in three pieces. He picked up the long pipestem. "His father, Chief Ay Ash Wash smoked this pipe during negotiations of Treaty Number 3 in October of 1873."

Later, I would read more about this land treaty between Queen Victoria and the Anishinaabe signed at the Northwest Angle on Lake of the Woods. It ceded vast tracts of land to Canada because the Crown wanted to build a transcontinental railroad.

"The red stone is from the pipestone quarry in southern Minnesota, and the black is found only at Buffalo Point," Don said. Buffalo Point is located across the Canadian border in Manitoba, on First Nation land, about a twenty-minute drive from Warroad.

Don fit the second piece, the bowl for the kinnikinnick, onto the long stone. He put the mouthpiece in the other end.

"What do you use for tobacco?" I asked as he handed the ceremonial pipe to me. It was nearly a foot and a half long, and its weight surprised me.

"We gather and dry different bark, herbs," he explained. "You can use tobacco, too."

I took a sniff of the pipe bowl and closed my eyes. When I opened them, Bug stood directly in front of me.

I smiled. She stepped back.

"Grandfather John traded this pipe with a Warroad businessman without his father knowing about it," Don said. "A tourist named Pat Howery bought it in 1940, and he died in 1986. His son inherited it, and he died in 2007. His brother, John, wanted to return this sacred object to its rightful owners. He's out in Oregon. He found me on Facebook."

"I did not know you had gotten the pipe back," Beth whispered.

I handed her the pipe to hold, and as I did Don's words sank in fully. "Wait. He found you on Facebook?"

He nodded. "John found the image of great-grandfather's peace pipe on a postcard I had put on the page for Kakaygeesick Bay. That's how he first connected with me."

"That's amazing. How long ago did this happen?" I asked.

"In the spring of 2010 he shipped it to me." He gestured to the pipe. "This pipe is a symbol of leadership in the Duck Clan. It belongs with our family and is part of our history."

Beth held the pipe, and her arm wavered with its weight. "Don, can we make a copy of these documents and get some pictures taken of the pipe for the Heritage Center? Maybe bring this into the museum for us to see?"

“Oh yeah, sure, Beth,” he said. “Happy to.”

“I’ve got my phone with me,” I said. “Can I take a few pictures now?”

“Ah, well, yeah, I suppose,” Don said.

Noting his ambivalence, I reassured him. “I won’t share these pictures; I just don’t want to forget the image of this pipe. I want to take photos of the deed and will, too—for research purposes.” I picked up my cell phone. “This is such a great story about getting your pipe back, and maybe I could write something to get published. I would talk to you first, and then we’d want to get professional photographs taken.”

“It’s a sacred object, Jill,” he said. There was a long pause.

In that moment I realized he cared less about the fact that Facebook had played a part in the pipe’s recovery and much more about the fact that the pipe—a piece of living history—had come home.

“You can take a few pictures,” he said, with some hesitation. “To help you remember.”

The fan blew hot air out the window in the living room, but it was still sweltering. Sweat ran down my nose when I leaned over to snap the picture.

I took photographs of the documents and the pipe on the coffee table to study it more closely under magnification. I resisted the temptation to take pictures of Florence, his mother, aware of how intrusive that would be. As I put my phone away, I noticed the clock on the wall said five thirty. The museum closed at five.

“Beth and I should get going, but I’d like to talk with you more about your family history and what happened with the will,” I said.

“Yes, that would be nice,” Don said.

I felt hot anger rise up in my throat thinking about how this altered will had been used to somehow swindle them out of their land. I didn't think much about why I was so angry that an injustice had been done, but I did observe the fact that Don did not look angry. Instead, he seemed calm and happy to have the pipe and the documents in his possession. He stood up to move his chair back into the kitchen. Bug escorted Beth and me out the door and waved goodbye.

The air had to be ten degrees cooler outside than in their trailer. Beth kept the windows of the sedan rolled down and let the breeze from the lake roll with us as we headed back into town.

I had a lot to think about. And it was hot. I wanted to get out on the lake, so I went to Doc's Harbor Inn, a bed and breakfast run by Janet Marvin, one of Beth's daughters, on the south shore of the Warroad River. In winter, they rented ice skates, snowshoes, and cross-country skis; in summer, canoes, kayaks, and paddleboards. I rented a pedal boat.

It was easy pedaling up the Warroad River toward the mouth of Lake of the Woods. I covered a couple of miles in twenty minutes and still didn't get close to the new construction of the casino.

The altered will had me confused, but the physical exertion and a light breeze helped me think. Who had changed the name of the beneficiary from Kakaygeesick's son to his daughter? And why? When was the will altered? And how would that have made it possible for Red Lake Reservation to take possession of the property to build a casino when Don held the allotment papers issued to his great-grandfather by the US government? Was this any of my business, to go butting in on his family matters? It wasn't my property. I wasn't Indian. I didn't live in Warroad.

I wasn't sure whether I was angry because it was unfair for Indians to evict other Indians from their land, because my maternal great-grandparents had homesteaded on Indian land, or because Mom had died. And Sam.

Enormous birds of prey, perhaps golden eagles, soared on the rising gusts of wind coming from the northwest. Thunderbirds. According to Ojibway legend, they are a symbol of power, protection, and strength; the beating of their wings causes thunder and stirs the wind, and lightning shoots from their eyes. I turned to follow their figures in the sky and saw a storm coming in. Turning the boat around, I started pedaling fast upstream against the current. My knees kept spinning, yet the boat drifted farther in the opposite direction. The rest of the sky was blue, while a rolling mass of dark gray clouds followed the Warroad River, headed directly for me.

Thunder boomed. I felt rain droplets falling—at first, gently. I knew it was dangerous being out on the water, and I wasn't getting anywhere.

A small fishing boat with an outboard motor raced toward me. As it drew closer I saw Janet at the steering wheel.

"See that dock?" she shouted. She pointed to a platform in the water in front of a palatial home with a private river view. "Tie the pedal boat there and wait. I'll turn around and be right back for you."

I did as she told me. As I grabbed the pole alongside the dock, the rain started coming down hard and fast. I crawled out of the pedal boat and tied it securely. Already dripping wet, I looked up at the new three-story brick home overlooking the confluence of the river and lake. I looked back and saw the new Seven Clans Casino under construction across the bay, where the thunderbirds swirled on the curls of the oncoming clouds.

Janet pulled up, and I jumped on board. In less than two minutes, we were pulling up at Doc's Harbor.

When I tried to get out of the boat onto the dock, I accidentally pushed the boat away and fell in shallow water with my cell phone in my pocket. My phone with which I'd taken the photographs of the pipe, the deed, and the will—dammit!

I stood up sputtering and walked onto the shore, sopping wet. Janet extended a hand, and I grabbed hold of it as she pulled me up onto the lawn in the downpour. We ran for the canopy cover of trees.

Beth stood on the covered porch. "Are you all right?" she called to me.

I nodded, laughing. "What a klutz I am."

She and Janet laughed with me.

"What about the pedal boat?" I asked Janet.

"Don't worry. That's my brother's house. Another one of us Marvins." She smiled. "I'll get it tomorrow."

The next morning, I drove to the public beach and walked along the shore. Looking at the cranes and trucks moving on the southern shore, I thought about what it meant to Don Kakaygeesick and his family to lose their land. I got back in the car and cruised past the trading post through the public campgrounds at the beach. In the same moment I turned my thoughts to Bug, she appeared before me on her bike in the street. I rolled my window all the way down and waved.

"Hi, Jill," she said. Both hands remained on her handlebars. She had the same calm and happy demeanor of her grandfather.

"Hi, Bug," I replied, and continued on my way to Caribou Coffee.

While eating a bowl of oatmeal with blueberries, I thought about how much Bug on her bike reminded me of myself at that age riding down Memorial Drive Parkway on my Schwinn, alone and free.

When I opened my laptop in the library and logged into Facebook, there was a message from Don. He wanted me to visit again to tell me more of their history. I was glad because I wanted to take a closer look at that altered will.

I told him I'd dropped my phone in the river and would need to drive over to Thief River Falls to get it fixed or replaced. I arranged to meet him the next day. The hour-and-a-half drive from Warroad gave me time to think. I kept my notebook open on the seat next to me and jotted down notes with my right hand while my left hand never left the steering wheel and my eyes never left the road. I knew I'd be the only one to decipher my notes, but the drive gave me the headspace to start thinking of questions to ask.

On my drive back from Thief River Falls with a new phone, I stopped to visit with Aunt Audrey. She and Mom had spent a lot of time, a lot of years, researching their family tree. Mom wasn't here to give me a tutorial on Ancestry.com, so I talked to my aunt about doing genealogical research. I learned there are separate databases to research lineage and kinship for American Indians. And some of the family records might be in Canada and not online. It might be more complicated than I thought to simply corroborate birth and death dates and establish the Kakaygeesick family tree.

That evening Shireen and her husband drove the thirty miles from their farm to go with me and Aunt Audrey to Arnesen's Rocky Point Lodge for supper.

The Arnesen family had lived and worked at Rocky Point on

Lake of the Woods since 1897. Originally, they fished with sail-powered boats and nets to catch sturgeon for the caviar trade, but then switched to walleye, first as a commercial fishery and then a sportsman's lodge. In winter, the lodge became the world's largest ice fishing operation. In summer, it was hands down the best restaurant for fresh walleye.

On the way to Arnesen's, we went past the old Kling farm.

"Pull over here," Aunt Audrey instructed. She pointed out Mount Carmel Lutheran Church on the right. "And that's where we went to school." The faded red one-room schoolhouse stood across the road from the church.

As we walked from the church parking lot to the school, a childhood summer memory of this place floated to the surface: playing with Mom in her old schoolyard as she ran alongside the metal merry-go-round while Barb and I hung on to the rusty handlebars laughing and spinning until we were dizzy.

"What a shame," Audrey said, when she saw tree saplings growing up against the foundation and shredded curtains hanging in the windows. "Somebody mowed the lawn, at least."

"What did they use the building for after the school closed?" I asked.

"Your grandpa attended Farmers Union meetings there. I don't know after that."

We looked in the schoolhouse windows and then crossed the road to the church and walked out to the cemetery and found the graves of my maternal grandparents.

I thought about how much younger Mom had been when her mother died than I was when Mom died. I remember how mad she got when I said her humming reminded me of Grandma Kling because she knew I knew how her mother's humming got on her nerves. She didn't want to become like her mother. And now I feared the many ways in which I had already become like my mother, right down to smoking menthol cigarettes.

What I feared most was becoming depressed and anxious. Thinking back over Mom's life, I could barely remember when she wasn't sad or suffering from low self-esteem. Grieving Sam, the love of my life, had made me feel like that sometimes. It seemed I had only just begun to pull myself out of a long dark mourning period of five years when Mom's health began to deteriorate.

As an adult I'd lived out of state, rarely visited, and kept in touch with Mom primarily by phone and email, but even from a distance I knew she experienced depression. Many of my best memories of her happy were when we were all together with her sister's family in Warroad when I was a child.

CHAPTER 6

I drove out to Don's trailer the next day. Bug greeted me at the screen door with a smile. Don's mother, Florence, and his sister, Karen, sat on the loveseat again, and Bug sat next to me on the couch. Don pulled up a chair from the kitchen. On the coffee table sat a large conch shell with a bundle of white sage.

Lighting the sage with a stick match, Don watched white smoke drift through the still air. First, he smudged himself, letting the fumes float over and through him. He held the sage over the conch shell to catch the ash and moved his arms toward and away from his torso, circulating the tendrils of smoke through the room in all four directions. He moved toward me. I smelled the sage and felt the smoke touch my hair and skin. He extended his arm in my direction, waving it left and right, up and down; the smoke wrapped its curls around me. As the scent met my nostrils, I felt calmed by its cleansing fragrance.

"Where do you get your sage?" I asked. I knew smudging to be a spiritual purification ritual. I'd bought my own smudge stick at Greenstar Food Co-op years ago and occasionally used it as an air freshener.

"My sister and I pick it," Don said. "Though you can't find it around here anymore. We drive down to Mille Lacs."

"You harvest it yourself?"

"Yes," he said. "There are many medicinal plants to forage, and white sage is one. We've been stopped many times by police or state troopers who assume we are after pot. We pick a lot of different plants for ceremonial and spiritual purposes. Pot is not one of them."

"How did you learn about these sacred plants? Who taught you?" I had so many questions.

"Kakaygeesick, my great-grandfather. And my father. Grandma, too. Also, my mother. They say Kakaygeesick was a medicine man, but not a man who healed sick people like a doctor. He belonged to the Midewin Society, and that's more a spiritual thing. Like our church."

"A secret society, right?"

"Secret in that it's sacred." Don looked at me like Bug looked at me: expressionless except for his eyes, which were open and curious. I could detect no anger, no tension or irritation.

"There are levels to the Midewin. At the most basic level, everyone learns about the plants and animals as part of the spirit world. It gets a lot more complicated after that." Don explained there are levels of apprenticeship as with karate or a hierarchy as in Catholicism, with its priests, bishops, and popes. "Kakaygeesick was a Grand Midewin. A spiritual leader to our people."

At this time I knew next to nothing about "the Way of the Heart," the spiritual beliefs and practices of Ojibway people, but in the years to come I would learn the Midewin Society is based on the Seven Fires Prophecy. The prophecy marks seven epochs in the life of the people of Turtle Island, the North American continent. The seventh fire is about the future, when the world and waters have turned bitter from disrespect and the people must choose between two paths. Spirituality leads to survival. Materialism brings suffering and death.

Don pulled out his files full of white paper: documents, legal depositions, and court decisions. He let me take photographs again of the altered will, the deed, the pipe. He began with the history of his great-grandfather's pipe, which had belonged to his father, the chief.

Chief Ay Ash Wash attended negotiations held in 1873 in the place now known as the Northwest Angle. This was when he signed Treaty 3, which ceded a tract of Ojibway territory north and west of Lake of the Woods to Queen Victoria. He brought the long black-and-red ceremonial pipe on the coffee table in front of me to the negotiations.

When the border between the United States and Canada was first established along the forty-ninth parallel west of the Mississippi in the 1783 Treaty of Paris, the source of the mighty river had not yet been identified near Itasca, Minnesota. Instead, Europeans erroneously assumed the Mississippi started from Lake of the Woods, more than 150 miles north. The treaty stated the boundary between US territory and British land to the north would run "through the Lake of the Woods to the northwesternmost point thereof, and from thence on a due west course to the river Mississippi. . . ." But these lands were not officially surveyed or marked when the border was first established. Back then, the simple task of drawing a straight line across the map sufficed.

When the remote territory was finally surveyed in 1824, corrections to the maps had to be made. The new survey created the Northwest Angle, which is the only place in the contiguous United States that is north of the forty-ninth parallel. This piece of land is also separated from the rest of the continental United States by Lake of the Woods. When you look at an outline of the state of Minnesota, the Northwest Angle is represented by the funny-looking chimney shape at the top of the map. Most of that irregular shape is water with a small patch of land across the northwest shore.

"When they created their border between Canada and the US, they took a knife and split me in two," Chief Ay Ash Wash told his son Kakaygeesick, who told this story to his grandson and great-grandchildren. The chief had pretended to stab a hunting knife into his heart and slash it down his torso ripping him in half.

This is how Don explained to me the rift created by the border which cut across Lake of the Woods. Both Canada and the United States denied his ancestors official recognition. The family of his great-grandfather's brother, Animikeese, remained on the Canadian side of the border. Kakaygeesick and his brother Naymaypoke and their family members were in Minnesota. The Kah-bay-kah-nong found ways across the water to continue summering on Buffalo Point in Manitoba and wintering on Muskeg Bay on the US side of the border.

Grain mills, lumber yards, and railroads brought the Industrial Revolution to Roseau County. Warroad continued to expand into a city. In 1905, when the federal government issued him an allotment south of the river across from the new bustling downtown, Kakaygeesick continued to walk his trapline, fish, and harvest wild rice as he had done for many years. In the winter, the townsfolk watched where he walked to know when it was safe enough to cross the river on the ice.

"I have strong memories of my great-grandfather when he was alive," Don told me as he held the sacred pipe. Don now brings the pipe every year to Treaty 3 Council meetings in Manitoba, where he represents his clan.

"I have strong memories of meeting your great-grandfather in the summer of 1968," I told Don. He told me more of his memories of his great-grandfather and how he visited him in his dreams.

Bug leaned against the back cushion of the couch. She folded her hands in her lap. She listened, too. It did not escape me in that moment that I met Kakaygeesick when I was about her age.

CHAPTER 7

Sifting through the history, treaties, and legal records from my home in upstate New York, my mind churned over the things I found in my research and the things Don told me. Months and months of research without getting any closer to an understanding of how this could have happened. It felt a lot like when my legs were spinning the pedal boat against strong winds and the river current into a rainstorm.

Had Kakaygeesick prophesied his family's dispossession from his land? I found the *Warroad Pioneer*, the local weekly newspaper, had published a letter to the editor on July 11, 1962, attributed to Kakaygeesick:

> *I want to ask you good people of Warroad to help me out. From what I understand they are going to take my home and land. I have a daughter and 10 grandchildren living on my land, and as you all know I am not young anymore and I know my time is short but it would make me very happy to know that I could leave that place to my own family instead of someone else take it. I have been a good citizen in this town all my life and so far the people of Warroad have always been good to me so I am asking you people to help me out so they will not take my land away from me. Thank you.*

Since Kakaygeesick did not read or write English, it is likely he dictated this to his grandson, George Angus, who submitted it to the newspaper. But it's clear evidence that he was worried his family would be left homeless when he died, and wanted to make sure the Bureau of Indian Affairs (BIA) at Red Lake Reservation did not remove his family. During most of Kakaygeesick's lifetime, the BIA couldn't be trusted to enforce treaties, respect deeds, protect sovereignty or hunting and water rights, manage records, or handle money. The BIA was run mostly by white bureaucrats, and Kakaygeesick worried they'd find a way to take his land.

That he'd written this letter six months before he was admitted into the hospital in January 1963, I found an interesting coincidence. I pieced together from interviews and local historical records what happened next. His daughter-in-law, Verna, had grown alarmed by his racking cough and weakened condition; she feared his advanced age meant he might not make it through another winter. Together, she and Mary, Kakaygeesick's daughter, convinced Don's dad, Robert Sr., to take his grandfather to the hospital and see Dr. Homer Ross.

Dr. Ross admitted Kakaygeesick into the Warroad Hospital early in January. His slow recovery from pneumonia was worrisome. Doc didn't want to release him and have him return to his wigwam during this long cold winter. Kakaygeesick was a local celebrity and claimed as a friend by many in the white community. He'd appeared in the Polaris catalog sitting on a snowmobile, posed for the cover of the *Minnesota Conservation Magazine*, and been immortalized on tourist postcards. For years he'd been the grand marshal of the Fourth of July parade, marching down the street in his full regalia. He was a living legend. Doc wouldn't let him go back out in the cold, so he transferred Kakaygeesick to the nursing home, a separate wing in the hospital building.

Kakaygeesick's family visited frequently. When great-grandson Donald was four years old, he sat on Kakaygeesick's lap in his room at the nursing home. Don showed me a Kodak snapshot of the occasion, dated June 1963. In it, Kakaygeesick is passing Don a wooden baton painted red. The old man told his grandson, Robert Sr., that his boy wouldn't understand what it meant now, but he would when he grew up to be a man: the passing of the Crimson Rod, Duck Clan history, and Midewin leadership would go to his great-grandson, Don.

The fact that Don Kakaygeesick was my age—less than a year younger—made me feel connected to Mom's hometown and my family history. Looking at that Kodak snapshot, the closeness between Don and his great-grandfather at this age reminded me of sitting on Grandpa Swenson's lap. But as Don continued to tell me his story, the similarities in our parallel lives seemed to end there.

Don's father, Robert Kakaygeesick Sr., returned from World War II to Warroad after surviving the Battle of the Bulge in 1945. Once home, he married Florence Cobiness. Don's eldest brother, Robert Jr., was born in 1948. Another brother, John, was born in 1951.

During the years after World War II, Don's parents worked seasonally at Red Lake timber mill at the Northwest Angle. Robert Sr. worked as a lumberjack, and Florence cooked for the camp.

They had seven more children, born in just eight years. Karen was born in 1956, Randy in 1958, Donald in 1959, and Stanley in 1960. Randy lived only sixteen months, and Stanley only four. Before his first birthday, Don had lost two brothers to pneumonia during a bitter cold winter. His sister, Martha, was born in 1961. Then came two more boys: Kenny in 1962 and Kelly in 1963.

The smell of melting snow tickled Don Kakaygeesick's nose as he looked out the open window of his second-grade classroom. The April sunshine had turned the playground to mud. Don's classroom was brand-new in 1967. Warroad Public School had added a third addition to the three-story brick schoolhouse, because enrollment had grown to almost seven hundred students. About thirty of them were Ojibway. The cinder block walls were painted bright white, and the chalkboard was green instead of black. Every morning, elder Tom Lightning passed by in his canoe on the Warroad River. As he floated by, he waved to the children on their way up the path to the front doors of the schoolhouse and called out the Ojibway greeting, "Boozhoo, Boozhoo."

In the middle of that April afternoon, Don heard his name called over the intercom, instructing him to come to the elementary school principal's office. There he saw his siblings: Martha, Karen, Kenny, and Kelly. They were told they would be going for a ride and nothing more. His parents, Robert Sr. and Florence, who were working at the Northwest Angle, were *not* notified.

A woman from the Roseau County Welfare Office put the five youngest Kakaygeesick children in her car and drove west on Highway 11. "There's not a single family in the county who can take all five of you," she said. "It is up to you to decide how to divide yourself between two foster families."

Karen, only ten years old at the time, was the eldest of the five children in the car. She doesn't remember it quite the same as Don, but what he told me is that she decided the two youngest brothers, Kenny, age five, and Kelly, age four, should stay together. They were left with the Eftas, a family living on a farm not far from Greenbush, about forty-five miles west of Warroad. The welfare lady then drove north of Greenbush and left Karen, Don, and Martha in foster care with the Kalinowski family.

They later learned their older brother, John, age sixteen, had also been called out of his high school classroom and sent to Badger, Minnesota, to live with a foster family. John returned to Warroad. He walked the thirty-five miles.

"I never ran away," he told me. "I walked away."

Their eldest brother, Robert Jr., had already left Warroad for college. Their mother, Florence, and her mother, Grandma Rose, had saved money for his tuition and sent him off to Wisconsin in a new suit. Robert wasn't too sure he wanted to go. "I just got out of school," he told Don. "I didn't know that I wanted any more of that." But he did go, and by the time his siblings were taken from Warroad Public School, he was already enrolled in his second semester of his freshman year.

Don repeated second grade at school in Greenbush. He and his sisters caught the school bus on the county road. Closer to town, the bus would pick up their younger brothers, Kenny and Kelly.

I asked one of Don's Greenbush elementary school classmates, Aliza Olson, if she remembered Don from grade school. "Yes, he would eat an entire apple. The whole thing! Core and seeds and all. We *all* thought that was strange." She said the other children didn't play with the Kakaygeesick children or interact with them. "They kept to themselves."

When Kakaygeesick passed four-year-old Don the Crimson Rod in 1963, the family was worried the old man would die soon. Four years later, he remained in residence at the nursing home and missed his great-grandchildren's visits.

Prior to admission to the hospital, Kakaygeesick had left home only once, in 1909, at age sixty-five, and it was not of his own volition. Edward T. Olsson and Julian Brown, concerned white citizens from Warroad, delivered Kakaygeesick on March 21, 1909, to the Roseau County courthouse, where they testified that Kakaygeesick had withdrawn and refused to see anyone during the previous two weeks. At 2:40 a.m., Judge Mike Holm committed Kakaygeesick to the Fergus Falls State Mental Hospital. There he was treated for "tremors" and "chronic intoxication" and made a quick recovery.

Clinical notes in his medical file found in the Gale Library at the Minnesota History Center reflect that Kakaygeesick was suffering from grief at the time. His first wife had died in 1891. Tuberculosis had taken his second wife, his eighteen-year-old daughter by his first wife, and several grandchildren by 1909.

His medical records from the 1960s also show he suffered from hardening of the arteries and peptic ulcers. He would *not* die from "hereditary alcoholism," as diagnosed on his admission to Fergus Falls sixty-some years earlier.

Six weeks after his admission, on May 9, 1909, the State Mental Hospital released Kakaygeesick with nothing more than a paper bag lunch. At age sixty-five, he walked the two hundred miles from Fergus Falls back to Warroad. His cure and safe return warranted a notice in the *Warroad Pioneer*. He never left his ancestral homeland again until his admission to the hospital in 1963, more than fifty years later.

In 1967, his great-grandchildren were taken into foster care and stopped coming to visit him. The only things Kakaygeesick had left were his medicine bag, his language, and his name on the deed to Allotment 3.

CHAPTER 8

When the nights began to chill in August 1968, Kakaygeesick knew his end approached. His nurse, Virginia, knew it, too, as she had taken care of him the past few years. By the end of August, she spoon-fed Kakaygeesick, his arms too weak to raise a fork to his mouth. He grew smaller. His days grew quieter.

On Saturday, September 20, 1968, Willard Leaf, a full-blooded Swede with the Bureau of Indian Affairs, drove up to Warroad from Bemidji with his wife, making their first stop on a two-week holiday, as I learned from reading the documents Don copied for me. Ronald Beaulieu, from Red Lake Realty Office, had called Friday to say he needed Willard Leaf to come up and notarize Kakaygeesick's will, according to his court deposition. Ron Beaulieu said he'd been notified the old man was getting ready to die. Beaulieu filled in the standard form. He typed in the name of Robert Kakaygeesick Sr. on the line as sole heir of the estate. Robert Sr., Don's father, was the grandson of Kakaygeesick and the only son of John Kakaygeesick.

Reviewing various accounts from legal depositions and interviews, I pieced together a coherent chronology of how Kakaygeesick's will came to be altered. When he arrived that Saturday afternoon, Willard Leaf met George Angus, George Kelly, and Ron Beaulieu in the lobby of the Warroad Nursing Home. George Angus was

Kakaygeesick's grandson by his daughter Mary. George Kelly, a twenty-year-old Red Lake forestry aide, came as a witness.

Ron Beaulieu had told Willard Leaf on the phone that Robert Kakaygeesick Sr. had called to request a will be prepared for his grandfather. But Robert was not in Warroad on September 20. He was at the Northwest Angle. And there was no telephone at camp.

Before they entered Kakaygeesick's room, George Angus told Mr. Leaf that his grandfather wanted the land to go to his daughter, Mary Angus, George's mother.

"What? I need someone to translate for me who isn't a relative." Leaf looked at George Kelly. "Can you?"

Kelly cast down his eyes. "No, sir."

"Ron, can you converse with Kakaygeesick?" Leaf asked.

Beaulieu looked at his feet. He couldn't. Even though he was a tribal member of Red Lake Nation, he couldn't understand the dialect of the Ojibway language that Kakaygeesick spoke. The language barrier was likely due to several factors. First, Kakaygeesick learned his language before the Civil War, and it had changed a good deal in the past hundred years. Second, the dialect used in the far north of Minnesota, and in Manitoba and Ontario, is different from that used a hundred miles south by residents of Red Lake Reservation. And third, they had been discouraged from using their language for so long that most people on Red Lake Reservation no longer spoke it fluently or considered it their first language.

George Angus suggested Maggie Lightning Aas translate. He noticed she had been sitting in the lobby when they came in. An elder and close friend to Mary Angus and her sister-in-law Verna Kakaygeesick, Maggie knew everyone in the Warroad Ojibway community. She agreed to translate and accompanied Willard, Ron, and the two Georges into Kakaygeesick's already crowded room.

Mary, Verna, and his nurse Virginia made space for the men and Maggie. Ron stood near the head of the hospital bed and pulled out the will he'd prepared from the inside pocket of his jacket.

"How much money did you make last year, Chief?" Willard Leaf loudly spoke at Kakaygeesick from the foot of the bed.

He didn't wait for a translation. Kakaygeesick held up two fingers and grunted at Leaf. Kakaygeesick thought Leaf was there to settle up for flood damage. When Canadians had constructed the Rollerway Dam in 1887 and the Norman Dam in 1894 on the north end of Lake of the Woods for hydroelectric power to serve the city of Kenora, Ontario, floods eliminated thousands of acres of wild rice habitat along the former shorelines. Of the original 102 acres listed on the deed for Allotment 3, floods had taken 96 acres. Kakaygeesick had joined the reservation's claim against the Canadian government for reparations.

"Two hundred dollars sounds right." Ron grinned.

"Nuh. Nuh," Kakaygeesick shook his head. He held up two fingers and shook them at Leaf.

"Sound mind, all right," George Kelly said.

"Two thousand," Maggie said. "Not what he made. That's not what he said. Two thousand is what he wants from you." Kakaygeesick wanted payment for flood damages.

"Do you want your land to go to your daughter?" Leaf asked Kakaygeesick.

Maggie Aas asked his question. Kakaygeesick spoke.

"He says he has only one surviving daughter, Mary," Maggie said.

"He wants my mother to be able to stay on this land," George Angus said.

"Is this your daughter, Mary Angus, who you want the land to go to?" Willard pointed his finger at the elderly Mrs. Angus.

Maggie translated, and Kakaygeesick pointed his chin toward his daughter.

To the right of Willard Leaf stood George Kelly, who opened an ink pad and pulled Kakaygeesick's right thumb toward him, then placed the pad of the thumb into the wet ink sponge. Leaf pushed the thumb onto the paper document. Maggie, George Kelly, and Ron Beaulieu signed as witnesses to the will, which deeded Allotment 3 to Robert Kakaygeesick Sr. As soon as the ink dried, Willard Leaf put the document in the envelope and tucked it in his briefcase and left town.

When Willard Leaf returned from his two-week vacation, he went straight to the Bemidji office, where he crossed out Robert Kakaygeesick Sr.'s name with typewritten X marks, according to his deposition statement. "Mary K. Angus" replaced Robert's name on the line above. Leaf put his initials, "W. L.," next to the change in the altered document. He approved the will with his stamp and postmarked it on October 8. He wrote an annotation in his file notes dated September 20 that Kakaygeesick wanted his only surviving daughter to gain title to the deed of Allotment 3.

Leaf sent the altered will off in the mail from Bemidji. The next day, October 9, the gift deed was approved in Minneapolis by the Bureau of Indian Affairs. It is possible the BIA used airmail in 1968. That is one explanation for how quickly it arrived and passed through two BIA offices known for delays and bureaucratic mismanagement and was rushed to be recorded with the Department of Interior in Portland, Oregon; the BIA stamped its receipt and approval on October 11, 1968. On October 17, Willard Leaf wrote Kakaygeesick a letter advising him the "transaction is complete and the land is now held in trust for your daughter." It is unknown whether that letter was received, though a carbon copy exists on file.

November 1968 brought heavy snows. The river froze on Thanksgiving. Days later, so did the lake.

"It's time for me to go," Kakaygeesick told Mary, Verna, and his nurse, Virginia, on December 2. They knew it, too. There wasn't much to do but wait with him for his spirit to take its four-day journey to Gaagige Minawaanigoziwining, the Land of Everlasting Happiness. When she came back the next day, Virginia found Mary and George, Robert and Florence, standing silently in Kakaygeesick's room. Slow and low she could hear Kakaygeesick chanting. His eyes were closed; he breathed in while he chanted. He breathed out while he chanted. Then there was silence for a long while before he would start again.

That second night, Virginia brought a tape recorder into Kakaygeesick's room. His eyes opened in the dark, pupils dilated. His voice grew stronger, and he chanted. Telling the stories not to be forgotten in a language no one else spoke. Then he sang and chanted a while longer. When the chanting stopped, he spoke clearly in strong declarative statements, though she could hear the weakness in his voice. Then silence. Virginia fell asleep in her chair only when she heard him chanting again. She did not leave his side.

Hour after hour. After three days and three nights, he was gone before dawn.

Don still had a copy of the tape Virginia gave the family after his great-grandfather's death, and he was able to send me the audio file. The sound quality was poor, full of static, but the barely audible low chanting of a dying man haunted me. I listened to the recording several times, and although I had no comprehension of the words he spoke, I noticed no struggle, no anger—only a meditation and calming recitation of his truth. Deep within his chest, the chanting sounded like a moaning, a lamentation, prayer. Kakaygeesick's voice split into two tones, one so low in the bass I felt it more than heard it under his soft baritone voice.

When I closed my eyes, I was pulled back to that moment when I met him.

When Dr. Homer Ross signed the certificate of death for Kakaygeesick at 3:50 a.m. on December 6, 1968, he didn't call Tom Thunder to come for the body and prepare it for a traditional Indian burial, as he had done so many times before for other Indian patients. Instead, he waited until 8 a.m. to call Roger Helgeson in Roseau at Helgeson Funeral Home. Then he called Rev. Lindholm, the Lutheran minister. The community would come together for a Christian memorial service for Kakaygeesick.

Nine-year-old Don was in the barn when he heard the news on the radio. Mucking the stalls, he listened to the radio at dawn doing chores. At first he wasn't sure he'd heard his great-grandfather's name. When the radio announcer said it again, then he felt certain. And sad.

While they were eating breakfast, a sedan arrived in the farm driveway. The welfare lady and a man in a suit stepped out and spoke to Helen Kalinowski about the children. Helen dressed them in their Sunday best and ushered them into the back seat of the vehicle. They drove them to Warroad.

The car pulled up in front of the school and stopped. The back doors flung open. Karen, Martha, and Don ran inside to find family. Kenny and Kelly were already there, as was their older brother John, who'd come from Badger. Robert Jr. arrived in the suit he was wearing when Grandma Rosie had sent him off to the university. The kids reunited with their parents, Robert and Florence, outside the high school auditorium.

Businesses in town had closed for the funeral on December 10, 1968. People from hundreds of miles around showed up for the service. The double doors to the gymnasium were closed, and the school hallway filled with a crowd.

Tom Thunder stepped out of the gym into the hall and made an announcement. The family had asked for his intercession to first allow them some semblance of a traditional ceremony.

"We want to give him a good send-off," Tom Thunder said. He asked everybody to wait while the family took a few moments for a private ceremony.

Don and his siblings stood right outside the double doors, too young to participate. Karen stood facing the doors, her back to the sea of strange faces surrounding them. Don peeked through the crack between the doors. He could see his mother and father. He could see Tom Thunder and Daniel Rain Cloud and other Red Lake elders. Don watched them turn the coffin four times. Rain Cloud and Thunder chanted and kept the rhythm with a shaker—one they'd had to make on the spot using a tin can covered with cloth. They put cotton work gloves and tobacco inside his coffin. Everyone sat in a large circle and quietly joined in the ceremony. Platters of food lay on white tablecloths on the polished hardwood floors of the basketball court. Then Tom Thunder uncovered a plate of wild rice. People passed around the plate. Each dipped a couple fingers into the manoomin and raised a few grains. Someone played a water drum, the heartbeat of Mother Earth.

When the doors to the auditorium opened almost an hour later, organ music of Christian hymns filled the cavernous room, and swarms of people holding their winter coats and stomping their snowmobile boots filled the bleachers. Rev. Lindholm stepped up to the microphone under the hoop at the end of the basketball court. He tapped the mic to make sure it was switched on.

"Thank you," he greeted the room. "Thank you very much. Thank you all for coming together here today."

As the reverend began the Christian memorial service, Daniel Rain Cloud, Tom Thunder, Red Lake elders, and members of the Midewin Society sat on metallic folding chairs near the Grand Midewin's casket in the middle of the basketball court.

Don saw his great-grandfather's corpse in a white man's suit laid upon white satin. Don felt sad to see he wasn't wearing moccasins. There was no feather behind his ear.

"Welcome, ladies and gentlemen. Please rise. Let us bow our heads in prayer," Lindholm said. He paused. "Our Father, who art in heaven," he began. Many in the audience mumbled the words together like a chant. Then they sang a few hymns, after which they filed out peaceably. Pallbearers, including Dr. Ross, the mayor, two former mayors, and two local businessmen, moved the satin-padded metallic coffin to the hearse.

Under gray skies and twenty-degree temperatures, the crowd quickly dispersed into the school parking lot. Hundreds of car engines idled, and each tailpipe emitted a cloud of winter white fog.

Uncle Al had parked along Riverview Drive after he closed up the post office at noon. He'd skipped the service and instead waited for the Kakaygeesick family to arrive at the old Indian burial grounds along the river. Before the hearse arrived, he leaned against the passenger door, smoked a Winston, and remembered fishing with Kakaygeesick. Many times. Many years. Watching and listening. Never needing words.

Uncle Al once told me a story about sitting silently fishing with the old man in a small boat one night. Along the western horizon, white lights rose in the sky and hovered above eerily. They didn't say a word to each other. But Kakaygeesick pointed his chin up at the lights when Al looked at him to see if he saw them too, and what they saw in the skies out over the wide-open waters had been mystical.

The Helgeson's hearse passed Al and pulled up onto the yard. There in the middle of the snowy lawn lay a plastic carpet of faux green grass for the family to stand on for the private interment.

Al dropped his cigarette butt on the frozen ground and stepped on it with his boot. The Kakaygeesick family gathered under the great maple trees by the last bend in the river. There stood three traditional low wooden spirit houses, simple pine boxes the size of a coffin that sat above the ground. Kakaygeesick would lie next to his brother Naymaypoke.

Cars pulled up and parked on either side of Riverview Drive for several blocks. A crowd gathered around the inner circle of family.

Nine-year-old Don searched the faces of strangers around the grave site. He felt his great-grandfather nearby. He remembered the times before Kakaygeesick went into the nursing home, before he was taken into foster care. Those memories of his great-grandfather lived inside him. Powwows on the summer solstice. Harvesting wild rice in the canoes. Hearing the stories as they sat around the campfire. Marching in full regalia for the Fourth of July parades. Walking his trapline. Sometimes his great-grandfather had visited him in his dreams when he was in Greenbush on the farm.

Uncle Al squatted down next to the hole in the ground where they let the casket down. He hugged his knees and rocked gently back and forth on his heels. He tipped his hat and caught young Don's eye at his level. "He was my friend, too."

CHAPTER 9

Dad hired Andy Buckanaga to work on Saturdays to help make deliveries for the furniture store after the grand reopening of Pearson & Swenson Furniture. Mr. Buckanaga was the tallest and strongest man I'd ever met. He could lift a sofa all by himself and carry it above his head. He worked Monday through Friday as a machinist, and after working for Dad on Saturdays, he drove north to his reservation to visit his wife and children for a day and drove back Sunday night.

My little sister, Barb, brought Mr. Buckanaga to school for show-and-tell. Her teacher, Mrs. Hay, asked Barb to introduce him. Mr. Buckanaga told her classmates how he'd grown up in the northern woods of Minnesota, liked to fish for walleye, and spoke another language, Ojibway. He taught the kids to say "thank you": miigwech. When he asked if there were any questions after his short presentation, he called on one little boy who raised his hand high.

"Did you scalp anybody?" the boy asked.

"Not today," Buckanaga replied.

Dad laughed when he heard what Andy had said. Dad laughed a lot when he was around Andy. I didn't always understand what was funny, but it was good to hear Dad laugh again. The way he did before Grandpa died.

—

Mom still worked evenings as a receptionist at Iten Chevrolet, but she spent her mornings at the furniture store answering the phone and greeting customers. Dad would go to the bank or run errands while she was there. Near the back of the first-floor showroom there was a display kitchen set. The Bunn coffee maker always had a fresh pot. Customers would sit and work out a deal there. Sometimes they'd stop by just to visit.

Mrs. Wyand, an older lady who lived in the neighborhood, walked by the store on her way to take her grandson to school. Sometimes she'd stop and look in the window if there were a new display. Mom always invited her in for a cup of coffee when she saw her there. Most days Mrs. Wyand would say no. Sometimes she would come in. Months went by, and soon Mrs. Wyand stopped in almost every day. Dad said Mrs. Wyand was never going to buy anything but might as well keep our mother company.

We didn't have school on George Washington's birthday, and that meant Barb and I went along that day to the furniture store. It was the first time we met Mrs. Wyand and her grandson, Michael.

She was short, otherwise I might have mistaken her for Andy Buckanaga's mother. Her hands were crippled with arthritis. She didn't talk much, but Mom had learned her son moved from Pine Ridge to get involved with the American Indian Movement. Her son and grandson were living with her a couple blocks away. Michael sat silently at the table and sipped weak coffee with lots of sugar and powdered creamer.

Barb and I ran up the flight of stairs playing hide-and-seek and then tag. Michael didn't play with us. Barb was "it" and chased after me around the second floor. I peeled around the corner, jumped on the wooden banister, and slid down to the first floor squealing.

"Jill Dianne! Barbara Dawn! Get over here!" Mom yelled at us.

She turned to Mrs. Wyand in exasperation. “My kids are a couple of wild Indians.”

I heard her say that. And as soon as she did, I saw her regret it. Wrinkled forehead, pursed lips, she shrank into herself.

Mrs. Wyand smiled. “They’re wild all right. But they’re not Indians.” She tucked her chin.

Mom told Dad at supper how embarrassed she was to have said that. Dad told her not to worry: “Mrs. Wyand will be back for more coffee.”

Sure enough, she did come back and usually brought Michael.

At the dinner table, the Swenson family belonged to the Clean Plate Club. You ate what was served on your plate, and you were grateful for it. Whenever I wanted some choice in what I put inside my body, those starving Korean children were invoked to make me grateful for the privileges my parents granted me. Eating canned peas did not taste like privilege. Dad stabbed our forearms with his fork if he saw our elbows on the table. If he told us to do something and we didn’t immediately obey, then his voice would thunder “*NOW!*”

One night, Dad caught Barb leaning back in her kitchen chair with the two front legs lifted off the ground, and he pushed her backward.

She fell and hit her head against the wall.

“Ow!” Barb yelled.

“It hurts, don’t it,” Dad said.

“You’re the doughnut!” Barb retorted.

Dad hadn’t expected that. He laughed. But he wasn’t laughing when he threatened to make me wear a pacifier around my neck if I didn’t stop chewing my nails. He made me so mad when he yelled at me about that, because he himself bit his nails to the quick. I had heard Grandma Swenson scold him for his "dirty habit" more than once. If he couldn't stop, why would he try to make me?

Mom stressed about money. She sewed all our clothes, canned vegetables from the garden, brought her own lunch to work, saved S&H stamps, and went shopping at garage sales. There were times as a child I knew my mother was lonely. Depressed. I heard her crying behind her closed bedroom door when she said she was going to take a nap.

In third grade I felt so bad for her that I organized a surprise kaffeeklatsch.

"Let's cheer Mom up," I suggested to Barb. "We can clean the house on Saturday morning before she wakes up and bake a coffee cake and invite her friends."

Barb helped me make party invitations with colored construction paper. "One for Auntie Har," she handed me the envelope for each. "One for Bev. One for Diane across the street. And one for Pat." I found the roll of stamps in the junk drawer. We sent the invitations in the mail.

Saturday morning I baked a streusel coffee cake while Mom slept late. Barb set the table, and I brewed up coffee in the percolator on the stove. I washed and she dried the dishes without argument. When the doorbell rang, Mom came out of the bedroom all dressed and her hair brushed, happy to have company. I'd felt so satisfied to have made her smile.

Many years later I learned my aunt had called her a few days in advance so she wouldn't be caught with curlers in her hair or put the kibosh on my baking project.

I'm not entirely sure when I began to feel responsible for my mother's emotional well-being as a child. When I think about it now, I can still see the world through her eyes—insecure and depressed—and I wonder whether I hurt her when I threw her a pity party. That I'd failed to carry out the daughter's role for making my mother less miserable, and in ways I hadn't even realized at the time, only really hit me after she died.

"Girls, I want to talk to you," Dad said one night as we finished eating supper when I was in fifth grade. "Go sit down in the den and we are going to have a conversation."

Barb and I went and sat in the orange recliners.

Dad stood in the doorway between the kitchen and den and crossed his arms. Mom cleared the table and started washing dishes. "Your mother works hard, and it is time the two of you start helping out more."

It felt like I was in trouble.

"The two of you are doing the dishes after supper from now on. I want you to keep your room clean. Once a week you will vacuum and dust the living room and dining room. And I do not want to hear any arguing."

I didn't know what I had done wrong.

"Do you understand me?" He said it like he didn't want us to say another word.

Barb and I nodded our heads. But I didn't understand at the age of eleven that the tension I felt was between my parents, both working full-time.

School took me away from family and chores. I couldn't wait to get there in the morning. Walking in the front doors a half hour before everyone else, I headed to the janitor's closet to get my bright orange flag. There I put on my official patrol belt with my badge pinned to the shoulder strap. I stood at the corner of Lake Drive in front of Lakeview Elementary as a proud member of the School Safety Patrol. First to arrive and last to leave. And on Wednesdays I could stay even later for my troop meeting. At school and in Scouts, good behavior earned rewards.

Teachers selected me for the Junior Great Books program, and once a week the best readers were allowed to leave the classroom for discussions of great literature. The books we discussed were even more special than we were. *Aesop's Fables*, *Grimm's Fairytales*, *The Silver Skates*, *Of Mice and Men*, *Little Women*, *Charlotte's Web*, *Treasure Island*, and the poetry of Langston Hughes and Christina Rossetti. I raised my hand to answer every question my teacher asked. I did not look forward to vacation.

The Monday after school let out for summer, Michael Wyand walked in the front door of the furniture store behind his grandmother. A large white muslin dish towel wrapped around his neck served as a sling for his left arm, covered by a white cast. His gaze did not leave the ground.

"Did you break your arm?" Mom asked him.

He didn't answer.

"He got it caught in the wringer-washer," Mrs. Wyand said. "He mangled his elbow and crushed his forearm."

Michael kicked one foot back as red flushed his cheeks.

"Oh no!" Mom said.

Grandma Swenson had the same kind of washing machine in her basement. If it was plugged into the wall, we weren't to touch it. Sometimes I watched her use it. She'd fill the ceramic tub with water, put the clothes in with laundry soap flakes, then plug it in and turn the agitator on. Paddles attached at the center splashed the clothes around and sudsed them up. Then she'd stop the machine and drain the dirty water out. And she'd fill it again with clear water using the hose attached to the spigot on the wall. She'd pull each piece of clothing out of the tub and toward the spinning rollers to wring out the wetness.

"Get back now. That thing'll take your arm right off!" Grandma warned us every time. If something got caught and jammed the machine, she'd reach over to the catch-release lever. The sound it made when it got jammed up scared me.

I couldn't help but imagine how terrifying it must have been for Michael.

Over supper that evening Mom told Dad about Michael's broken arm. I wanted to make him feel better. It seemed the Christian thing to do. But I don't recall any discussion of replacing Mrs. Wyand's washing machine with one of the dozen floor models at the store. Instead, the discussion focused on what *I* might do for Michael.

Suddenly, an idea occurred to me: "A bike!"

"How can you afford to buy him a bicycle?" Dad asked me.

"A bike with a cool banana seat, Dad," I insisted.

"How much money do you have?"

I looked down. "I don't have any."

"Well then," Dad said, "if you want to get him a bike, you'll have to figure out how to earn the money to buy him one."

I don't know where I got the idea from—and I cringe now—but what I came up with in order to earn the money for Michael's bike was "Slave Days." I offered my services, for a fee, doing anything someone else in the neighborhood didn't want to do. Clearly, I didn't have any idea of what slavery meant and likely stole the idea from some other fundraiser in our white-flight community. I made a pledge to myself to spend the summer doing work for hire and put my earnings toward the purchase of Michael's bike.

First thing I did was Tom Sawyer all my neighborhood friends into doing Slave Days with me. I rounded up Julie McChesney, Wendy, Cookie, the Martin girls, two of the four Levine kids, and my sister, Barb, in the backyard, and we made a plan.

"We can go door to door," Julie suggested. She and I had sold a lot of Girl Scout cookies together in our neighborhood that way.

"We can explain what happened to Michael," said Wendy, "and ask if they will pay us to work to earn money for his bike."

"Let's go!" I led my group of friends to the front door of the older couple next door and rang the bell.

When she heard our pitch, the neighbor booked two hours the next afternoon. "You can iron my husband's hankies and work shirts."

"I'll pay you five bucks to wash and polish the Mustang," offered Bill McChesney, Julie's dad.

We mowed lawns. Weeded flower beds. Hung out laundry on the line and folded clothes. Cleaned kitchen cupboards. Swept out a garage. Polished silver.

One lady hired me to harvest her sage. Her plants grew big as bushes in front of her house, and she showed me how to clip their leaves with a tiny scissors and put them in a big flat basket to dry.

Touching the gray-green velvet leaves gave off a musky smell. I spent hours in the sun cleansed by the sweat of my labor.

In the middle of August, Mrs. Wyand came in to the furniture store for coffee and told Mom the cast on Michael's arm would soon come off. Mom told us at supper when she got home from work. "Maybe we can invite Michael and Mrs. Wyand over to our house then," Mom suggested.

"Do you have enough money to buy a bike yet?" Dad asked me.

We counted up all the bills and coins, and Dad agreed to take me and Barb and Julie to Sears at the Brookdale mall on Saturday afternoon to shop for Michael's gift. We found the perfect bike: a purple Deluxe Sting-Ray with monkey handlebars.

The last Sunday in August, Dad delivered Michael and his grandmother to our house. All the kids in the neighborhood rode their bikes over when they saw Dad's car pull into the driveway, and we went into the backyard, where there were hamburgers, chips, and Kool-Aid on the picnic table. We could hardly wait to surprise Michael.

Dad pulled the bicycle out of the garage and presented it to him. "This is for you from these kids," he said.

Michael looked at his grandmother, his face stricken with confusion.

"Michael, say thank you," Mrs. Wyand said.

"Thank you." He threw one leg over and jumped on. Michael rode his own bicycle round and round on the concrete patio.

"C'mon," I shouted. "Let's go for a bike ride!"

"Grandma?" Michael looked at Mrs. Wyand.

She nodded. "Yes, go."

With that, a pack of white suburban kids and one little Indian boy, all on their bicycles, rode down Grimes Avenue, from one end of the block to the other.

There is much I don't remember clearly about my summer of charitable efforts and the start to my white savior complex. Like how the idea of "Slave Days" came about. Like how I knew Michael didn't already have a bike or that he wanted one. What I do remember is how much fun it was working together with my neighbors for something beyond myself. How good I felt when Michael rode his bike that day on Grimes Avenue, just like any other kid in my suburban neighborhood.

I never saw Michael again. Mrs. Wyand came to the furniture store sometimes, though not as often, for coffee. Michael went home to Pine Ridge. I hoped he'd brought his bike.

Not long after that, the City of Minneapolis unveiled an urban renewal plan that would expand Interstate 94 through the north side of the city. While Dad hoped for the best, day after day there were fewer and fewer sales. Then fewer pedestrians walked the street, until almost no one besides the mailman came in the store anymore. One by one, retail businesses on West Broadway closed. Lila's Fashions. Cy's Menswear. Even Mickey's Diner. Less than two years after the grand reopening of Pearson & Swenson Furniture Store, Dad closed the business and sold the building. Most of the old neighborhood simply disappeared. The entire block where my palace of fine home furnishings had once stood was leveled to the ground. Today it's a strip mall parking lot.

CHAPTER 10

Karen, Don, and Martha were returned to their foster parents immediately after the funeral service for their great-grandfather in December of 1968.

"Clem sure did a lot of ear-pulling. You might get your hand slapped," Don recalled about his years on the farm. "Helen would grab Karen around the upper arm and leave bruises and scratches from her iron grip." He said their foster parents didn't spank them, but they were strict. "The welfare lady came and brought us children down in the basement to talk to us. Karen's arms were bruised, and she spoke up."

Karen remembered the social worker was concerned enough after that meeting to move her to a different foster family in Crookston, one hundred and forty miles from Warroad. But this was painful for Karen, because she wanted Don and Martha to get away from there, too. The social worker had found her a safe home, but there was only one bed available. That family had children of their own, plus two other foster children. Karen suffered for years from guilt, knowing she'd left her siblings behind with the Kalinowskis.

Don and Martha lived in a state of terror. It scared them to watch Clem spank their youngest of three sons, Wayne. They tried to do everything they were told, but never seemed to do it right. They were not allowed to use the indoor plumbing and had to use the outhouse, even in winter. Don and Martha both peed in their beds regularly, which enraged Helen. They faced daily humiliations for it. Once a week, Helen scalded and scrubbed their skin in a big metal tub.

At Christmas time, Robert and Florence Kakaygeesick were allowed to visit their children on the farm and brought them presents. They had continued to work at the lumber camp on the Northwest Angle and couldn't convince authorities to release their children back into their custody.

"One year I got a model garage with cars. But I only got to play with it that one day," Don recalled. Helen picked it up after his parents left, and Don never saw it again. In 1970, his parents brought him an Apollo 11 model kit for Christmas. He studied the box and all the parts and looked forward to working on it. Again, Helen took it from him, and it disappeared.

The last day twelve-year-old Don spent on the Kalinowski farm, knowing he would never have to return there, he told me he went down into the cellar and covered the walls with a red crayon used to mark lumber, leaving his rage behind.

I am struck by the fact that this is the only time Don ever spoke to me of feeling anger. My own reaction to learning about his childhood, like my reaction to knowing they lost their land, was fury.

In 1971—after five years in foster care—Don, Martha, Kenny, and Kelly were returned to their parents. Karen came home a year later. It's not entirely clear why they were taken from their parents in the first place, nor why they returned home when they did. I could find no official documentation but interviewed family members and local sources to corroborate accounts. I searched in vain for the woman who worked for the welfare agency at the time in Roseau County.

What I have since learned is that their story was not unusual. When Bertram Hirsch, a New York attorney, was sent in the late 1960s to North Dakota by the Association on American Indian Affairs (AAIA) to assist with a kinship dispute, he discovered child welfare workers were forcibly removing children from family members and placing them in white homes. Hirsch and AAIA collected data from adoption and foster care agencies and audited the records of the Bureau of Indian Affairs, which had the authority to place children at that time. By the late 1960s, *one-third* of all Indian children in the United States had been removed from their homes, and 85 percent of these children were placed with non-Indian families. The Child Welfare League of America and the Bureau of Indian Affairs had initiated the Indian Adoption Project in 1959, advocating children be adopted by non-Indian families.

The Kakaygeesick children were not the only ones in Warroad taken from their parents; nor were they the first, or the last. One of the first had been Maggie Lightning Aas, who had translated for Willard Leaf at Kakaygeesick's bedside for the signing of his will.

Her grandfather, Honest John Lightning, had been married to one of Kakaygeesick's sisters-in-law. But in the 1920s, when his son, Tom Lightning, wanted to send his children to school in Warroad, he was told they were Canadians and would be charged tuition. Even though they had a house in town, the Lightnings spent time at Buffalo Point, a few miles across the Manitoba border. Tom Lightning sent his children—Hans, age twelve, and Margaret, age seven—to a boarding school in Shoal Lake, Ontario, Canada, likely the Cecilia Jeffrey School, run by Presbyterian missionaries. The Truth and Reconciliation Commission in Canada has in recent years released many documents related to the poor living conditions, overcrowding, lack of medical care, and physical, sexual, and emotional abuse suffered by students at Cecilia Jeffrey School since 1901. The Presbyterian Church has also issued a formal acknowledgment and apology for these acts of cultural genocide. There are at least sixty unmarked graves on the site.

I found the gravesites of Margaret and Hans Lighting at Riverside Cemetery in Warroad when I went to find Uncle Al's headstone. Uncle Al was close to the river, immediately off the paved lane on the curve of the riverbank, and a marker identified his grave as that of a veteran. Back far from the waterfront under a grove of old cypress trees, the number of gravestones in the section for the Lightning family surprised me. I searched for the older markers. A round sunken stone with her name and birth and death dates marked Maggie's grave.

When Warroad High School teacher Grace Landin had interviewed her in 1972 for her graduate thesis on Warroad's original three families, Maggie said that instead of being taught to read and write, they were given chores and housekeeping tasks at the Indian boarding school. When her father found out she and Hans were still unable to write their names after the first year, they were transferred to another school she described as a prison. Her father brought them home to Warroad, where they lived in town with their grandmother. The following year, Maggie and her brother attended Warroad School, but it wasn't easy for them.

"I never liked school very much," the elderly Maggie Aas told Grace.

Her answers to Grace's other questions are not a surprise to me, based on what I know now.

"The white children would tease me all the time," Maggie said. "They would call me all kinds of names, and I wasn't one to fight back. They would call me a 'dirty Indian.' Maybe they thought my skin was dirty when it was darker than theirs."

Maggie Aas was the earliest case I found in my research of Warroad's Ojibway children who were taken away from their family and tribal way of life.

On Red Lake Reservation, St. Mary's Mission School was run as a boarding school by Benedictine nuns who made the children collect, clean, and sort chicken eggs, by the thousands each day. The mission school started in the late 1800s, and the priests did not consider learning to read and write or study mathematics a priority over making the farm profitable.

Uncle Eddy Cobiness, the brother of Don's mother, took his family to Buffalo Point across the border rather than risk having his children taken from him by Roseau County Welfare. Several years after the Kakaygeesick children were taken from school, their classmates, the Sargent kids, disappeared from Warroad into foster care. Their father had left. Their mother had lung cancer. The county welfare department believed placement with white families working on farms would be better for them rather than staying with extended family. It wasn't much different from the "placing out" system started in 1884, which relocated Native children "to learn the value of work and the benefits of civilization."

Reading survivors' accounts from across the United States and Canada of how these school policies were implemented made me realize it was *much* worse than I could have ever imagined. While public education lifted me up and out of my personal circumstances, the education system for Indian children was intended to extinguish their identity.

CHAPTER 11

Dr. Martin Luther King Jr. spoke in April at the University of Minnesota three months before the violence on West Broadway in 1967. It was not his first visit. He had been in the Twin Cities in 1961—I was three years old—and returned in 1963, before the bus boycotts across the country started. While integration had stalled in some cities, Blacks from Detroit, Gary, Chicago, Saint Louis, and Milwaukee were migrating further north, moving to Minneapolis and settling on the near north side. During his 1967 visit, Dr. King talked to the three thousand in the audience at Northrup Auditorium about the unfinished work the civil rights movement faced. His voice and urgency for action resonated with the audience.

No one I knew attended that event. I didn't know anything about Dr. King's visits as a child or understand how my life experiences might be colored by the fact that I was a white girl. And as for Black people? I didn't know any, except for one friend Dad had from River Falls who came to Sunday dinner sometimes.

Dad liked to tell the story of the first time that friend came to visit us in north Minneapolis when I was four years old.

"Go wash them hands again, Mister. My mom wants both sides clean," I had told my parents' dinner guest.

Mom blushed and shushed me. I learned quickly I wasn't

supposed to talk about skin color. The silence around whiteness began at home.

The only other Black people I saw were when I went grocery shopping with Mom at the Red Owl (which Dad called the Dirty Bird). Or walking the sidewalk on West Broadway, riding the city bus, or at the State Fair. Oh, and downtown at Dayton's, where Black ladies in black dresses with white aprons and collars handed me a white cloth hand towel after I washed my hands in the fancy restroom.

I didn't know any Jews in my early childhood either. Or not that I knew of. On WCCO I had listened to the news stories about the stores targeted by looters, and someone said it was like a pogrom. Twenty years after World War II, nobody talked about what had happened in Germany or Poland or Czechoslovakia or Hungary, and the silence in response to my questions about pogroms didn't make much sense to me. The night of the fires after the Torchlight Parade, news reporters said Blacks had started them, deliberately targeting the stores owned by Jews with Molotov cocktails.

This confused me, but the focus of my life in seventh grade involved very different things: Luther League and Aqua-Robbins, the synchronized swim team at Robbinsdale Junior High School. Church and the public library, which were within walking distance. Plus, I had my Schwinn.

Friday evening, heading west from Baudette toward Warroad, Mom drove the lonely stretch of open road into the setting sun. Out the passenger side window, I could see the train tracks running parallel to the road. On the driver's side, looking past Mom at the wheel, there were only open fields.

Mom and I had left Barb home with Dad earlier that day to drive up north; it was June 1970, and I was going to spend six weeks with Aunt Audrey and Uncle Al. Better there than another hot summer in the Twin Cities, as far as I was concerned. Mom planned to stay the weekend and drive home in time for work on Monday morning.

Out of nowhere an unmarked metallic gray aircraft pulled alongside us. It hovered so close to the ground next to us I thought we would be killed in a crash. Mom looked to her left and saw the silent, windowless object with wings, and no wheels. She screamed.

I screamed.

"Shut up!" she screamed at me.

I threw myself into ramrod perfect posture, facing the front with my seat belt safely latched. The aircraft kept pace with the Chevy at 55 mph. Chills and sweat and a wave of fear hit me. Mom burst out crying. Tears ran down her crinkled-up face, and she gripped the steering wheel hard. I expected to die.

The aircraft veered left and up. I watched it bank into the clouds across miles of open cropland. It disappeared from view in seconds. We were the only ones along this stretch of highway.

Mom slowed down and pulled off the road. Sobbing. She slammed the car into park, unbuckled her seat belt, and swung open the door. She jumped out, pulled her pants down, and peed along the side of the road. Then she jumped back into the car.

"Don't tell anybody what we just saw," she said. Then she started to laugh hysterically.

"Why not?" My immediate thought had been to tell *everyone* I knew.

"People will think I'm crazy." She turned toward me as she buckled her seat belt again. She looked into my eyes and pleaded, "Don't you dare say a word to anybody about this. *Ever.* Do you understand me?"

I thought about all the times she'd cried in front of me. Confiding in me her insecurities and emotional sensitivities. Her hissy fits. Hiding in her bedroom crying, ranting into her pillow against a cruel and unfair world pitted against her. "Depressed" and "lonely" weren't words I would have used for her, but I knew that is how she felt inside her petite body and head of strawberry blonde curls. The last thing Mom needed was people thinking she was crazy. Only crazy people claimed to see UFOs. Mom wasn't crazy. But no one else had seen it. Except me.

"Yes, Mom." I knew something, and I had to keep my mouth shut. For her, I would do it.

And I did. I kept my mouth shut. But I remembered what happened. Many years later I learned the US Air Force had a station forty miles away and played a significant role during the Cold War in border surveillance and testing new technologies. There had been lots of unexplained sightings along the same stretch of highway in the 1970s. Uncle Al's stories about lights over Lake of the Woods were similar to other accounts reported to authorities.

What we didn't know.

What was left unspoken.

What we didn't talk about.

My family watched *CBS Nightly News* together after supper every night. Walter Cronkite delivered a different message to me than to my Republican parents. Mom and Dad saw a world threatened by godless Communists in Russia. I saw teenagers, American Indians, Blacks, and the Vietnamese threatened by dogs, fire hoses, police batons, napalm, and M16s. We watched the same events but made sense of them in different ways.

CHAPTER 12

When their children were returned to them in 1971, Robert and Florence Kakaygeesick rented the stucco house next to Florence's mother in town, and the Kakaygeesick kids reenrolled in Warroad Public School.

Don completed tenth grade but did not finish high school. He and Vern Sargent, another Ojibway classmate, had to put up with a lot of bullying in school. The Markovich kids were relentless. Their father was the Department of Natural Resources Officer in Warroad, and the tensions over Indian fishing, hunting, and trapping rights found expression in the teenagers' taunts at high school.

Vern and Don had each other's back. They were in classes together and tried to fit in as best they could. This meant even if Don knew the answer to the question the teacher asked, he would not raise his hand to answer it, because then he'd stand out, and others would think he was showing off.

Their teacher, Dick Roberts, said something to Vern and Don when he caught them goofing around one day: "We put everything on a silver platter for you people, and all you do is spit on it."

Don never forgot that. And he took it to heart.

It surprised me to hear this about Dick Roberts. It was a name I recognized. A friend to Dad. A friend to Uncle Al and Aunt Audrey. A local hockey legend as player and coach. It surprised me—but then I thought about how I'd heard my own mother call me a wild Indian in front of Mrs. Wyand. I believed Don.

At the end of the school year, Vern told Don they were the only two who hadn't passed, and they would be held back a year. Neither Vern nor Don returned to school that fall. No one from the school ever followed up to find out why.

It would be years before Don learned Vern had lied to him. Don *had* passed. Only Vern hadn't.

Grace Landin had been teaching in the Warroad schools for more than twenty years by the time she started collecting archival materials and conducted personal interviews to complete her thesis for a master of science degree in education at Moorhead State College. *A Study of Three Chippewa Families at Warroad, Minnesota and Their Historical and Cultural Contributions* was submitted and accepted in May 1972, and it included accounts of the Kakaygeesick, Lightning, and Thunder families.

"The Indian drop-out rate at Warroad has been high, with only six students out of twenty-two completing their high school training in the past ten years," she wrote.

Don's eldest brother, Robert Jr., had been one of those six to graduate. Nationwide, the school dropout rate for American Indian students was slightly higher than 45 percent, and more than one-third of all working-age Indians were unemployed.

Grace Landin took a personal interest in the families of her Indian students and appreciated the paintings and drawings, beadwork and basketry of their parents and grandparents. She recognized their intelligence and cultural contributions had been overlooked by her white community. She reported Indian students were only 5 percent of the total enrollment, yet constituted 19 percent of students referred to the school social worker. Her intent for her thesis was to preserve family history and give them greater pride in their heritage with new educational programs.

My cousin Shireen took a class in beadwork from some of the elders during her junior year of high school. I asked Audrey if she remembered when Shireen took the class.

"Yes, Georgina Prevlitz was the teacher," she recalled. "Wait a minute, I want to show you something." Audrey went into her bedroom where she kept her jewelry box.

I heard the lid lift and the jingling of rings and bracelets. She walked back to the dining room table clutching something in her hand.

"Georgina gave this to me. Back when your Uncle Al and I were young parents." She showed me a beautiful necklace. A round blue-beaded medallion hung from a thin white-beaded strap. She had kept it as a precious gift all these years.

It was Grace Landin who helped launch these first American Indian Education programs in Warroad. She was also part of a much larger national focus on better serving the educational needs of Indian children in public schools. The first gathering of American Indian scholars met at Princeton University in 1969, followed by a subsequent meeting in Minneapolis in August 1970, to incorporate the National Indian Education Association. In Warroad, Landin convinced many of the Ojibway parents and elders to teach classes about their traditional ways and customs.

After Don dropped out of high school, he was employed at $1.20 an hour to assist with these Indian programs during the summer. He recalls learning how to gather birch bark and construct a wigwam. He worked with his father and Uncle George Angus on the projects. Maggie Aas and Verna and Florence Kakaygeesick also taught many of the beadwork and basketry classes.

There is a big manila folder full of newspaper clippings and a thick photograph album in the back office of the Warroad Heritage Center about the early days of the American Indian Education Program. Grace Landin's thesis, I discovered, is easily found online. But only at the Heritage Center can I see samples of the beadwork by both teachers and students from those inaugural years of the American Indian Education Program.

The Warroad Indian Education Program remains an integral part of the programming at Warroad Public Schools. In November 2019, at the request of the Kakaygeesick family, students in the Indian Education Program and a shop class worked together to replace the spirit houses marking the graves of Kakaygeesick and his relations. The weathered, rough-hewn wooden boards had disintegrated naturally. Today the Indian burial grounds are designated as a cemetery but are surrounded by the lawns of private residential homes. Marking the site occupied by their ancestors, Don and his siblings wanted the spirit houses to remain intact to symbolize the relationship and history of the Kah-bay-kah-nong band to Warroad. The students contributed their skills, labor, and materials, for which the family expressed deep gratitude. As community elders, they shared with students their history, conducted a smudging ceremony, and followed protocol in accordance with their teachings. Students built an extra spirit house to represent and honor the unmarked sites of those who have journeyed on.

In the years after Kakaygeesick's death, the family continued to tell the stories about him. Don told me he had fond memories of going with him in the summer to help him gather his medicine on Buffalo Point. He remembered sleeping on the floor of his wigwam there with his siblings, like logs lined up end to end, when he was a young boy. Don said Kakaygeesick thought it was a funny game for him to play while they were asleep, trying to dance over the rolling logs. He didn't know if it was a dream or if his great-grandfather actually did it, but he heard Kakaygeesick calling him awake one night—not as "Don" but with a different name, a sacred name. Even in his sixties, Don's memories of being there remained strong: sturgeon bladders, hollowed duck bone, elk teeth, a tin full of bear grease. From the maple sapling rafters overhead hung healing plants and herbs to dry: cedar, sweetgrass, white sage, pin cherries, and chokecherries.

Kakaygeesick had worn a necklace made with bear claws. He said it had been his father's, Chief Ay Ash Wash, who won the necklace in combat against the Dakota in the 1840s.

The Dakota had attacked the Ojibway, and Ay Ash Wash needed medicine to defeat them. He prayed and fasted, and he had a vision. Great Spirit would turn him into a bear during battle. Kakaygeesick had been asleep with his brothers and sisters, mother and father inside a birch bark tipi on Muskeg Bay when a Dakota warrior crept up on them in the middle of the night while they slept and assaulted Kakaygeesick's mother after slicing his father's scalp.

From deep inside Ay Ash Wash's chest came a feral growl. Shape shifting into a bear, he stood up on his back legs and roared in rage. Ay Ash Wash's claws slashed the Dakota warrior's side through his rib cage, and he let him escape. The warrior ran to tell the others that when he'd scalped the chief, Ay Ash Wash became a ferocious bear who could tear them all apart. The bear claw necklace represented the transformation from being attacked into defeating his enemy. Kakaygeesick passed down this family history in his many tellings to his grandchildren and great-grandchildren.

Seeking full-time employment as a young man, Don took a job working for Marvin Windows like so many other people in the Lake of the Woods area. There he met Shirley, a white woman from Baudette who was a year younger than him, and they started dating. Not too long after, Marvin Windows fired her. She convinced Don to quit then, and they traveled around together for a while.

Don had one suit in his suitcase, and when he and Shirley arrived in Crookston, he changed into it to apply for a job at the Crystal Sugar factory.

"You want to work?" the guy asked when he showed up at the employment office. "I'll put you to work. Follow me."

They put him to work below, in the furnace area, where he felt suffocated in his suit by the heat. He quit after the end of that first day.

After that, Don and Shirley went back to Baudette and lived on her family's farm to save up for college. Don didn't really want to get married, but she didn't want him to leave for college without getting hitched. So, he traded in his 1977 Arctic Cat Jag 3000 snowmobile for a Buick Regal and proposed. Don worked for her father, a sheep and cattle rancher. They made plans to attend college in International Falls.

Don and Shirley moved there in 1979 and enrolled at Rainy River Community College, part of the Minnesota State Colleges and Universities system. An admissions counselor told Don to take the GED exam first. He did and passed the test easily. Don had saved enough money to pay for full tuition. After he was admitted, he learned he could apply for grants to help cover expenses. He took classes in art, psychology, and mass communications. He worked as a night janitor on campus and excelled in his art classes. His art instructor, Professor Dick Weis, hired him as his apprentice, and Don assisted him with the preparation of classes and art supplies. Weis encouraged him to paint.

Don and Shirley rented a small apartment on Main Street, upstairs from the downtown pharmacy. They didn't have much, other than a mattress on the floor and an old couch. Cardboard boxes served as end tables. He remembers how she would stretch out nude on the couch for him to sketch. He was living the life of an artist and happy. Near the end of his second year of coursework, they decided to quit school because she got pregnant. He worked full-time as a janitor on campus but remained one semester shy of his associate's degree. Then she had a miscarriage.

He was deeply saddened, and she pulled away from him. He thought it was her grief. Before the end of their third year of marriage, they were divorced.

Don moved to Bemidji in 1981 and took a few classes at the state university. While his parents never said anything against his marriage, he knew his father had not approved of him marrying a white woman. When he headed back to Warroad to visit his parents, Don had to come through Baudette, Shirley's hometown. As soon as he saw the radio tower there, he'd get a tight feeling in his chest and have a hard time breathing.

It wasn't long before he moved back home to Warroad. He stayed with his parents out in the trailer at Muskeg Bay and in the evenings went to the local bars, which is where he met Ronda.

"Your wife is whomever you sleep with," his father had always told Don. "And you don't sleep with just anyone."

So Don called Ronda his wife, although they lived together without a marriage license. Ronda wasn't a Red Lake tribal member—she was originally from Wyoming—but she was part Cherokee. She and Don had two children, Barbara and Curtis.

Don went to work at Marvin Windows. Again.

Don disclosed these personal details of his life to me over the course of several years. I scheduled face-to-face interviews with him during my now annual end-of-summer road trips to visit Warroad. We stayed in touch using Facebook Messenger and email as I tried to make sense of how Red Lake Nation ended up building a casino on Allotment 3. There were times I reflected on his friendship and the trust he placed in me to try to tell the story of what happened. Was it warranted? Why should he trust a white woman to tell the truth?

While I questioned my own motivations and intentions, I also worried that Don had unrealistic expectations for what a book could do: it seemed unlikely he would get the land back. We had agreed that if he would tell me his story, then I would do research, try to figure out what happened, write about this case, and possibly find someone interested in publishing it. He shared with me scanned documents, photographs, family history, and answers to my every question. But if I wanted to get to the truth, I knew I had to learn more about Red Lake Nation and the history of the reservation where Don's granddaughter, Bug, lived. I kept reading more history and sending Bug postcards from various states I visited: Texas, Ohio, Virginia, Wisconsin.

CHAPTER 13

"What did the president know, and when did he know it, Dad?" I stirred up dinner conversation after spending another day of summer vacation watching the impeachment proceedings of the House Judiciary Committee. "Even Howard Baker thinks Nixon is involved in a cover-up."

"Rose Mary Woods *accidentally* erased the tape on the Dictaphone when she reached for the telephone," he replied. "Don't believe everything you see on television, young lady."

His condescending tone got under my skin, and my anger spread like a rash. He hadn't watched the hearings that day, so what did he know. He hadn't watched because he was working. Dad landed a new job managing the cafeteria at the corporate headquarters of Kimberly Clark. We had moved into a new house in the late Senator Joseph McCarthy's hometown, Appleton, a conservative Wisconsin community where paper factories along the Fox River provided middle-class incomes.

"Nixon is a crook!"

"That's not true, Jill. Your president didn't commit a crime. The people who worked for him did; he just protected the people who worked for him."

Our disagreements over politics would escalate during high school. Since puberty, the friction between us had grown. His teasing—from "potato chips go right to your hips" to "Jill, Jill, from Garbage Hill"—no longer felt like affection. He had threatened to disown me dozens of times for daring to have my own opinions. It made me furious that he thought I was wrong about Nixon.

After supper, Dad went in the living room and turned on the nightly news. I rinsed the dishes, and Barb loaded them into the dishwasher. Mom put away the leftovers in Tupperware. Seething with rage, I tried to hide my tears facing the sink.

"Why don't you join the debate team at your new high school?" Mom whispered, softly putting her hand on my back between my shoulders. "You like to argue."

"I can't win arguments," I hissed.

"Your dad told me you said something to him," Mom said, "something that made him quit smoking cold turkey."

That stunned me. I didn't remember what I had said. I still don't know what I said that persuaded him, but now I realized he had quit shortly after we moved to Wisconsin. I remember the way Mom made me feel in that moment—influential when I felt so inconsequential.

"Maybe you want to be a lawyer," Mom said as she rubbed my back. "Debate would be good prep." Mom worked with lawyers at her job in the Honeywell office in Appleton. Her typing and shorthand skills had kept her employed as the steady breadwinner since the store burned down. When Dad closed the business, he had several jobs in food service management that hadn't lasted long.

Standing at the sink in the kitchen, she spoke softly so Dad couldn't hear us over the television set in the living room. "Have you thought about what you want to do after high school? Which reminds me—I need to get you signed up for classes at your new high school this week."

"Should I take a shorthand class?" I'd taken a typing class in ninth grade and already could do sixty words per minute.

"You do not want to take dictation from men all your life," Mom said. Dictaphones had all but replaced shorthand stenographers by the mid-1970s.

"But if I can type, I'll get a job."

"If they know you can type, that's all they'll expect of you," she warned me. "Don't ever think you can depend on a man. And you're going to need more than typing skills to keep a roof over your head."

It was some of the best advice she ever gave me. Even though I have spent more of my life at a keyboard than I would have ever imagined, I thought I understood what she meant. She hadn't been able to depend on my father. I had witnessed her enough times as unmistakably miserable when I'd watched Dad bring her to tears with his teasing and personal criticisms. Now he directed his criticisms toward me, too. I told her more than once to get a divorce.

"If I had the money for a divorce attorney," Mom said, "I wouldn't need a divorce." She loved him, and only decades later did I understand they were perfectly happy being miserable together.

When the phone rang after supper, Dad answered it. Then from my bedroom I heard him calling from the kitchen: "Jiiiiilllll. Telly-fone. Oh, Jeee-alll, it's a *boy*!"

Humiliating me seemed his idea of fun. And I felt humiliated when the boy in my class only wanted to know what answers I had for the homework assignment and not whether I wanted to go to homecoming with him that weekend.

When I joined debate team, my partner, Sharon Schwab, became my new best friend. I still couldn't win arguments with my father, but I found an ally who shared my views and opinions.

"Should the United States decrease its dependence on fossil fuels?" This was the topic for high school teams to debate in 1974—the same year the United States experienced its first oil crisis. Sharon and I spent months conducting research into the feasibility of nuclear, solar, and geothermal energy production and running projections on oil consumption and the depletion of reserves. Reducing demand for gasoline meant fewer cars, and nobody wanted to hear that. I wonder how it is that I have been marshaling the evidence and arguing the facts since high school, and I still can't seem to win with some people on the facts about the planet's nonrenewable resources.

"Achtung!" Frau Graf called the class to order. A petite woman with short salt-and-pepper hair, our German teacher was originally from Switzerland, and she started promptly when the bell rang.

"Guten Tag, Frau Graf," we replied in unison.

Sharon and I took the advanced-level German class together. Sharon had told me she and her grandmother in Florida exchanged weekly letters in German.

"Guten Tag, Meine Damen und Herren," Frau Graf greeted us with a smile. She announced a new exchange program with a school in Germany. "Their students will come here in the spring, and then I will take a group of students from here to their school in Bavaria this summer."

A trip to Germany seemed a fantasy escape from the tensions at home.

"You will need your parents' permission to sign up for the trip," Frau Graf said.

“What if they can’t afford it?” someone asked. It wasn’t me, but I was worried about the same thing.

“No one will be denied for financial reasons. You will stay with host families. German Club has a budget,” said Frau Graf, “and we will raise money to cover airfare.”

“Car washes,” someone volunteered. “I’ll bring buckets and brushes and extra hoses.”

“Who wants to come to my house and learn how to make Bavarian pretzels you can sell at school?” Frau Graf asked. Four of us girls raised our hands.

“We can have weekly bake sales,” Lynn said.

“Hey, bratwurst fundraisers at tailgate parties,” Pete chimed in.

“Maybe a school dance benefit?” asked Beth.

I convinced my parents to give their permission and applied for my passport.

“My parents aren’t going to let me go to Germany,” Sharon confided in me.

I didn’t understand why.

“My mother and grandmother in Florida were liberated from a German concentration camp.” Sharon explained it was one thing to learn the language so she could converse with her grandmother, but a betrayal to travel there.

In that moment I was sad my friend couldn’t go abroad with me. I didn’t fully comprehend why she wasn’t going until I went to Germany.

"Sit next to me," Mimi said as I got on the tour bus. We watched the rural countryside out the window on the way to Dachau, a concentration camp less than an hour away in the rural countryside.

"Where is Gabi?" I looked around the bus for the girl whose parents were hosting me. The Zaglauers owned a Gasthof—a small hotel, bar, and restaurant. I'd been enchanted by the Bavarian culture and found it fascinating to be in the restaurant kitchen and involved in their family business. When I saw Gabi near the front sitting next to her cousin, I sat down beside Mimi.

We arrived at the concentration camp by driving through the metal gate with the ARBEIT MACHT FREI ("Work Sets You Free") sign above our heads. The tour guided us around the camp, through the munitions factory, the clinic where they conducted medical experiments, the barracks, the ditches, the guard towers, the crematorium, all of it surrounded by barbed-wire fencing.

The horror of it.

Silent. Silenced.

For days after our school field trip, I kept to myself and wrote in my journal. I'd seen the evidence of genocide. From what little I'd gleaned from my high school textbooks and World War II movies, I knew we had led the Allies to victory. But I had little grasp of the scope and sweep of the evil and depravity until then.

On Saturday morning, I came downstairs for tea. I'd slept through breakfast. I took a seat at the family table off the restaurant kitchen and was surprised to see Frau Graf there.

"Guten Morgen," Frau Graf greeted me.

"Gruss Di," Herr Zaglauer said, and tipped his head. He poured me a cup of tea from the pot and set it in front of me.

"Morgen. Zucker?" Frau Zaglauer pushed the sugar bowl in my direction.

"Guten Morgen," I said.

"Frau Zaglauer is worried about you," my German teacher said in English.

"Me? Why?"

"She told me you seem unhappy all of a sudden. She is worried you don't think they are good hosts because they are always working in the Gasthof," Frau Graf said softly in English. She turned to Herr and Frau Zaglauer and spoke to them in German with a smile.

"Oh, no, it has nothing to do with the Zaglauers. They have been wonderful. I simply can't stop thinking about what we saw at Dachau." I couldn't reconcile how Germans had to have known what was happening. They let it happen, and it seemed as though nothing happened as people went on with this perfect picture-postcard life.

I don't recall how Frau Graf translated and mediated the conversation over tea, but I remember the word Frau Zaglauer used: Heimweh. The pain or ache you experience when you can't go back home to the way things used to be.

"If you want to go to college, you're going to have to earn your own way," Dad told me at supper a few weeks after I came home from Germany. He'd changed jobs, again. During the week, he worked in Minneapolis and stayed at his mother's house in north Minneapolis. On the weekends he commuted home to Appleton.

"I'll save all my money, and I'll get a summer job," I told him. Just because he wouldn't pay for college didn't mean I wasn't going. The school librarian had hired me to babysit part-time, and she encouraged me to apply to the local liberal arts college where her husband was on the faculty.

"Don't expect me to foot the tuition bill," Dad warned me.

"I can get student loans and grants and scholarships, Dad." Why did I have to debate him about going to college? I couldn't see at the time how financially insecure he felt—only how I felt he considered any investment in my future unworthy. What I couldn't grasp then was the larger context of stagflation and an 8 percent unemployment rate and that in order to find work he had to move and leave his wife and daughters.

"I got in!" The offer of admission arrived in April with a financial aid package that made college my decision, not Dad's.

"We're going to put the house on the market," Mom said. "Don't worry. We won't close on the house until school is out." They planned to move back to the Twin Cities.

"What am I supposed to do?" I felt confused. I wanted my independence from my father, and I feared losing the security of home and my mother. "I can't move on campus until September."

"If you can find a summer job, I guess you can find an apartment," Mom said.

"Can you get me twenty dollars in cash from your bank?" Dad asked me Sunday afternoon as they were getting ready to leave after Parents' Weekend of my freshman year. "I don't want to have to charge gas on the credit card."

Every time I go to the bank in Appleton, I replay that ATM transaction when I was eighteen and my parents needed me to help them out with gas money. Time rewinds—the memory rewritten, reshaped, re-recorded to serve the story I'd like to think was true about me: that I put myself through college.

Yet Barb reminded me after Mom died that there are canceled checks from 1976 to 1980, and she sent them to me. Lots and lots of twenty- and fifty-dollar checks Mom made out to me that I cashed at the Bursar's Office. Checks for tuition bills. While I never felt Dad supported me, Mom made me feel she had. It hurt to think Mom held on to these receipts all these years, as though they were my unpaid debts for her love. It hurts even more to realize too late that Mom could never have written those checks unless Dad knew and that I hurt him by never acknowledging his help.

"Show me the way to go home, I'm tired and I want to go to bed, I had a little drink about an hour ago and it went right to my head . . ." The girls sang a camp song on the bus I was driving that Saturday morning.

I had not wanted to go "home" the summer after my freshman year to my parents in Minnesota. Instead, I took a job as a counselor at the Youth Conservation Camp at Mecan River in central Wisconsin. Aldo Leopold had written *A Sand County Almanac* from his observations of this landscape. I'd loved the book and wanted to live where Leopold had. The way Leopold had.

"Sing it again, girls!" I called out from the driver's seat to the teenagers I was taking to town after a week on work crew. Campers on my crew rebuilt breeding habitat for brown trout on small creeks and streams. They felled tamarack trees, stripped the bark off, and laid the skinned poles end to end, reshaping the creek's edges into tight zigzag curves ideal for spawning.

On Saturday, it was my turn to drive the bus of campers to the nearest town, Princeton, for the afternoon. Earlier that morning after breakfast, I learned to drive the orange Bluebird bus and practiced on the long dirt camp road in the woods. Girls climbed on board, and I pulled out onto Highway 23 and drove five miles into Princeton, Wisconsin.

"The A&W! Let's stop for root beer!" a girl behind me yelled.

In the rearview mirror I could see the girls pointing off to the right ahead and cheering. "A&W! A&W!"

I coasted off the road and gently applied the brake. Ever so gracefully did I come to a stop with the screeching of metal on metal: the overhang of the A&W roof now sat on top of the roof of the bus.

That wasn't my last fiasco with a state vehicle. A couple weeks later the camp director asked me to take the Farm-All station wagon into Portage. "I need you to drop this vehicle off for repairs at the DNR garage. The brakes are going on it, so be careful."

I was extra careful, going no faster than 45 mph through the state forest. I pulled into the back of the Department of Natural Resources regional headquarters and found four big bays of a garage with all the doors up and a vehicle already in each stall. I pulled toward the edge of the parking lot away from the garage. I coasted in between two other dark green state cars and left the vehicle in neutral when I stopped and let the clutch out. I got out and walked toward the garage with the keys in my hand—proud of myself for accomplishing a dangerous mission.

Three guys came running out waving their red grease rags and yelling at me.

I waved back. "Hi, I'm delivering"—crunching gravel, shushing grasses, and the sounds of tumbling behind me—"this vehicle from Mecan River."

I turned around to see tall pine trees swaying gently. Then I noticed. The Farm-All had disappeared. I ran toward the empty parking space and followed the tire tracks to a precipice. About a hundred feet below in the creek bed lay the wrecked vehicle.

I didn't get to drive a work vehicle again. And I didn't get the job when I applied the next summer. The bonfires and stories of Indian lore, the legacy of Leopold, listening to the loons at night, waking to the wild screech of herons, identifying wildflower species, hiking geological formations, re-creating a fish habitat, transforming minds and bodies with good hard work, and swimming and bathing in the small gorges of spring-fed creeks. What romantic notions I entertained about the nobility of my work.

Why wasn't I held accountable for the damages to vehicles? I don't recall feeling any sense of responsibility for those mistakes. To be young, female, and white in Wisconsin.

CHAPTER 14

"Want to go to the Grill and study for the Anthro midterm?" Alice asked me after seminar on Wednesday in Stephenson Hall.

"Sure," I said.

It was a short walk past Main Hall to the student union. I ordered a grilled cheese sandwich, and she got a chocolate shake. We sat at a table by the windows overlooking the Fox River.

"What are we supposed to know for the test about Chippewa customs?" Alice pulled the pencil from behind her ear and turned to a new page in her notebook. "I haven't finished reading that Densmore book yet."

"Did you know the Chippewa still live in northern Minnesota? That's where my mom's family is from," I said.

"Do you have Chippewa blood?" she asked.

"Yeah, maybe," I said.

Why would I claim to be part Indian? There are no Indian ancestors in my family. Why had I wished there were? Absolution from the guilt by association of my skin color for the sins committed by settlers and soldiers in American history? What would I have gained from being identified as Indian? Some sort of cultural cachet or prestige? I didn't think about what it meant to make such a false claim of Indigenous identity. My textbooks made Indians the object of study from a vanished past and I was too ignorant to imagine the real-world implications of my white lie. The more I learned to think critically, the more I wanted to dissociate myself from the history of colonialism. I thought I'd be cooler if my peers thought I was part Indian. It hadn't impressed Alice, so I don't remember doing it again. I know I am not the only one who has made such claims.

My embarrassment now at having been a Pretendian is uncomfortable, yet necessary. But it is entirely insufficient. Humiliation does little more than make me feel as though I am a victim, and while that might offer me a door to empathize with others who have been subjugated in some way, my shame silences the part of me that must be accountable. If in my shame I look away, then I miss the point of learning what I did not know, adding insult to injury.

What I didn't know was the complicated history of blood quantum. Instead, I knew all the lyrics to Cher's smash hit of 1973, "Half-Breed," and liked to wear a bandanna headband. The cultural appropriation in the 1960s and 1970s counterculture in which I grew up made being an Indian seem cool and groovy. Assimilation, integration, urbanization—euphemisms used to suggest inclusion masked the intended goal of extermination.

The folk logic that blood determined racial identity seemed questionable, and yet I didn't have reason to question it. The one-drop rule had been used since the days of slavery, when one drop of Black blood meant a person would be considered subject to enslavement. I hadn't learned how early colonialists attempted to enslave Indian people. That didn't go well, but it created the demand for the Atlantic slave trade and rationalized the violence against Indians.

Slavery ended after the Civil War, but racism remained. Blood quantum as it applied to Indians became federal policy—a policy based on the pseudoscience of eugenics. Blood quantum policies became a passive form of genocide. Indians would literally breed themselves out of existence and rid the federal government of their treaty obligations.

The Indian Reorganization Act of 1934 introduced the rule that tribal status must be determined by kinship and lineage. The US Congress did so for the purposes of limiting federal benefits or annuities paid under treaties that ceded Indian land in exchange for payments. Not until 1860 were Indians even identified in the US Census. Starting in the late 1880s, the federal government used blood quantum to decide who was Indian and who was not. White census workers in the late nineteenth century made those determinations based on their racialized perceptions, which focused on the size and shape of a person's skull, the tone of their skin color, the language they spoke, and the clothes they wore. Some were recorded as 4/4 or full-blood Indians. A check mark in one column indicated a person could speak English, and another check meant they could also read and write. Many census takers believed they were doing a favor if they designated a person as less than full-blooded, since they believed the closer approximation to whiteness would be of greater value for the person's future standing in a white world.

It doesn't take long to extinguish a bloodline. If your great-grandmother was 4/4 Indian, and your great-grandfather was white, then their daughter (your grandmother) would be only one-half Indian. And if your grandmother married a man who was not Indian, then their daughter (your mother) would be only one-quarter Indian. And if your mother married a man who was not Indian, then you would be only one-eighth Indian.

If you marry a man who is not Indian, then your daughter would be only one-sixteenth Indian. But in order to be a registered tribal member of Red Lake Nation, a person must be at least one-quarter blood quantum. In short, you and your daughter would not qualify to be registered as tribal members. But it's even more complicated than that. To be considered for tribal membership, Red Lake Nation specifies the blood quantum must come from registered Red Lake tribal members and not from any other tribe.

Why would a tribe *not* want to include as many members as possible? Why would they make membership so difficult to establish? The federal government disburses funds annually in fulfillment of its treaty and trust obligations to Indian nations. The fewer the members, the more the tribe can spend per capita on providing housing, healthcare, education, infrastructure, and law enforcement. Federal policy created incentives toward self-extermination.

In searching the Indian Census Rolls to see if I could establish any records of tribal enrollment to document Kakaygeesick's blood quantum, I found Kakaygeesick and his daughter Mary and son John recorded as 4/4 full-blood quantum in the count of Red Lake Indian families on Lake of the Woods in the 1926 Indian Census.

Kakaygeesick's children married. Mary wed John Angus, a Red Lake tribal member. John married Verna, whose grandfather was a Métis fur trader, making the blood quantum of their only child, Robert, 7/8. Robert's wife, Florence Cobiness, had been born in Canada at Buffalo Point, but she had no papers to prove she was 4/4. Red Lake Nation never issued Robert Kakakygeesick or his family official tribal membership, and none of them had ever been on the annuity rolls to receive annual payments. The Kakaygeesick family didn't live on the reservation, but Red Lake Reservation considered the land where they lived as theirs.

That Don Kakaygeesick and his family would lose their land to a tribe which did not recognize them seemed wrong, an injustice. But who was responsible for this? When I first started the research, I assumed the fault lay with Red Lake. Indians against Indians. But what did I mean by Red Lake? I didn't realize the slippage in my thinking about Red Lake Reservation as land, the Red Lake bands of Ojibway as people, and Red Lake Nation as a sovereign national government.

Reservations are under federal registration and tribal control with a system called "trust land." The Ojibway people of Red Lake share a common language, culture, and way of life. Red Lake Nation is the sovereign land of the people who are registered tribal members and governed by tribal laws. Not all tribal members live on the reservation. Not all Red Lake Indians have tribal membership.

Red Lake Reservation is a closed reservation. It is not land to which Indians were forced to relocate. Instead, the federal government acknowledged this place—where these people had resided before settlers arrived—would be designated as their land, as property. The tribal government has full sovereignty, which means state courts and local government have no jurisdiction there. In 1918, the Red Lake General Council Constitution was ratified, and the land surrounding Red Lake was reaffirmed to be held in common rather than as private property divided up in allotments held by individuals. The tribe claimed the land by aboriginal rights.

In some respects, this could be considered a major victory for the Nation of Red Lake. Especially when you consider that between 1877 and the present, more than 1.5 billion acres of land in the United States, spanning from ocean to ocean, was transferred into the hands of whites. One of the methods by which the federal government severed land from its original residents was the allotment system established in 1887 with the Dawes Act. But Red Lake

Reservation was exempt from allotments, and exempt from parts of the Nelson Act of 1899, which forced the relocation of all other Chippewa people in Minnesota to White Earth Reservation so that the vacated reservation lands in northern Minnesota could be sold, primarily for the purposes of harvesting timber. There were not supposed to be any allotments to Red Lake Indians.

Except there were.

Three.

The more I explored the history of Red Lake Nation, the more I realized my ignorance was dangerous. Not knowing what I didn't know shielded me from considering I might be wrong about who was to blame.

In the 1950s, new tribal leaders wrote a constitution to establish a democratically elected chairman and tribal council. The hereditary chiefs continued in an advisory capacity. The tribe elected Roger Jourdain as its first chairman, and he was reelected again and again until 1990.

Jourdain battled against the Bureau of Indian Affairs and the Department of Interior for tribal sovereignty for forty years. He wrested control from the Washington bureaucrats and consolidated the power of Red Lake Nation. In the 1960s, he approved tribal council legislation that gave preference to tribal members for employment on the reservation. Jourdain reclaimed land that had been ceded to the railroads and sold off in small parcels to non-Natives as private property. He also built roads, housing, a school, and a library. He delivered running water to residents on the reservation, created jobs at the timber mill, opened a gas station and trading post, and established a hospital and health clinic. He oversaw the creation of Red Lake Fisheries Association, which processed more than two million pounds of fish by the mid-1970s. Red Lake became the first tribe to issue tribal license plates.

Jourdain's greatest contribution had been helping the 1975 Indian Self-Determination and Education Assistance Act get passed. For the first time, tribes had authority over how to administer the federal funds allocated to them. The act reversed years of attempts to sever treaty obligations and terminate the legal standing of tribal nations.

Jourdain's frequent appearances in Washington, DC, and the Minnesota capital of Saint Paul, testifying at congressional hearings and lobbying politicians, made him a familiar face to many people off the reservation. Perhaps the most memorable example of his brash style came at the national commemoration of the bicentennial in Philadelphia in 1976. As the long lineup of speakers droned on, his friend Wendell Chino, chair of the Mescalero Apache, chided him that he ought to get up there and tell people how things really were.

Jourdain reached into his briefcase and grabbed a Gideon Bible he'd swiped from his hotel room, stormed up the stairs, and grabbed the microphone.

"You have two constitutions here in the United States," he boomed. "You've got this Bible, and you've got the Constitution. And you've never lived up to either one of them." He held the Bible above his head, then slammed it down to the ground and stormed off the stage.

As chairman of Red Lake Nation, Jourdain established political connections with Hubert Humphrey, Walter Mondale, and President Jimmy Carter. But when Reagan was elected in 1980, there were fewer opportunities for expanding Red Lake sovereignty.

When Congress passed the 1982 Nuclear Waste Policy Act, power companies solicited tribes for permission to store waste on their lands. The Red Lake tribal council adopted a policy to forbid any nuclear waste on reservation land. In 1986 the Bureau of Indian Affairs began to advocate opening Red Lake Reservation to white business development to address the problem of low employment rates and poverty. And the *Minneapolis Star Tribune* ran a series of stories critical of Red Lake tribal courts because reporters could not gain access to their court records through the Freedom of Information Act. In response, Jourdain pushed through a tribal resolution requiring tribal lawyers and judges to conduct all legal proceedings in the Ojibway language.

My understanding and appreciation for Red Lake Nation history come from reading secondary sources, particularly the work of Anton Treuer. Treuer teaches at Bemidji State University, where he's perhaps best known for his efforts to save the endangered Ojibway language. It is primarily his scholarship of Red Lake Nation history on which I rely.

Jourdain's autocratic style served the interests of Red Lake Nation in asserting sovereignty, but during his last twelve years as chair of tribal council the growing rates of unemployment, poverty, alcoholism, violence, addiction, and suicide presented new challenges. Jourdain faced growing opposition. When his home was burned to the ground, Jourdain's wife feared for their lives and they moved into the city of Bemidji. When he came up for reelection in 1990, the opposition candidate, Butch Brun, called for greater transparency and accountability. When the votes were tallied, Jourdain lost but immediately called for a recount. The tribal constitution had a residency requirement, however, and when Brun challenged him on it in tribal court, he cooperated in a peaceful transition.

The last major political accomplishment of Roger Jourdain was to get the reauthorization of the Indian Self-Determination Act in 1988 with new language about honoring broken treaties. What Jourdain wanted most was the return to Red Lake Nation of all the land that had been seized during the last century. Land on which my great-grandparents had homesteaded. The legislation passed.

The Bureau of Indian Affairs was established in 1824 by Secretary of War John C. Calhoun—defender of slavery and advocate for Indian removal. Without congressional approval, Calhoun created the agency as a division within the War Department. After the Indian Wars and forced relocation to reservations, BIA switched to implementing twentieth-century policies of assimilation: allotments; boarding schools; and prohibitions on using Indigenous languages, religious practices, and customs. Mid-twentieth-century assimilation policy took a new turn: urban relocation. Termination and assimilation policies had not fully succeeded in the eradication and extinction of Indians. The economic, social, and political conditions of American Indians had become insufferable.

What started in Minneapolis the same summer I was raising money to buy Michael Wyand a bike became the American Indian Movement (AIM). In November 1969, a group of protesters occupied Alcatraz Island for nineteen months, bringing attention to the serious issues faced by Indian people. In 1972, about five hundred protesters organized by AIM occupied the BIA headquarters in Washington, DC, demanding the enforcement of treaty rights and improvement of living standards. The protesters vandalized the building after a week of being ignored by President Nixon. In 1973, activists occupied land for two months at Wounded Knee calling for the impeachment of their tribal leader, Dick Wilson, who had amassed his own private militia using BIA funds. Opponents of Wilson protested his sale of grazing rights to local white ranchers at low rates and his decision to lease the reservation's mineral-rich lands to private companies. They protested his practice of nepotism in employment and contract decisions on the reservation and his close affiliation with white BIA officials. Wilson evaded impeachment when the federal government publicly asserted it could not remove an elected tribal official because—in a contradictory reversal in logic to its customary policy—the Oglala Sioux Nation had sovereignty.

Wilson remained in office, while the country watched Nixon resign from office. Today it is no secret that the FBI COINTELPRO program infiltrated, disrupted, and sabotaged civil rights organizations, including the American Indian Movement.

In June 1975 at Pine Ridge, an armed confrontation with the FBI escalated irrevocably. Two agents were killed; Leonard Peltier, a member of AIM, was convicted of their shootings. He remained incarcerated for forty-eight years, until the commutation of his life sentence to home confinement in February 2025.

After Gerald Ford signed the 1975 Indian Self-Determination Act into law, Red Lake tribal council submitted an Indian Community Development Block Grant application to secure more housing for tribal members. Under this program, the Kakaygeesick family was included. Apparently, they were Indian enough then. At the end of January 1976, under the block grant program, the US Department of Housing and Urban Development sold the family two 1972 Liberty

Mobile Homes for $610 each. Don sent me a copy of the original agreement.

Verna, John Kakaygeesick's widow, had signed the loan papers from the Security State Bank of Warroad for one of the trailers for fifteen installment payments of $45.75. Florence Kakaygeesick, Don's mother, signed documents for the other trailer and paid the $4 registration fee per trailer to the Minnesota Department of Public Safety–Motor Vehicle Services Division. The trailers were delivered to Kakaygeesick's land on Muskeg Bay. Robert and Florence, with their youngest children, Martha, Kenny, and Kelly, lived next door to Verna.

It wasn't the first time Red Lake Nation recognized Kakaygeesick and Allotment 3. I remembered reading in the court depositions something about flood reparations when Kakaygeesick signed the will in August 1968. I asked Don to explain. He said his older brother, Robert Jr., had written Red Lake Nation in April 1968 at his great-grandfather's request to join with the reservation's claim on the Canadian government for flood reparations.

Willard Leaf, the full-blooded Swede who ran the Red Lake Realty Office for the Bureau of Indian Affairs in Bemidji, had read Robert Jr.'s April 1968 letter and had to have examined the copy of the 1905 land patent issued to Kakaygeesick for Allotment 3. Willard Leaf must have known there weren't supposed to be any allotments for Red Lake Nation. Yet he assigned George Kelly, a Red Lake forestry aide, to survey the land lost to flooding. The same George Kelly who would be a witness to Kakaygeesick putting his thumbprint on the will four months later.

Tasked with surveying Allotment 3, George Kelly walked around the small parcel on Muskeg Bay with George Angus, Kakaygeesick's grandson. Angus knew the land well. He had never married, and after his father, John Angus, died in 1952, George and Mary moved off the reservation to Warroad, and George looked after his mother. They lived in a house they rented on a small plot adjacent to the Cherne farm and a short walk from Kakaygeesick's home on his allotment. George and his mother came over every morning for coffee and cigarettes. Even though Don grew up calling him uncle, George Angus was his second cousin. Mary Angus, George's mother, was Don's great-aunt.

George Angus and George Kelly measured the land. Where the lake ended was not demarcated by a sandy beach; instead, the willows, reeds, and wetland grasses created a mucky and muddled shoreline. Muskeg Bay is named after this type of marsh or bog, from the Ojibway word mashkiig, which creates a false bottom to the lake. It consists of decomposing plant life, a type of peat that acts like a sponge and provides habitat for muskrat, beaver, and otters. One of the Ojibway names for the lake is Babiikwaawangaazaag'igan, or "Lake with Uneven Sand."

Kelly and Angus would not have ventured further from shore than the tops of their boots. Muskeg is similar to quicksand, and they knew better than to get sucked in. They stood and looked out at the big lake. The two Georges walked the perimeter of the lot and recorded their measurements. They put in a detailed report to Willard Leaf and the Bureau of Indian Affairs on the ninety-six acres Kakaygeesick lost to flooding.

Willard Leaf wrote George Kelly on October 29 to request he affirm an affidavit of the flood damage to Allotment 3 estimated at two thousand dollars and forwarded it to the Minneapolis field office for approval.

There is an enigma here in that Red Lake Realty recognized Allotment 3 for the purpose of flood reparations, but Red Lake

Nation would not provide official recognition of Kakaygeesick's descendants as tribal members.

I have found no evidence that Kakaygeesick ever received a check for flood damages.

CHAPTER 15

My research took me to Saint Paul, the city where I was born, to visit the library at the Minnesota Genealogical Society. Having scheduled an interview with an expert on researching Ojibway lineage, I drove to the office building in South Saint Paul, and it seemed eerily familiar. When I entered the lobby, I recognized the midcentury-modern architectural layout as the old Farmers Union building, where Dad had once managed the cafeteria before I was born. To the left of the elevators and behind glass doors I could see waxed linoleum floors and an empty dining hall.

I stepped inside the elevator and pushed the button for the third floor. I looked down and saw the basement button. It made me think of Dad telling us the story of how Mom had been hired as a telephone switchboard operator in 1956 here at the union hall, and her windowless office was in the basement. She'd eaten in the cafeteria on her first day and caught Dad's eye. He'd found an excuse to go down and walk past the pretty new girl's office door. But the only other thing down there was the janitor's closet, and she knew it. He had to turn around and walk past again. He stuck his head in her office, introduced himself, and struck up a conversation.

Searching for genealogical records related to the Kakaygeesick case, I found myself thinking about Mom. She had taken such interest in researching our family ancestry, and I had never appreciated how much knowledge she had gained doing it. Knowledge I wished I had now about how to do this kind of research.

Digging up the past, sorting through the facts, corroborating the evidence, and putting things in chronological order should lead me to figure out what happened. Fulfilling this urgent need to know is my habitual coping strategy for problems I can't solve.

There had been three allotments. I had to track down the other two. Which meant I had to work on the kinship tree I had started for Kakaygeesick. I'd gleaned a lot of information in the three-ring binder about the three original families in the Warroad Heritage Center, but I had spent countless hours trying to corroborate birth and death dates and to fill in the rest of the tree. Transliteration from Ojibway to English meant a lack of consistent spelling. Ka-kay-geesick. Ka-kee-ka-kee-sick. Ka-ge-gi-jig. Ka-kay-geezhig. Kagige-gijig. This confounded my search efforts, which was the reason I was now seeking professional expertise. Once I had the family tree sorted out, then I thought I could sort out the real estate problem.

Chief Ay Ash Wash (1790–1899) had two sons living on the US side of the border, and each one had been issued an allotment. Another son, Animikeese (Little Thunder), lived across the border in Canada at Buffalo Point on Lake of the Woods, which is a First Nation Reserve today.

One of the chief's sons in Minnesota, Naymaypoke, received an allotment on which white settlers had already built a school in the center of Warroad. Another allotment went to a Kakakeese, at the Northwest Angle, which is largely uninhabited Red Lake Reservation trust land today. The third allotment went to Kakaygeesick. Where Seven Clans Casino now stood.

The US Congress enacted the Indian Gaming Regulatory Act, known as Public Law 100-497, on October 17, 1988. Red Lake Chief Roger Jourdain had supported tribal gaming because it offered a new revenue stream to help support his community, though he opposed this specific legislation because he saw how state governments would lay claim to the proceeds. Congress passed the bill, but Jourdain's objections had an impact on Minnesota politicians, who signed a compact for *no* revenue sharing with state government and *no* sunset clause for renegotiation. He'd won his last battle.

The Indian Gaming Regulatory Act of 1988 included one important item of note. The new law prohibited gaming operations on lands acquired in trust after the date the law passed unless such lands were located within or contiguous to the boundaries of the reservation of the Indian tribe.

Only months before Congress passed the legislation, in August 1987, Red Lake Realty had purchased the old Booth fishery building on Lake Street where it ends near the public beach and campgrounds in Warroad. Right where Kakaygeesick's old trapline used to be.

Commercial fishing on Lake of the Woods coincided with the arrival of European immigrants in Indian territory. In 1893, more than a million pounds of sturgeon were caught, and the yield of caviar amounted to nearly one hundred thousand pounds. By 1909, the sturgeon had virtually disappeared from commercial fishing records of Lake of the Woods—and with it, the caviar market. Sturgeon are slow-growing fish and could not survive under such heavy hauls. Whitefish and walleye, however, became important, and Warroad boasted three fish-packing companies until the 1940s. In the early decades, Kakaygeesick's daughter, Mary Angus, and his daughter-in-law, Verna Kakaygeesick, earned money making seam nets for Selvog and Booth Fisheries. But commercial fishing on Lake of the Woods had largely come to an end by the 1960s. The last commercial fish harvest took place in 1985.

As the commercial fishing industry faded, sport fishing took its place. When Cal and Beth Marvin established Cal's Resort in the 1940s, John Kakaygeesick worked as his fishing guide. He knew where the fish ran. He navigated a steamboat at night by the stars through the confusing and often shallow channels between Warroad and Kenora, Ontario. He met his wife, Verna, in Kenora.

In October 1957, John Kakaygeesick, age seventy-seven, was working the sugar beet harvest near East Grand Forks, Minnesota. It was hard work, paid well, and lasted only a couple of weeks. October 8, the harvest finished; he was paid in cash. John spent some of his money on something to drink, something to warm him up inside. The temperatures had been in the forties for the past week. Pulling beets all day in the cold wet mud had left him exhausted and weak. The night before it had gotten down to thirty-seven degrees, and Tuesday was their last day in the fields. He was glad to be going home. He sat down on a bench waiting for the bus, had a few sips, and fell asleep. He never woke up.

Don never met his grandfather, John Kakaygeesick. But when John was alive, everyone in town admired him for his skill and expertise with fish. When I was a kid, the old Booth fishery stood close to Cal's Resort. Cal Marvin catered to the sportsmen who came for walleye. He and his wife, Beth, rented rooms and had a small restaurant for their guests. Many of their guests flew in with Don Hanson, who owned Hanson Flying Service. Don was a bush pilot who had an amphibious plane, and he delivered mail and supplies to the Northwest Angle. He would also fly in white wealthy sports fishermen from Lake Calhoun, Edina, or Minnetonka.

Don Kakaygeesick recalled Hanson taking his father, Robert Sr., up for a ride to check on the wild rice paddies near Buffalo Point. How he would swoop down low to the water. His father would retell the story of how this let him determine whether the wild rice was ready to harvest or not. Then he'd laugh and laugh at flying over it with a bird's-eye view.

When the rice was ready, Robert Sr., George Angus, and the Kakaygeesick boys would take canoes out to the paddies and hand-harvest the crop. They gathered rice along Harrison Creek and the Reed River, and sold bags of it to Charlie McKeever of McKeever's Flag Island Resort.

The Kakaygeesick family didn't remember hearing about Red Lake buying the old fishery. They were still mourning the deaths of Kenny and Kelly. It was Memorial Day weekend of 1987 when Don's two younger brothers died in a head-on collision west of Warroad out on the pine ridge. Kenneth Wayne, age twenty-four, and Kelly Curtis, age twenty-three, had spent the evening of May 28 in Roseau with their cousin, Billy Prelvitz, and Craig Hamilton. Sometime around 4:30 a.m. on May 29, a pickup truck driving west from Warroad toward Roseau collided with the old Chevy Vega. Kenny, Kelly, and Billy died on impact. Craig Hamilton lived a week longer, in a coma. The driver of the pickup truck broke his arm but lived to tell the police and a reporter what happened: a car full of drunk Indians ran into him.

But Kelly didn't drink. Driving east, halfway between Roseau and Warroad, the highway begins to curve slightly near the intersection with 544th Street. It is likely Kelly simply drifted off to sleep as dawn crept over the horizon, and the car crossed over the center line.

Uncle Al served during the Korean War with Billy Prelvitz's dad.

Aunt Audrey's eyes drooped, and she spread her hands flat on the table across from me when I asked her if she remembered the accident. "I felt so bad for Billy's mom, Georgina. And her sister, Florence," she told me. "It was a terribly sad thing." It happened shortly after Audrey and Al moved from north of the window factory to the pine ridge. In the past twenty years there have been other head-on collisions at the same spot, less than a mile away. "One not too long ago," Aunt Audrey told me, while we talked over coffee and her blueberry pie.

Don said Kenny told him about a dream he had three times before he died. The first time Kenny dreamed it, he was in the Twin Cities. Then twice when he was in Warroad in the month before the accident. In the dreams, he stood where the old fishery stood. He saw a sacred person—with long loose hair standing next to a white buffalo across the river—who waved at him so he could be seen. Something or someone urged him to walk across the water. He looked down at his feet and saw he wore moccasins. He started across and felt filled with great joy, excitement, and wonderment on how this could be. He crossed the river still walking on water toward the old man and reached out to touch the white buffalo before he woke up. When Kenny told Don about this recurring dream, Don thought about what it could mean. The white buffalo signifies peace and new beginnings, a turn toward spirituality and conscious awareness.

Indian gaming in the form of bingo and pull-tabs became a popular form of entertainment in the 1980s, especially among white communities in Wisconsin. A group of grandmothers on the Oneida Indian Reservation not far from Appleton introduced bingo in 1976—my senior year of high school—as a way for the tribe to raise money to pay the light bill at the struggling civic center. Within a few years, bingo financed vital health and housing services for the tribal elderly and poor. The Oneida may have been the first in the nation to recognize gaming as a means for generating operating revenue for the tribe, but many were to follow, some tribes more successfully than others.

The Indian Gaming Act of 1988 sets forth strict regulations and reporting obligations for different classes of games. Class I games are defined as social, and prizes are of minimal value. They are considered part of traditional Indian culture, and individuals participate in them in connection with tribal ceremonies or celebrations: dance competitions at powwows or wagers on a friendly game of lacrosse. Class II gaming referred to games of chance, like bingo, pull-tabs, or drawings for those who purchase a ticket for a chance to win a prize. Class II did not include card games such as baccarat or blackjack, nor did it include slot machines. Those belong to Class III gaming, and Class III gaming was authorized for the first Seven Clans Casino operated by Red Lake Reservation in the town of Red Lake, a hundred and ten miles south of Warroad.

As soon as that casino opened, Red Lake tribal council began to plan for casinos in Thief River Falls and Warroad. They started construction first in Thief River Falls, where Red Lake River and Thief River meet, eighty-five miles southeast of Warroad.

Thief River Falls is where a large Ojibway village known as Negiddahmitigwayyung (Where the Two Rivers Meet) once stood.

Monsomo (Moose Dung), the chief of the village, and his son Miscoconoya (Red Robe) had both signed the Old Crossing Treaty of 1863. The treaty delivered eleven million acres of real estate in northwestern Minnesota and northeastern North Dakota to the US government in exchange for six hundred and forty acres reserved for Monsomo and his people.

The only chief who refused to sign the Old Cross Treaty was Maydwagunonind of the Red Lake Bands. He left the treaty negotiations and walked from Red Lake to White Earth, where he appealed to Episcopal Bishop Henry Whipple to intercede on their behalf with the federal government. Maydwagunonind objected to the treaty for its concession of lands and refused the notion of removal to reservations with land allotments. After Monsomo died in 1872, more white settlers began to arrive in the Red River Valley. His son, Miscoconoya, began to lease out or sell parcels. By 1901, he had lost almost all of the six hundred and forty acres, and whites saw no need for Indians to live among them. In 1904, whites forced the villagers to move to Red Lake Reservation to the east. The Indian cemetery was dug up, and remains from one hundred and fifteen graves were put on a barge up the Red Lake River and then dumped across the reservation line.

What little property remained from the original six hundred and forty acres reserved for Monsomo and his people was then put into the Red Lake Reservation trust land. The city of Thief River Falls grew from about two hundred people in 1870 to nearly nine thousand today. Home to the snowmobile manufacturer Arctic Cat, which ceased production in 2025, Thief River Falls is known today for Digi-Key, the electronic parts distributor, which is now the largest employer. Red Lake Nation opened a casino there in 1991 where white people came and spent their money.

Within a year after the casino opened in Thief River Falls, Red Lake Nation opened the Seven Clans Casino in Warroad in the renovated fish-processing plant. The building still looked like the old fishery from the outside, but inside, the black walls and blinking lights of slot machines made some forget whether it was day or night when playing games of chance. It was something to do in the winter besides ice fishing and hockey, mostly for the white tourists.

I'd begun my research thinking Red Lake Nation had no right to take the Kakaygeesicks' land for a casino. Slowly, I was beginning to see how complicated the history of this land was. My great-grandparents homesteaded on the diminished Red Lake Reservation, which implicated me in the loss of Indian land and the allotment issued to Kakaygeesick. The more I learned about the legal dispute over real estate, the less it had to do with Indians and the more it had to do with the history of white settlers. As I learned more, I began to see things differently.

But I kept coming back to the fact that sixty days before the Indian Gaming Act became law on October 17, 1988, Red Lake Realty had quietly purchased the old fish-processing plant property and placed the parcel into Red Lake Reservation trust land.

CHAPTER 16

Three Arabic-speaking women and two toddlers came out the sliding glass doors of the Women's Community Center building. The kids ran to the baby pool, and the women sat down under the shade of an umbrella at a nearby table.

Rarely did anyone swim in the Olympic-sized pool. It made my job as lifeguard easier, though it wasn't easy to endure the heat of an eight-hour shift in the Saudi sun.

I watched the women remove their abayas in the privacy of the twelve-foot-high fence surrounding the pool. From what little I knew about Arab Muslim women, I had expected to see Amish plain faces behind their veils. Their glamorous makeup and stylish Western clothing astonished me.

The women watched me slather my nose with white zinc oxide and giggled.

"Why do you burn your skin this way?" one of the women asked me in English.

"I don't want it to burn," I replied. "That's why I put this on." I showed her the tube of cream.

"No, I mean, why do you want your skin to be dark?"

I hadn't expected her to speak English. I hadn't expected her to interview me about the customs of my culture. I was there to conduct fieldwork for a master's thesis in the graduate program I would start in the fall.

"We try to make our complexion light," she added. She put her palm to her face to show me how creamy the foundation on her cheek looked compared to the back of her hand.

I didn't have a good answer to her question. Why didn't I like my skin white?

Immediately after I graduated from college and my sister from high school in June 1980, my family had flown together to Saudi Arabia. Dad got me and Barb summer jobs working as lifeguards in Yanbu, where he had worked the past couple years providing food service management for the kingdom during the construction of this new industrial city in the desert on the Red Sea. Granted family status as an executive, Dad convinced Mom to move to Saudi instead of facing an empty nest alone at home in the Twin Cities.

I had read everything I could on Arab Muslim women from my college library before I arrived. I came with a lot of assumptions. I assumed wearing a veil meant women were treated as subservient to men. I wanted to know why women went along with this.

"We wear it to command the respect we deserve from men," a young Egyptian mother at the pool told me. She had learned English studying for her law degree. "I prefer men treat me by the quality of my character, rather than my physical appearance."

My perspective on wearing an abaya widened with the experience of living where men and women cover themselves from head to toe for a practical reason. While I did not wear an abaya, I gladly adopted the custom of wearing full-length long-sleeved caftans because they protected me from the sun, and the evaporation of perspiration created a natural form of air-conditioning.

Conversations poolside, interviews in the Women's Community Center, observations on the bus, in the library, at the markets, and in the countryside where I visited a Bedouin village at the base of Hejaz Mountains—my experiences challenged my assumptions about Arab Muslim culture to reveal deeper questions about my own culture.

I asked an intimate question about marriage rituals that I had read about. "What about the custom of showing the bloodied sheets to prove the bride's virginity?"

Laughter erupted around the poolside table.

"You don't think mothers and daughters couldn't coordinate dates with the bride's monthly cycle?" a woman replied.

"A stick pin will draw blood," said another woman.

They helped me understand that in the same way wearing a white wedding dress is not a diagnostic test of virginity, a bloodied sheet is symbolic. And the conversation revealed my own assumptions about marriage and sex. I had mistakenly believed this ritualized evidence of virginity came the morning after the wedding because having sex for the first time would leave bloody evidence. But I had it all wrong. The custom of the bride presenting a bloodied sheet happens on the morning of the wedding—before the ceremony.

The male anthropologists who I had taken as authoritative sources on Arab Muslim women had not been privy to women's private lives. I had assumed women had been relegated to the private sphere because the public sphere was more important, until I saw that nothing much happened in public except men sitting around smoking khat from hookahs and drinking tea. All the real action happened within the realm of the family, where women had influence as wives, daughters, mothers, and aunties.

"But what about men having more than one wife?" I had asked these mothers at the pool.

"It depends on the wife," one woman said. Another woman chuckled.

"It depends on his mother," said the other woman.

We laughed together.

I could only imagine the disadvantages. These Arab women argued that one clear advantage to polygamy is that wives outnumber their husband and can become effective allies in decision-making, particularly if his mother joins in allegiance with her son's wives, and especially since a husband is required to treat each of his wives equally according to the Quran. I wasn't convinced that a man outnumbered by women in his own home couldn't be a tyrant. I'd grown up in such a household.

"Come in," his muffled voice called out behind the office door.

When I walked into Professor Marvin Zonis's office, I found him sitting behind a large desk in front of a wall of windows, the telephone wedged between his ear and shoulder. He didn't look up at me. I stood there waiting, silently.

Putting one hand over the mouthpiece, he whispered through his mustache, "Sit down. I'll be just a minute."

I sat in the chair directly across from him.

He held up his index finger for me to wait one more minute. He shook his head from left to right as though trying to hurry the person talking on the other end of the line. "Yes, yes, I agree. I'll look at that before we go on the air tonight." He hung up the receiver and disentangled himself from the long phone cord.

Then Marvin Zonis sat up straight, looked me in the eye, and gave me his undivided attention. He recognized me from his class, and I told him I needed a thesis adviser.

"Tell me about your summer in Saudi," he said. He listened, asked questions, and agreed to be my adviser. "By the way, I need to hire a research assistant. Do you need a part-time job?"

"Yes!"

He put me to work. I read translations of foreign radio and television news broadcasts, filed newspaper clippings, and reviewed government documents and white papers from policy think-tanks and foreign policy experts. Marvin appeared nearly every weeknight providing analysis and commentary on the ABC late-night news program *Nightline* when American hostages were held in Iran. While gaining research skills, I earned money for living expenses.

What I hadn't realized when I walked into Marvin Zonis's office that September afternoon in 1980 is that I had found a father figure who encouraged me to ask critical questions and supported my efforts.

Dad arranged for Barb and me to get our summer jobs back as lifeguards in Saudi, and I had a second summer of fieldwork on which to write my thesis when I returned to Chicago.

"Whose puppy?" I asked when I looked at the room for rent. An adorable mixed terrier like the one on *Petticoat Junction*. It had just peed on the freshly mopped hardwood floors.

"That's Bob; the last tenant left him behind. I'm Reggie," said the attractive six-foot-tall man whose ad in the classifieds I had answered. "Yours, if you want him. Comes with the room." He showed me the rest of the four-bedroom apartment he shared with two graduate students, one from India and one from Poland. Walking distance to campus, the place had an enclosed sunporch where I could write.

"I'll take it." And I wanted the puppy.

"Come here, Bob," I heard my own voice sounding exactly like Mom calling Dad by his first name. I tied a red bandanna around his neck. Bob quickly learned to follow my every command.

Reggie collected the rent. I learned he grew up in Hyde Park. His Jamaican-born father worked on campus as an electrician. On Saturday nights from midnight to 2 a.m., Reggie deejayed a program on the university radio station playing the best tunes heard on Chicago's South Side—from Marvin Gaye to Gil Scott-Heron. I became his most avid fan, and within weeks he became my lover.

"I'm meeting your dad in Bangkok next week," Mom said, when she called me Sunday afternoon. Dad flew her to a foreign country every three to six months, and they vacationed together.

"Thailand?" I wasn't sure where they would go next. They had been to see the changing of the guard in London, toured Spain, and ferried from Copenhagen to Helsinki.

"I hope it's like the Philippines," she said. "Hot tubs, fresh shrimp, and shopping."

These were good years for Mom. Dad spending money on her—gifts of jewelry, tailored clothes, five-star restaurants, souvenirs, and pricey knick-knacks—this was his way of showing affection and showing off. She had moved back to the Twin Cities, got a new job at Honeywell, and took luxury vacations in foreign countries. Dad kept working in Saudi, and Mom kept their finances. And she never seemed happier in her marriage to my father. They wrote letters to each other every day they were apart.

His chest to my back with his arm swung over my waist, Reggie started to snore. Our bodies slick with sweat after sex in the late afternoon during a June heat wave, we lay there naked in front of the fan. Two years together. He'd recently lost his job delivering pizzas on his bike and started delivering weed instead, while I had been admitted into the doctoral program and spent most of my time working in Marvin's office on campus.

I rolled out from under his arm and off the bed, headed for the shower. I turned on the water and stepped in. Reggie opened the bathroom door.

"Grab your own towel," I said.

He shut the door, pulled the shower curtain back a little, and stepped in behind me.

I looked down and saw my crotch crawling with bugs. I bent over to look closer and saw movement in my pubic hair. And I felt him hard behind me.

A jolt of rage swept through me. I leaped out of the tub. "What are these?" I picked at them and it felt like scabs under my fingernails.

Reggie shut off the water and pulled back the shower curtain. "Looks like lice. Let me see."

He stepped out of the tub and looked at the bug on the tip of my finger I had shoved under his nose. "You got crabs, babe." Then he looked down at his own crotch.

I couldn't see them against his dark skin. "If I have them, then you have them."

"Shit." He poked his groin and pulled one off with his fingernail.

"What whore gave you crabs?" I was mad. "You did this to me!"

"Shut up, bitch," he yelled.

"No!"

Reggie punched me in the upper left cheek, and I fell against the bathroom door, hitting the back of my head.

"Stop it!" I screamed.

He hit me again.

I fought so hard for so many years to forget what happened then that I don't have many memories—except in shards. The peach-colored bathroom walls and white porcelain sink, looking in the mirror without recognizing myself. My Polish roommate putting a steak on my black eye. The apology, the vow it would never happen again, the tender kisses. It did happen again. Someone called the police, because he was arrested. Somehow I took Bob the dog and left.

"Do you remember when we played Lincoln Logs together at Aunt Audrey and Uncle Al's house?" I asked my cousin Mark.

"No, I don't remember that." Mark had spent some of his childhood in Warroad, and some of his childhood in the Twin Cities. Aunt Shirley and Uncle Howard divorced when we were kids. Mark had just arrived in Chicago on a postdoc fellowship and agreed to share the rent on a two-bedroom apartment on Harper Street, close to campus. "I really don't want to talk about the past."

Neither did I.

"Do you want to watch *Purple Rain*?" Mark asked, showing me the new video he bought. He had a large-screen monitor set up in the dining room, where we didn't even have curtains on the windows yet.

"Yes," I said, "and I'll make popcorn."

Mark turned the volume up loud. We enjoyed watching the Prince movie, and I think some of the neighbors did, too.

"Mark! Open up, please!" I had come home the next afternoon with my arms full of groceries, Bob on the leash, and an urgent need to pee. I had unlocked the front door and the deadbolt, but the sliding chain lock on the inside blocked my entry to the apartment.

"C'mon," I said. I heard scuffling inside, down the hallway. Sounded like a couple people rushing around, maybe trying to put on clothes. Did Mark have a woman here for a rendezvous in the afternoon? "This is ridiculous," I called out.

Then I heard the back screen door slam.

"Mark? Mark! Open up!"

No answer. Inside my chest, irritation morphed into anger tinged with fear. I shoved against the door and broke the chain off. Furniture in the living room knocked over. My room looked like it had been ransacked. Closets open and boxes tossed around. Then I saw the video monitor was gone from the dining room. The kitchen back door stood ajar. Out the window I could see a couple guys running behind the Co-op toward Fifty-Fifth Street.

When I called 911 to report the break-in, my hands shook.

"So nobody's hurt?" the dispatcher asked.

"No, but the front door is busted," I said, "and they stole my cousin's big-screen TV."

"Anything else?"

"No, I don't think so." The truth is we had nothing worth stealing. I had a used mattress on the floor, boxes of books, and a typewriter. The thieves had ransacked through everything we did have.

"We'll try to send an officer out there today," the dispatcher said. "This is a nonemergency call, so I don't know when they will get there."

I felt so violated, so exposed, sitting alone in an apartment house with a broken front door. Mark came home before the police arrived. We filed a police report.

When I called the property management company to arrange for them to come fix the locks, they refused. "The tenant is responsible for the repair and any damages," the woman on the phone said. "Read your lease. Any damages will be taken out of your security deposit."

Mark fixed the door.

Because we'd called the police, Ace Realty sent us an eviction notice. They didn't want tenants who called law enforcement to their properties. Mark and I both looked for other housing. He found a one-bedroom on Hyde Park Boulevard in a building out of my price range, and I moved in with a friend in Wicker Park on the north side.

It would be many years before I learned the property management company had won a judgment in eviction court against me for breaking the lease. The fact that I was white had meant it hadn't affected *my* attempts to secure housing. No one had ever run a background check on me for arrests and convictions. It wasn't until forty years later that I wondered whether Reggie's arrest record for domestic violence had made it difficult for him to get housing or employment.

For decades I thought of myself as a victim. I was able to convince myself my experiences made me exceptional. Like the knife at my father's throat coming from the back seat of the Impala for his wallet. Like my father's throat spewing his rage at me. Like his daughter who had to be told to lock her door and roll her window up driving through this neighborhood. Like I deserved it.

I had believed back then that I had deserved it. The victimization. The trauma. The drama. Without Dad playing that role in my life, I found Reggie to replace him. Even though I'd let myself fall head over heels with someone as different from my own father as I could possibly imagine, I'd accepted a dynamic even more toxic and dysfunctional.

CHAPTER 17

When Seven Clans Casino opened in Warroad in 1992, Don Kakaygeesick got a new job working as a machine technician.

"My job was to keep those slot machines running," Don told me.

The repurposed Booth building had plush new carpeting, digital slot machines, and flashing electronic lights everywhere; it didn't look or smell anything like a fish-processing facility on the inside anymore. Seven Clans Casino made good money from bingo in their other facilities. But in Warroad, bingo was upstairs on the second floor, and the first-floor casino was their cash cow.

"Is that where you met Charlene?" I asked Don. He'd told me the casino opened a couple of years after he and Ronda broke up.

"Yes. Charlene worked at the casino as a cashier," Don said.

Charlene Rose Martin, whose Ojibway name was Mushkoways (To Be Strong), had been born in Red Lake the same year as Don: 1959. "When I was a teenager," Charlene had told Don years later, "there were days my heart raced so fast it scared me." Other times she felt short of breath even though she'd be sitting perfectly still. The tightness she sometimes felt in her chest matched the high numbers of her blood pressure. She was diagnosed with pulmonary hypertension. But she graduated from Red Lake High School in 1977, went on to nursing school in Detroit Lakes, Minnesota, and graduated in 1985.

Charlene had worked at the Jourdain-Perpich Extended Care Center on Red Lake Reservation before she moved to Minneapolis. "There she was employed at Cedar Pines," a nursing home in the center of the Indian urban community, Don told me.

Charlene's heart compensated for the disease by thickening its walls and expanding its chambers to increase the amount of blood it could hold. She didn't have any symptoms when she was resting, and she experienced shortness of breath and chest pain only when physically active. Even though her doctors recommended she not have children, she ignored them and had a son, Shawn, and two daughters, Cheyenne and Lisa.

"Charlene worked for Cash Systems in the Twin Cities for eight years," Don told me. "She applied for the position of cashier when she heard Seven Clans Casino opened in Warroad."

Charlene moved north with her three children. She took her medications and monitored her health carefully. She knew she would never get better, but she tried to get sicker slower. And she worked steadily.

The new casino brought in people from outside Warroad. Tour buses filled with seniors arrived from Winnipeg during the middle of the week. Without a movie theater in town, the casino became one of the only venues for entertainment other than the bars and churches. Unlike Las Vegas gaming establishments, Seven Clans Casino did not serve alcohol. With dim lighting and dark carpeting, the bright flashing lights and rollicking sounds of gaming machines transformed the old building where fish were once processed.

Charlene gave her heart to Don, and in 1994 they had a daughter. "Dakota was born prematurely and spent two months in the neonatal intensive care unit," Don said. When Charlene's health began to deteriorate, she had to take more medicine and be careful not to overexert herself. "I helped care for Dakota in a way I hadn't with my previous children." He bought a used manufactured home and parked it at a trailer park north of Warroad.

Don's parents, Robert Sr. and Florence, still lived on Allotment 3 in one of the two trailers financed through Red Lake with the HUD block grant in the 1970s. Don's sister, Karen, and her husband lived in the other. Don and Charlene spent time together with his parents so they could enjoy their new granddaughter.

"Charlene went back to work at the casino for a couple more years, but eventually she was too sick to continue working so hard," Don said. She stayed home with Dakota, and Don went to work for Marvin Windows again. For a while he drove one of Marvin's tractor trailers on long hauls across country.

Early in the morning of June 17, 1998, Don's dad, Robert Kakaygeesick Sr., went out to the van while he waited for his wife, Florence, to get ready because they were going into town. Robert had plans to meet tribal officials from Red Lake. Don's recollection is that Red Lake Realty had offered his father a loan and wanted the deed to Allotment 3 as collateral. What he needed a loan for is unclear, but at his age he would likely be unable to repay it on his monthly veterans benefits. That would have been an easy way to have laid claim to the deed.

When Florence came out to the van, she found him slumped over the steering wheel. She called to Karen for help. Karen and her husband moved him to the middle of the bench seat, and her husband drove them to the hospital in Roseau.

"I remember there was a big white envelope on the seat next to him," Karen said as she recalled finding him unresponsive. She's not certain it was the deed.

They arrived at the hospital where they resuscitated him and ran tests. The doctor said he'd had a heart attack and recommended he make an appointment in Grand Forks for more tests. He would likely need surgery for a blocked artery.

"Not a good day," Robert Sr. told his son, Don, after they admitted him to a hospital room. He spent four days there, but refused to schedule an appointment in Grand Forks, and they discharged him on Father's Day. Karen brought him a card, a cake, and a gift. "He really enjoyed the beanie baby," Karen said.

Their father wanted to get back home for the Warroad powwow the next weekend, but he wouldn't live to attend.

Around 3 a.m. on Wednesday, Florence came rapping on Karen's trailer door. She needed help. Robert Sr. was up wandering around the living room hollering. Karen gave him one of his new nitro pills. It didn't seem to calm him down any. Then he suddenly slumped to the ground. Karen grabbed under his head before it hit the floor. She held his head in her lap and got him to swallow a second nitro pill. Florence called an ambulance.

"It's going to be okay, Dad," Karen said to him. "They're coming." She kept talking to her father until they heard the sirens.

The EMTs put him on a stretcher and into the ambulance. Karen asked her mother if she wanted to ride in the ambulance, but no, Florence made Karen get in with him. As they drove west on Highway 11 to Roseau, Karen noticed streaks of color above the horizon running northeast to northwest. Aurora borealis. The spirits of ancestors dancing in the heavens readied to greet her father. Karen's husband and her mother followed the flashing lights to the hospital in the van. Karen recalled the EMTs gave him CPR en route. In the emergency room they spent nearly an hour with defibrillator paddles shocking him before declaring time of death.

He was born on August 4 in 1922, and he died on June 24, 1998, at the age of seventy-five. A mere coincidence that June 24 was the date of President Roosevelt's signature in 1905 on his grandfather's allotment papers.

When Don's father died, his mother moved to the trailer next door with Karen on Allotment 3. And Karen's husband moved out. Don and Charlene spent more time visiting his mother, especially during the summer months.

The 160-acre agricultural parcel next to the Kakaygeesicks' land was owned by Anthony Cherne. Cherne was a wealthy man who had created a multimillion-dollar contracting business that flourished in Minnesota and Michigan. In the 1960s, his company built the Minneapolis–Saint Paul airport in Bloomington.

Anthony Cherne hadn't lived on the land for many years, but someone from the family had always remained in residence. The farm had been in the family for more than a hundred years. There was a cemetery on the property where Anthony Cherne intended to be buried. Marvin Windows had tried several times to purchase the Cherne land to build another factory, but Cherne had always refused.

In 1999, Red Lake Realty approached Cherne. Anthony Cherne had been a good neighbor to the Kakaygeesicks. Don had mowed the lawns around the big Cherne barn during his teen summers. Mr. Cherne always remembered Don's great-grandfather fondly. He wanted to make sure the Kakaygeesicks kept the land they'd always lived on. So, when the tribal realty officials told him their purchase of his land would provide permanent housing for the descendants of Kakaygeesick and protect their legacy and status in the community,

Mr. Cherne agreed. Cherne sold the land for $590,000 on August 16, 1999, and the transfer of deed to Red Lake was recorded in Roseau County on September 11, 2000, with two thousand dollars paid in taxes.

What Red Lake Nation intended was to build a new and bigger casino in Warroad with a luxury hotel and resort facilities across the river from the original casino. The old fish-processing facility had grown too small, and while they'd expanded years ago by repurposing an old Quonset hut attached to the front of the fishery for slot machines, the casino lacked tourist appeal. They had already begun construction in Thief River Falls on a new water park and resort hotel at the casino. When Cherne sold, no public or official announcement of the land transfer was made except in the county clerk's office with the register of deeds.

Red Lake Realty acquired the 160 acres of Cherne land situated between Highway 11 and the waterfront. The only way in and out of Kakaygeesick's land was along the Cherne property line.

Now all Red Lake needed to secure a vacation destination location for a new resort casino was the missing piece: Allotment 3. The land where Karen lived with her mother, Florence. The land where Don kept his trailer. The land they called home.

In the spring of 2000, after Robert Sr. had died and the Cherne land had been sold to the tribe, Red Lake tribal officials invited the Kakaygeesick family to Lakeview Restaurant and bought them dinner. Lakeview Restaurant was owned by the tribe, as they'd continued to purchase waterfront properties from the old casino up to the public beach. They'd built Warroad's only upscale restaurant with a wall of windows facing the waterfront and served first-rate meals with fresh walleye, fresh-baked cranberry bread, and hand-harvested wood-parched wild rice. Robert Jr., John, Karen, Don, Martha, and their mother, Florence, attended the dinner. The conversation during the meal was polite; everyone was cordial. But Don knew they would never have approached his great-grandfather about sitting down to dinner together like this. Kakaygeesick had never trusted Red Lake officials and had died convinced they would try to take his land.

"Are you done with that?" the waitress asked Don.

"Yes, thank you," he replied, and sat back in his chair as she leaned over to take his plate. Don turned to Harlan Beaulieu, who sat next to him. "So what's the reason for this meeting?" Don appreciated the free supper, but he knew there must be strings attached.

It was then Harlan stood up. The entire table fell silent. As an officer of Red Lake Realty, he offered to buy the Kakaygeesick property. Beaulieu talked about building permanent housing for the family members and even discussed offering them tribal membership.

"We'll think about it," Don told Harlan.

The next morning, Harlan Beaulieu showed up at the bay. He knocked on Karen's door.

Karen opened the door and saw who it was. Beaulieu stood in the lawn, looking around at the property, facing away from her trailer, his chin pointing from oak to oak around the perimeter of the property. She stepped into the doorway and didn't invite him in.

He turned toward her. "Wouldn't you like to live in a real house instead of this ol' trailer?" he asked her. "We'll build you something better than this." He jutted his chin toward her home and tried to catch her eye.

"I love my trailer. I love this place. Go on!" Karen shut the front door behind her. She stood there with her back to the door. She listened and waited a long time before she heard the door of his vehicle slam shut and him driving away. Then she went outside to walk the land, to face each of the four directions.

Don and his siblings talked with Florence about Red Lake Realty's offer. His mother was adamant that they should not move. Red Lake tribal officials had verbally reassured them during their previous dinner that they would not have to relocate. The Kakaygeesick family then heard it would be part of a housing development, not custom home construction. And tribal membership never materialized when Red Lake put their offer in writing six months later. Neither did any cash offer; only the in-kind value of life use of Red Lake housing. Bottom line: Florence Kakaygeesick and her children had no interest in selling the land or moving.

The Kakaygeesicks did not respond to Red Lake Realty's offer. No response meant no. Don anticipated an attempt to take the land, but he didn't anticipate that it would be through probate court.

In December 2001, without the knowledge of the Kakaygeesicks in Warroad, the Bureau of Indian Affairs in Red Lake submitted to probate court the estates of Albert and George Angus, who were the sons of Kakaygeesick's daughter, Mary. Probate court sent letters to the descendants of Mary Angus, to determine whether they had an interest in the matter, but not to the descendants of Robert Kakaygeesick. Since Don and his siblings knew George Angus had a will and knew Robert Kakaygeesick to be the sole beneficiary, the Kakaygeesick family was quite surprised to discover George Angus's estate would be probated. The court had not notified the heirs of Kakaygeesick despite their interest in the estate of their father, Robert Kakaygeesick Sr.

Don Kakaygeesick knew they needed legal advice, but attorneys cost money. Finding the right attorney wasn't likely in Warroad, so he went to Bob Marvin and asked for his help. Bob agreed and contacted Marianna Roca Schulstad, a lawyer with Leonard, Street & Deinard in Minneapolis, the firm that had handled Marvin Windows' legal matters for many years. Bob paid her retainer fee. She began her investigation into the facts of their case.

Mary Angus had died without a will in 1974. Because she had no will, there had been no challenge to the inclusion of Allotment 3 in her estate inventory back in 1978 when the probate courts settled her estate. That she did not have the allotment papers, nor a copy of her father's will, was not taken into account in the court's determination.

Kakaygeesick had kept the deed to the allotment in a safe in the jewelry store of Julius Anderson in downtown Warroad for decades. George Angus had taken possession of it when Anderson closed the jewelry store for good, in the early 1980s. George had given it to Don shortly before he passed in 1990.

Albert Angus died intestate in 1976. But long before his own death, George wrote a will designating Robert Kakaygeesick Sr. as the beneficiary of his estate. Dated August 16, 1982, the original and two copies were sent to Red Lake Nation. But when Red Lake Bureau of Indian Affairs submitted the estates of George and Albert Angus in December 2001 for probate, no will for George Angus was presented. Further, there was no indication anyone had ever challenged Kakaygeesick's will of 1968, which had been altered from the original to make Mary Angus the sole beneficiary. But, according to Anton Treuer's reading of Red Lake tribal archives, someone *had* objected to Mary's gift deed to Red Lake Reservation in 1973, though who that person was isn't clear. Treuer noted only that Allotment 3 as a gift to Red Lake Nation was blocked by the objections of other heirs. When I emailed him to ask about the footnote, he wasn't able to offer any additional information.

Red Lake Nation documents submitted to the probate court asserted Mary offered to give the land to them in 1973 shortly before her death, but Don did not recall that their family ever heard Mary planned to gift deed the land to Red Lake Reservation. He and his sister Karen told me Red Lake Realty came out to the land in the mid-1970s, after Mary died, and poured a foundation, saying they planned to put a house there for George Angus. I asked Don if he thought George might have been the person who objected in the Red Lake Council records. Don couldn't say, but he did remember his dad telling him that Tom Lightning had gone to Red Lake tribal elders and said if they built George a house, they needed to build housing for Verna, and for Robert and Florence Kakaygeesick, too.

No house was ever built there.

In probate court in 2001, Red Lake tribal council claimed to have lost George's original will. The judge would not recognize copies as legal evidence, and the proceedings moved forward as though the only will that mattered was one that had been altered in 1968 bearing Kakaygeesick's thumbprint.

In April 2002, attorney Marianna Schulstad, on behalf of the Kakaygeesick family, wrote to the administrative law judge to request they be included on the service list for the probate of George and Albert Angus's estates. The letter did not state why they were interested in these estates and made no mention of Allotment 3. It received no response. On September 6, 2002, Judge Lambrecht received a second letter from Schulstad that explained their intent to contest title to the property and provide evidence that Allotment 3 should have passed to their father, Robert Kakaygeesick Sr., through John, the son of Kakaygeesick, instead of his daughter, Mary Angus.

Schulstad researched the case and put forward a number of Freedom of Information Act requests for documents, and discovered that Kakaygeesick's will had been altered. She confided in the Kakaygeesick family that they lacked avenues for legal recourse.

Don had written to Senator Paul Wellstone on August 18, 2002, asking for his help. The popular Minnesota senator, known as "the conscience of the Senate," advocated for poor and rural communities. Don hoped he might find a way to intervene at the federal level on behalf of Don and his family. After the court hearings began in September, Wellstone's staffer called Don to set up a meeting. It never happened, however, because Wellstone died in a plane crash on October 25, 2002.

Judge Lambrecht first held a hearing in the fall of 2002 to determine the heirs. Albert Angus had seven children, one of whom had preceded him in death. The only child of the deceased seventh child, Albert's grandson, was also identified as an heir. George Angus had no children.

After the heirs were identified, the court determined who received what share of the inheritance. Any debts or assets held by the deceased were recorded in an estate inventory.

For a long time, I believed Red Lake Bureau of Indian Affairs held the position that Allotment 3 shouldn't be included in the estate inventory because it belonged to Red Lake Reservation as trust land. I believed this when I read that they had argued Mary had tried to gift deed Allotment 3 to the tribe before she died in 1973. I believed this because they had tried to buy it from Florence after Robert Sr.

passed away. I believed this because their most recent intention was to build a casino there, and that could only happen on trust land.

But that was before I understood it was in the best interest of the Bureau of Indian Affairs Red Lake Agency to argue for the inclusion rather than exclusion of Allotment 3 in the estate inventory—because the Angus heirs were amenable to selling the land to them.

CHAPTER 18

The engine turned right over despite the subzero temperatures and blustery winds. I let the old Subaru warm up while I hauled my dirty laundry and detergent out to the car. The January cold snap had kept me home writing my dissertation during the semester break.

"C'mon, Bob," I called the dog to jump in the car. The snowbanks were already waist-high, and there wasn't anywhere he could run or even poop. I took him to the laundromat, where I could walk him along the edge of the parking lot at the strip mall. Bob had moved with me from Chicago when I accepted a one-year teaching appointment at the University of Wisconsin–Green Bay.

The radio reported the temperature at forty below with windchill. I parked and hauled in my laundry. Bob came inside with me. It was warm and humid with the dryers running. I loaded up four washing machines and plugged them full of quarters.

"C'mon, Bob." I walked out the laundromat door.

The second that blast of cold air hit my glass lenses, they exploded. I decided right then to look for a permanent position in a warmer climate.

I took off my winter coat and boots before I left Hartsfield airport. The shuttle drove me to Athens, where the beauty of the cherry blossoms took my breath away. Walking across the lush green campus of the University of Georgia in February felt like a Valentine to myself. Right down to the red velvet cake served at the fancy faculty club for lunch.

After two days of interviews for a full-time tenure-track position teaching broadcast news in the Grady School of Journalism, the university made me an offer.

"That tastes good!" Mom finished her first Bloody Mary fast. The long drive, the heavy lifting, the heat—we were both thirsty. She ordered a second Bloody Mary before the first had taken its full effect.

Mom had agreed to drive down with me to Athens to help me move my things; then she'd fly back home. It was the first trip we had taken together, just the two of us, since we'd encountered that unidentified flying object almost two decades earlier. It was also the first time she and I smoked cigarettes together. She had been surprised when I pulled out my pack and lit up. She pulled out her stash and made me promise I wouldn't tell Dad she hadn't quit. I never did. And I never let Dad see me smoke.

We'd just spent two days on the road with all my worldly possessions piled into the bed of my pickup and tied down with ropes. When I'd caught her humming the tune to *The Beverly Hillbillies*, we laughed. After unloading the truck into the duplex I'd rented off Nowhere Road just outside of town, we were sitting at a restaurant bar, waiting to be seated for dinner.

Sipping on a draft Rolling Rock, I realized I'd never been in a bar with Mom before. We sat on stools side by side.

She turned to me and looked at me as a thirty-year-old woman—not a child anymore. "You remind me of my sister, Shirley."

"Shirley? How so?" I didn't see how I resembled Shirley, but I felt almost flattered she considered me more like a sister.

"You took away my youth, the same way she did," she replied and looked down into her drink, mostly ice left in the glass. "I always had to take care of her kids. Then you came along; I had to stay home and take care of you."

As my father's little girl, I knew I'd often stolen her thunder and been the focus of his attention and affection. My arrival nine months after marriage hadn't been something she'd planned. "So why did you decide to have another kid?" Barb came more than three and a half years after me.

"I didn't decide. It just happened."

Barb more recently explained her understanding of how it happened. Mom had one ovary removed when her doctor found a cyst, and Mom didn't think she could have any more kids.

"Once you have one kid, it's all the same," Mom shrugged. "Your Aunties Carol, Harlene, and Jenny—we were all pregnant at the same time, and I was thrilled. At least, Barb wasn't a breech baby like you." The Bloody Marys had loosened her tongue. "But you're all grown up now, and this is the last time I have to take care of you. Getting you set up down here in Georgia."

The server came over then and offered to seat us; we ordered our food and ate dinner mostly in silence.

I didn't think she had intended to hurt me. But I felt sad and abandoned. The next morning, I drove her into Atlanta to catch a flight back to Minnesota. The next time I saw Mom was in Chicago for the graduation ceremony in Rockefeller Chapel. I hoped finishing my PhD would make her proud of me.

"What on earth is everyone staring at?" I demanded.

"It's not customary to see a university vehicle out in these rural parts," Bill said. "But it's more unusual for a woman to be driving if there's a man in the car. Guess we're giving them something to talk about."

Bill Griswold taught print journalism at the University of Georgia, and we'd teamed up because I was helping conduct a research project on rural economic development. My role was to head up a piece of the project examining the role of local news media in twelve communities, and I needed someone who would have credibility with Georgia journalists and community leaders when we visited to conduct interviews and focus groups. Bill had grown up in Georgia, and he was finishing his dissertation for the University of Minnesota. He'd previously worked at the *Atlanta Journal-Constitution.* He'd arrived a year before I had, and he had the right accent and the right gender to be taken seriously by our sources.

We had visited a number of small towns throughout the state in a white university vehicle with the red-and-black school logo on the passenger doors, and the stares we got when I drove and Bill sat in the passenger seat startled me. This wasn't Saudi.

I shook my head. "What year is it again?"

Seated next to me on one side of the desk, Bill began to interview the publisher of a weekly newspaper that had served the people of Blakely, Georgia, near the Alabama border since 1859.

"I grew up inside the newspaper office," Billy Fleming told us. "Fourth generation to run it. I consider my daddy, W. Hoyle Fleming, the publisher emeritus."

I'd been reading the local weekly newspapers from small towns across the state in the course of our research, and one article in the *Early County News* kept nagging at me. The story was about a trailer home that burned to the ground, and the local fire department had not tried to put it out. The corpse of a child had been found stuffed inside "a chester drawers."

I didn't know how to ask the publisher directly, so I'd said I wanted to ask him about a story that caught my eye because of the typo.

"Oh, I didn't catch it. I'm going to blame that one on Judy," he said. His wife, Judy, worked as general manager, sold advertising and proofread editorial content.

"What happened after you reported this story? Was there any kind of investigation into the child's death?" I couldn't let it go. I knew the publisher had served terms as mayor, county commissioner, and head of the chamber of commerce, Lion's Club, and Rotary. Blakely was a town of about six thousand people, about 40 percent Black. The city council had never had a Black member, and the appointed school board had only one Black resident serving. Six-year-old Antavious Williams died in that 1987 fire to which the city's fire department had not responded. The fire chief was also the city building inspector responsible for condemning unsafe housing. But none of that was in the news article.

"There had been a similar death the year before," Fleming said. Another Black child, seven-year-old Charles McCoy, died "in a fire the city fire department did not respond to promptly."

While I wanted to know how and why this could happen, Bill Griswold knew how to ask the question in a nonthreatening way to elicit an answer.

"The troubles started when Mr. Benjamin Cawthon came home to Blakely," Fleming said. Cawthon, a twenty-year retired veteran of the US Army, organized a Black citizens' group who "raised a fuss" about the difficulties Blacks faced trying to vote. The group sued under the Voting Rights Act, which led the all-white city council to scrap an at-large election system and establish council districts. Then Cawthon and his group sued the fire department, and in going to court they forced the resignations of three full-time members, including the chief, who admitted they had been members of the Klan's local klavern. None of this had been reported in the *Early County News*. Why not, I wanted to know.

Bill turned to Billy Fleming and smiled. "She's new to Georgia," Bill said to the publisher. Bill knew what to say and how little to say.

"I couldn't stay in business if I reported that, ma'am. I earn my living from selling advertising. Nobody who wants to read that kind of news has any money to advertise." Billy Fleming was honest. "Darling, my family has been running this newspaper since before the Civil War. Things don't change much around here."

He said that like it was a good thing.

When we visited Sparta, another rural community, Bill and I walked into a one-man newspaper operation. The *Sparta Ishmaelite* began publishing in 1889. The publisher agreed to meet with us because Bill had asked. He treated me like I was the secretary taking notes for my boss. The pudgy, bald white man chain-smoked cigarettes behind his desk, his plate-sized ashtray full to the brim with butts.

"Well, it doesn't look like you're getting rich running a weekly newspaper here," Bill said to him. Sparta has a total area of less than two square miles. It is the seat of Hancock County and the site of a state prison. In the late 1980s there were about 1,700 residents, about 90 percent Black, and 35 percent lived below the poverty line.

"Well, you might be surprised at how rich I am," the publisher replied. "I can't have people here thinking I've got money."

"How do you stay in business?" I asked. "Do you also print the church bulletins?" He gave us a tour of his printing operation. There was an enormous cold press circa the 1950s that took up half the building.

"Naw, the Black churches around here don't have no money for me. None of 'em will buy advertising neither. But they read the paper, if they can read."

"Well, what do you print then?" Bill asked.

"Well, Bill, I make most of my money printing Klan material," he said. "I've got the contract to publish their newspaper, all their posters and handbills. Mighty lucrative."

I had to pick my jaw up off the floor and close my mouth. Bill gave me the side-eye, and I kept it shut.

When I got behind the wheel of the university vehicle and Bill shut the car door, I asked him again, "What year is this?"

It seemed impossible to think about future economic development in rural Georgia when the shameful and ugly past remained so much a part of the present.

"I'm worried you're making it difficult for yourself, Jill," a well-meaning female colleague said to me after the faculty committee meeting. "I thought you wanted tenure here."

"What do you mean?" I replied. "I do."

"Then why did you agree to be the faculty adviser to Students Against War?" she asked. "The news coverage of their tent encampment on the quads is not going to win you any brownie points with the administration."

"Because the students asked," I said. One of my smartest undergraduates had approached me after class with several other students. She had said they needed an adviser to the student group to apply for a permit to protest on campus. She was the kind of student who cringed when her classmates barked at me in Friday afternoon class, as Bulldog football fans tended to do.

"Jill, it's not only that," my colleague said sweetly. "This is the South. You wear Birkenstocks instead of heels and lipstick."

In that moment, I realized it wouldn't matter how much research I published or what my student evaluations looked like, because I didn't belong there. I started looking for teaching jobs in the North, at small liberal arts colleges like the one I had attended.

The real estate agent, Cathy, picked me up from the hotel in downtown Ithaca and drove me around the city to look at housing options.

"Let me show you a place outside of town," Cathy said. She went up the hill, heading west on Highway 79. "The owners of this house made an offer on one of my active listings. They don't want to sell this house to buy the second one, but they need rental income to close the deal." She drove down a long country lane and, after the pavement ended, turned into a short driveway.

A small two-story gable-roof home sat back off the tree-lined lane. On the north side of the house was a porch facing a field of waving grass against a backdrop of undulating hills. Inside was an open floor plan with an enormous kitchen and two bedrooms upstairs with an open loft space and skylight windows. I didn't yet have a job offer, but I was ready to put down a security deposit to live in this beautiful place on eleven acres of land.

I wasn't back in Georgia more than a week when the job offer came. Before I accepted, I called Cathy, the realtor, to find out if the house was still available. It was. I signed a lease for an August 1 move-in date.

My first night at my new country home, I sat on the back porch watching a field of fireflies dance as dusk arrived. I could see the stars overhead, and the sky seemed as endless as it had been when I was a kid on Lake of the Woods. I went inside and fell asleep on the floor.

Something woke me up. When I opened my eyes, I could only see a bright shining light coming in the bathroom window to the east. Was that a car out there with its brights on?

My heart thumped, and the rush of fear forced me into high alert. Alone in the country in the middle of the night, and I didn't have a landline connected yet. I frantically groped around on the floor searching for my glasses. There was no place to hide.

Bob the dog just lay there, sound asleep.

When I put on my glasses, I burst out laughing. The light was a full moon, beaming down at me through the window.

I wasn't the only faculty member who wore Birkenstocks in Ithaca. Four years later, I delivered my files to the dean's office to be reviewed by the tenure committee.

And as soon as I did, I drove up and out of Ithaca and back to the land where I made my home. I went out to the deck, lay flat on my back, and shut my eyes to everything except the sound of the breeze in the trees. My bones hurt. My organs felt inflamed. My skin felt raw. Even with my eyes closed and my breathing calm, tears leaked from my eyes. I got up and called the doctor's office.

"Dr. Endo can see you Friday morning," the receptionist said.

The pain and exhaustion had been building for months with my relentless efforts to earn tenure. I didn't know what was wrong with me, but I trusted my doctor.

Dr. Endo examined me and asked a lot of questions about sleep, stress, and my symptoms. "Let's order some lab tests."

I returned to his office to discuss the results the week before fall classes started.

"I am putting you on a medical leave for the fall semester, Jill," Dr. Endo began. "You have fibromyalgia, and rest right now is required because you are spiraling down."

"I have what?"

"It is a disease of the fascia, the connective tissue. The fascia is how your body holds itself together," Dr. Endo explained. He handed me a pamphlet. "Your muscles, bones, organs, and skin all get glued together with fascia."

"So how can I get better?" I asked.

"You need to change your lifestyle," he said with a smile. "Less stress. Take this time and get into a good sleep cycle."

"I can't let you take a medical leave this fall," was how my department chair responded to my phone call. "Classes start next week."

"I'm not asking; I am letting you know. Doctor's orders." I ended my conversation and made another call to Human Resources. I let them handle it. I heard from my colleagues who needed copies of my syllabi because they were told they had to cover my classes. My medical leave added to their workloads, risking votes on my tenure case. But I was so sick, my entire body inflamed and in pain. I could barely stand to walk, and I didn't care anymore.

Doing nothing was exactly the remedy I needed. Sleep became my medicine. I took daily walks with the dog and met my neighbors.

The woman who lived around the corner on Buck Hill Road stood up from her flower bed when Bob the dog and I walked by. She took off her garden gloves and extended her hand. "I'm Nancy." She invited me in for a cup of tea and the first of many conversations.

We were watching *Martha Stewart* on the TV in her sunken living room one November morning when Nancy said, "You need to meet this friend of ours."

"Who?"

Nancy got up from the sofa to add pellets to their stove. "He built his own cabin and raises goats. Oh, and he lives by himself."

Her back was to me so I couldn't read her expression. *This must be her husband Jack's idea.* "Uh, I don't need you or Jack to play matchmaker," I replied.

"Do you want to come with me to the carol sing at Cayutaville Methodist Church tonight?" Nancy asked when she called on Christmas Eve morning. "Jack and the kids don't want to go, but I do."

"Okay." I didn't want to spend the holiday entirely alone.

"I'll drive," she volunteered. The roads were slippery with freshly fallen snow that night. We arrived a few minutes late.

As we approached the doors, I had a déjà vu moment. I felt like I'd been there before. Except I hadn't. We slipped into a pew in the back. People turned their heads and nodded or waved at Nancy. A young woman played piano, and the community sang. It started snowing on the way home and didn't stop until New Year's Eve morning.

Nancy called all the neighbors up and down the road and invited them over to play board games and ring in the New Year. Jack had the woodstove going and a houseful of guests when I arrived.

I'd taken a few sips of hot cider when in walked a tall handsome stranger.

"Sammy," said Jack. They bear-hugged.

Sam wore Carhartts and a cap on his head with earflaps that covered his long blond curls. Round spectacles. Strawberry blonde beard and mustache. And he smelled like goats.

I was smitten.

"Where do you live?" he asked me.

"Around the corner on Enfield Center Road."

"Do you have a dog?"

"Yes."

He smiled. "I've seen you walk that dog up and down Buck Hill."

"Where do you live?" I asked.

"Down back behind my parents." He'd been a truck driver hauling hazmat but had returned home to the family farm. His parents lived next door to Nancy and Jack.

And then it dawned on me. This was the farmer Nancy had wanted to fix me up with. She told me he lived like a hermit. She hadn't mentioned he was a mash-up of Kris Kristofferson, Grizzly Adams, and Jeremiah Johnson. I'd never met a more attractive hermit.

But at quarter to ten, he was already done. "Time to go," he said.

"What? You only got here."

I was disappointed he left the neighborhood party right when I was starting to have fun. But I would see him again; I would make sure of it.

After New Year's and before I returned from medical leave to teach again, I had plenty of time on my hands to become obsessed with Sam. The next day I walked with Bob the dog up and down our road hoping to run into him. Past his parents' house there was a driveway I hadn't paid attention to before. There were sawhorses at the end of it with a hand-painted sign: DO NOT ENTER.

Bingo! I made my way down the unplowed lane in search of Sam. There was a little barn—more like a shack—on the left, and a cabin on the right. No vehicle. Though I could see tire tracks. This secret compound could have been where the Unabomber hid out.

I didn't trespass just once. I did it again. And again. Early morning. Before, during, and after the lunch hour. Right before dusk. Five days of a thirty-nine-year-old woman's life. Crazed by cabin fever, stalking a bachelor goat farmer. No bunnies were harmed, but I had to admit I felt a bit like Glenn Close in *Fatal Attraction*.

Then I sat down and wrote him a love letter. A long letter. But self-doubt set in. Sam didn't strike me as a man of many words. So I started over and made it short. One page.

On what must have been my fifteenth act of trespassing, I finally knocked on the cabin door. No answer. I pulled the love note out of my coat pocket and read it over one more time.

"I want to see you again. I want to be a gentle-woman farmer and raise vegetables, fruits, flowers, and write books in the winter by the fireplace. I love goats and wish you'd let me make feta cheese. I have read all of Thoreau and Emerson and admire you enormously. Call me. I'd like to have you over for dinner."

It was ridiculous! I tore off the right bottom corner with my name and phone number and put just that scrap of paper in the envelope. With three condoms. Then I tacked the envelope to the door and ran home.

Later that day, I watched the sun set from the back deck and heard the phone ring.

"Hello, Jill?"

"Yes."

"Or is it Jim?"

"What?"

"Jill or Jim? Because this hen-scratching looks like J-I-M. Jim. I had to call Nancy and Jack to figure out who would play a trick on me like this. You're a college professor, and your penmanship looks like this?"

"Oh, no! Nancy and Jack know?"

"Yes. I asked Jack if he knew who Jim was. Nancy recognized your number."

"Uh, oh, so, do you want to come up here for supper some time?"

"Sure. How about tonight?"

"Really?"

"Yeah. I need to let my dog out and take a bath. I'll see you in an hour."

About fifteen minutes later a truck pulled into the driveway, and Sam waltzed into my kitchen.

"Hey darling, you got a tub with hot water?" He had John Deere green sprayed on his face and hands.

After he stepped out of that claw-foot tub, Sam and I were inseparable.

CHAPTER 19

Sam pulled the orange Allis Chalmers tractor into the machine shed when he saw the car pull down the lane.

Dad, Mom, and Aunt Audrey got out and stretched next to the vehicle. Mom pointed to the windmill next to the pond, Audrey pointed to the solar panels on the roof, and Dad leaned against the car door looking at the waterwheel.

Bare-chested and in jeans, Sam walked up to Aunt Audrey and gave her a hug.

Audrey gasped. "Oh my! He looks just like Krist." Audrey smiled, her deep dimples showing. I knew it wasn't only the long blond hair, beard, and mustache but also his lanky bow-legged way of carrying himself that reminded her of my cousin Krist. Mark's younger brother, Krist had lived on an island in Lake of the Woods with an Ojibway woman working as a fishing guide when he died of a sudden heart attack at age forty-two. What I remembered most about Krist is what my Uncle Al said when he crossed back over from Canada. He had dodged the draft, and when he returned to the United States, he walked the six miles from the border to their house barefoot.

"Jesus, Krist!" Al said. The kids had thought for sure the Lord arrived.

Audrey winked at Mom. We all went inside the cabin.

Mom sat next to Sam on the bench at the table. The color of their hair matched as the sunlight from the windows backlit the two of them. Strawberry blonde in soft curls.

"Well, I see where Jill gets her looks." Sam put his arm around Mom.

Dad sat rather uncomfortably in the rocking chair in the corner where my mother-in-law always sat when she visited us. Dad looked around at the rough-cut interior of the ten-foot-by-twenty-foot cabin, stunned by the rustic surroundings. He shuddered when he saw the cat walk across the table. I knew he would never eat here.

They were on their way from Minnesota to a timeshare in the Poconos and had stopped to visit for a few hours. It was the first time my parents had met Sam, though I had moved to the farm more than two years earlier.

"Come out with me to see the baby goats," Sam said to Dad. He grabbed hold of Dad's right hand and pulled him up from the rocker. Dad followed Sam out to the barn. I didn't know how that would go until later.

When Sam got Dad inside the barn, he picked up a kid goat and tried to put it in Dad's arms. Wearing a cream-colored sweater, Dad refused to hold the hay-covered, smelly, four-legs-kicking-in-all-directions animal.

"What are your intentions toward my daughter?" Dad asked Sam.

"Well, you better ask your daughter what her intentions are toward me!" Sam replied.

"You need to protect your assets from his ex-wife," said our attorney, Mariette Geldenhuys. Sam sat next to me at a conference table in her office to discuss our situation. Sam's parents had decided to sell their land to us for a nominal dollar, but both our names would go on the deed because they didn't want Sam's ex-wife to get her hands on their land.

"How does she protect her assets?" Sam asked. We weren't married even though he had proposed several times. I never saw the need for a wedding. He'd been married twice before, so I knew a marriage license offered no guarantees. His ex-wife had named her son Sammy Jr., and Sam had paid child support for him the past nine years even though Sam and his ex were separated when she got pregnant.

"Each of you needs a will," Mariette said. "We'll set it up so that if you die, Sam inherits your estate, and if Sam dies, you would inherit his." We had her make our sisters the executors of our wills.

With our wills and the deed recorded, by the end of August 2001, this tenured professor had become a landowner.

"Sam, I can't find my keys." I called him at home on my flip phone. The past twenty minutes I had frantically looked in every pocket, retraced my steps from the Eight Square Schoolhouse to my parked car and back again, gone inside to rummage through every cupboard and drawer in search of my car keys. I felt frantic.

"Well, where did you leave them?" Sam asked.

"If I knew that, they wouldn't be lost! Grrrr!" I snapped back. I could tell from the tone of his voice I had interrupted him. But I was stranded. The school bus full of fourth graders had pulled away after their field trip, leaving me in the 1892 schoolmistress costume I wore in the living history program.

"What do you want me to do?" he growled back.

"Come get me. Come start my car," I whined.

"I'm not going to drive all the way out to Dryden," Sam said. "You need the key to start the car. You need to find your keys,"

"I can't," I protested.

"Yes, you can."

Then he hung up on me.

Fury filled my lungs. I called back. He let it ring and didn't pick up. I was so frustrated, I started to cry and sat down on the front steps of the schoolhouse and wept with self-pity. Then I got angry with myself because he was right. I kept looking until I found the keys, lying in the grass not far from the steps, where I must have dropped them.

"Where did you find your keys?" Sam asked with a smile when I arrived home.

Too embarrassed, I couldn't quite admit to myself that I had reacted as though I were a victim of my keys and I had expected to be rescued or saved.

The field of sunflowers, as if on cue, bowed their heavy swollen heads full of seeds and bent their necks to look down at the ground. An eerie silence. The world had gone quiet—no planes overhead, no traffic in the distance, no electrical hum. I finished picking ripe tomatoes and peppers until the sun was nearly overhead, I walked to the cabin for something cold to drink and found Sam inside with the TV on.

"The second plane hit the North Tower at 8:45 a.m.," the reporter said. On the screen were images of rubble in Manhattan.

When I learned what had happened on that eleventh day of September, I went back out to the fields and picked beans all afternoon. Dragging a bushel basket down the row, I thought about how

I wanted to spend the future. The previous year on my sabbatical I had worked making Christmas tree wreaths for the New York City green markets, taught knitting lessons at a yarn shop, helped launch the Trumansburg Farmers Market, sold produce to local grocers and Moosewood Restaurant. Sam had convinced me we could do more with less. As I scootched along the row of beans in my overalls, I decided it would be my last year at Ithaca College.

"We keep our stock in the barn," Sam used to joke. "Playing the stock market is like gambling at the casino." Sam built more fencing, a bigger barn, and raised deer, elk, and buffalo for breeding stock. We even raised a couple litters of puppies from a pair of dalmatians—payment for a welding job Sam had done.

Christmas morning I put the water on to boil and rewrapped the Hostess fruitcake that had been in the freezer for a year. I had been so mad at him the year before for gifting it to me—crap from the convenience store at the nearest gas station—that I froze it and planned to regift it to him.

"Open it up," Sam said, as he walked in from morning barn chores on Christmas with a large box with a red bow on top.

"What is it?"

"Open it!"

Inside, I found a traditional-style spinning wheel. I hadn't known how much I wanted one until he surprised me with the perfect gift for me. It was as if he knew me better than I knew myself sometimes.

Living off the land was part *Little House on the Prairie* and part *The Last Alaskans*. Creating a sustainable small-scale farm was risky—a dangerous romantic adventure. We didn't have health insurance, but my health had never been better. I stacked firewood, baled hay, spun wool into yarn, gathered eggs, knit mittens, pickled cukes, bottle-fed kid goats, shelled peas, baked bread in a wood cookstove, and midwifed puppies.

"Girl, you've got it made," Sam whispered in my ear. "Do you know that? It can't get any better than this." He stood behind me with his arms wrapped around me and nuzzled his beard on the back of my neck after skinny-dipping in the pond under a rising moon at dusk.

When I woke up naked next to him the next morning, I looked out the window at the edge of the pond and watched the sun slowly burn off the cool of the night. The fog lifted into light.

I slipped out of bed and into a dress.

"Where are you going?" Sam asked.

"I thought we were going to court today," I replied. His ex-wife had petitioned to extend child support payments beyond age eighteen for Sammy Jr. But if Sammy Jr. wasn't enrolled in college, Sam's legal obligation ended, and our attorney, Mariette, told us she expected the court to see it that way.

Sam was mad. "It's the same thing over and over again with Colette." She'd been trying to get more money from Sam since the divorce.

"That boy is not my son," Sam always said. He couldn't contest it: the courts had sealed the case on the question of the child's paternity because he was married to her at the time the child was born.

When I first met him, he had been paying day care and support payments for years only to find out the child hadn't been in Colette's custody. She'd left her son with an older brother when she was arrested and sent to drug court.

"Don't wear that," he said. "It will just get her jealous and all riled up."

I was flattered he thought I looked good. He hadn't slept nearly as well as I had. Tossing and turning, not a lot of snoring. I knew he was in pain. One of his bison cows had nailed him hard in late June—snapped both his wrists and broke a few ribs. Afterward, he had sold the buffalo to a guy starting his own herd near Trumansburg. I thought he was bummed about having to sell his mamas. But the pain hadn't lifted for Sam this morning. The skin cancer on his back had come back with a vengeance: a deep patch between his shoulder blades that he wouldn't let me see or touch. He wouldn't go to the doctor. He was exhausted before he'd finished his coffee.

"Let's leave for town now," Sam said. He wanted to be early for his 9 a.m. family court hearing in Ithaca.

There were a lot of other people across the country in courtrooms on September 15, 2009. After the worst of the economic downturn they called the Great Recession, people were losing their homes in foreclosures with the collapse of the subprime mortgage market. People filing for bankruptcy. Nine months before the Affordable Health Care Act became federal law.

I pulled over to park the car at a meter on Aurora Street.

"Stay in the car," Sam said. "Wait for me here." He didn't want her to see me. At all. The de-escalation strategy made sense to me. I waited outside the courthouse for an hour and a half.

Sam opened the passenger door and slid in the front seat. He buckled his seat belt.

"So, what happened?"

"Nothing." Sam slumped down in the car seat.

"What do you mean nothing?"

"I mean nothing. Big waste of time. She brought college papers saying he's going to be a student at the community college."

"What does that mean?"

"I don't know. Nothing for now. Drive. I want to get home." He was sullen. I drove west on State Street. "Pull in here and go get me some beer and a pack of cigarettes."

I turned right into Pete's Gas & Groceries in the west end. I went inside where it was air-conditioned. It was only 10:30 a.m., but it was already hot. I filled a paper cup with ice and Coke, opened the cooler to grab a cold twelve-pack of Natural Lite, and stood in line at the counter. "A pack of Marlboro reds."

"Any gas?"

"Nope."

Outside the passenger window, I handed Sam his beer and cigs. Then I got in the driver's seat and started for the farm.

It was like any other end-of-summer day. I went swimming when we got back from town. Then I worked in the field pulling onions and setting them to dry on plywood boards, curing their necks in the sun. Picking peppers, sweet and hot. Fall green beans. I swam again mid-afternoon and came inside to snap and freeze beans.

Sam had company. A friend his dad's age who lived a couple miles away stopped by to visit him. Sam gave him the tour of the animal pens, and I kept busy freezing beans.

"I'm going up to my mother's house," Sam came in to tell me after his friend left. It was moving day for his parents. Sam had wanted them to live out their lives in the farmhouse, not move into town. He'd moved back almost a decade ago thinking he'd help care for his retired parents. But his mother had other ideas. She had her heart set on a senior apartment in Trumansburg. I don't know what they talked about that afternoon. But he was not happy when he got back. And I knew he did not want to talk about it with me.

Sam waited inside the cabin that afternoon for Geoff to show up at the farm at five o'clock to pay him the money he owed. It was hot inside from steaming green beans to freeze. I still had time before supper to drive over to the four tiny cottages at the other side of the pond to get the sleeping bags and supplies out of the empty cabins before the mice took over. We didn't anticipate any more campers this season.

I opened up the doors on the first two cabins and grabbed the sleeping bags and threw them in the car. I went back to haul more camping gear. Inside one of the cottages while deflating air mattresses from the bunk beds, I thought I heard a gunshot.

What? I ran outside and ran to the end of the pond where I could see our cabin. I didn't see or hear anything. *Where is Sam?*

I ran back to the cottage and grabbed the air mattresses and started shoving them into the hatchback.

"SAM!" I yelled a few times. *Ugh! He can't hear me.* I didn't see anything. I noticed the door of the cottage was still open. I ran over to slam it shut. I got in the car and drove back over to the cabin. No Sam in sight. I ran inside the cabin. He wasn't there. And his rifle was gone from its hook on the wall. I ran back outside and into the barn. Calling for him. I clambered up the ladder to the hay mow and peeked over the edge but heard and saw nothing. I scrambled down and checked all the goat pens. I couldn't find him. I went down to the root cellar. Nowhere.

My eyes scanned the property lines. Then I saw at the top of the field a car driving down the lane. Fast. Then the driver saw me, and the SUV slowed down. Three of Sam's drunk friends.

"Where is he?" John stumbled out of the passenger seat of the dusty vehicle. Rosie was driving. Her boyfriend, Jeff, got out of the back seat.

"I don't know. There was a gunshot. I can't find him."

John stopped in his tracks and looked at me. "He called me."

"When?"

"I don't know. Ten minutes ago?" John looked to Jeff.

"Half hour?" Rosie said.

"What did he say?"

"He was killing himself, and come clean it up before you saw it," John said.

It was then I howled.

And then a board creaked. John, Rosie, and Jeff walked toward the animal chute facility. The one place I didn't look. Because I never went in there. It's so stressful for the animals when the vets come or they are moved onto trailers. It's like a turnstile in a subway. Five-eighths of an octagonal outbuilding intended to corral stock without spooking them. There's only one way in and one way out. I heard shuffling inside the chute and yelled, "Sam. No. Don't do this."

Jeff reached the door first and discovered Sam had locked it from the inside. Locked it with a chain over the beam overhead.

Then the gun went off. I heard his blood spatter across the pine wood boards. My knees buckled. I collapsed on the ground. It felt as if I'd been shot in the back, right below my left shoulder blade.

"Get a crowbar," John yelled. Jeff rushed back to the SUV in search of one.

When I realized I wasn't shot, I scrambled up and ran into the cabin and called 911. The Schuyler County sheriff's department sent a deputy and an ambulance. The dispatcher kept me on the line until I opened the front door and recognized a neighbor's daughter, who seemed all grown up. She wore the yellow jacket as part of the ambulance crew.

She hugged me tight. "Are you okay?" She walked me outside. Somehow, she got me to my in-laws' house at the top of the lane until the sheriff could talk to me.

While I waited inside the house where Sam grew up, the rest of his family moved furniture into a rental truck. His mother directed the traffic of boxes from each room in the house to where it should go in the new apartment. Niece, niece's boyfriend, nephew, brother-in-law, and Sam's sister, filled the truck with furniture and boxes.

"Can't this wait until tomorrow?" I asked as if I were the only one shocked by his death.

"After what Sam did, do you think I could sleep one more night in this house?" His mother pointed her index finger at me.

When the sheriff finished interviewing me, Sam's brother-in-law and nephew moved the dining room table out to the truck and wanted to pack the chair I sat in.

"Can I go home?" I asked the sheriff.

"We're done down there for tonight. I know your dogs are inside the cabin. Kinda stressed." He looked at me, and I saw pity in his eyes. "I don't see why not." He drove me down the lane and watched me go in and turn on the light. He didn't use his cherry lights leaving up the lane or down Buck Hill Road.

I let the dogs out and walked around the pond. I howled again, raging against the moon in the sky.

First, I called Barb. Then I called Mom and Dad. I don't remember much about the conversations except they were short. It was after 10 p.m. I couldn't stop crying. Barb and her family were about to leave for a family vacation to Germany. She promised to be back by the funeral.

"Your dad and I are on our way, Jill," Mom reassured me on the phone. I may have fallen asleep for a few hours. They drove across country all night.

Bird and Annie, the neighbors, arrived with apple cider and doughnuts in the morning. I took two sips and a bite. Then I threw up. And cried for hours. They stayed and sat with me. Sam's sister came and cried. She told me the family would gather at her house to figure out about a funeral that evening.

I called Tina in Trumansburg. She called my two best friends, Amy and Mary. Amy and her husband made plane reservations from Madison, Wisconsin, immediately. Mary booked a stay for a few weeks later in the fall arriving from Atlanta. Tina called everybody else and took over my email and let people know what was going on because I simply could not function. I turned into a snot factory. Gasping to breathe, sobbing, relentlessly.

Mom and Dad arrived at the farm bleary-eyed from driving straight from Minnesota to New York. I settled them in to guest accommodations in Trumansburg with friends who generously offered.

"I can't forgive him for what he did to you," Dad said in the car on the ride to my friends' home.

I couldn't see what there was to forgive Sam for; he hadn't done anything to me. He was the one who was dead. Not me.

Then I was terrible to both of my parents. They thought I should make plans to leave the farm after the funeral. Clean start. Come home to Minnesota. I felt like a child who had misbehaved and been sent to my room. The farm was my home. I couldn't leave. Every moment I cherished with Sam was on this land.

Mom and Dad didn't know how to help, and I didn't know how they could help. Mom had a limited oxygen supply. They brought all her tanks in the car. Her COPD meant they wouldn't be able to stay until the funeral the following Saturday.

When they drove away on Thursday, I was relieved I didn't have to be drowned by their grief for me while still struggling for air on my own.

On Friday, Amy and her husband, Tracy, arrived from Madison in Elmira, New York. Standing outside the airport next to my car waiting for them curbside, I picked up a rock lying in the median strip. I held the rock in my hand; it fit perfectly in my palm when I wrapped my fingers around it. I put the rock in my pocket and kept it.

I got lost leaving the Elmira airport and ended up on a dead-end road.

"Pull over." Amy spoke quietly. I turned the car around and shifted into park.

"I don't know where I am."

"No shit."

Tracy giggled nervously. I burst out sobbing.

"But you know who you are," Amy said.

"No, I don't even know that anymore."

"Well, I do. I'll remind you. We've got a funeral tomorrow. Now we've got plenty of time to get there. So, no stress. We can have a road adventure. Let's go that way."

I looked around and realized I'd gone through an intersection where I should have turned left but didn't. How had I gotten here?

Sam died.

Amy and Tracy got me to the church on time.

The last song was accompanied by piano: "You Are My Sunshine." Whenever we'd taken a drive in his pickup together, I'd sung this song to Sam. Whenever I was a kid on long car rides, Dad used to ask Mom to sing it. Sam's mother had not selected this piano piece; I had. And I was glad to have been seated in front, turned away from everyone else, because my face was so red and splotchy. I sang along, probably off-key. I don't remember who was there or what was said.

After the funeral service, they served coffee in the basement of Cayutaville Methodist Church. There may have been food. I don't remember. His mom and the church ladies took care of all that. Banquet tables with folding chairs full of people who knew Sam. I stood at the end of the line, which backed up the stairs from the sanctuary. When I turned the corner on the landing, I scanned over the top of heads into the crowd. At the far end I saw Sammy Jr. for the first time since he was ten years old, when we'd flipped the script on Sam's ex-wife and sought joint custody and visitation. The boy's mother had allowed one visit to the farm, and then she refused, saying he didn't want to have to see Sam again. It wasn't fair to the boy, so Sam dropped it and sent his weekly checks.

I hadn't considered he might show up for Sam's funeral.

Sammy Jr. stood looking at photographs of blue-eyed curly-blond Sam on the memory board propped on an easel. Six-foot tall, dark brown straight hair, built like a linebacker, old enough to enlist. He looked nothing like Sam. I understood in that moment Sam had been right to question paternity and why she hadn't allowed any contact. The thought slammed me hard: Sam had gone to his grave without knowing who the biological father of his namesake was.

Then one of Sam's friends walked over and stood next to Sammy Jr. Same stance. Same height. They turned sidewise simultaneously. I recognized the silhouettes of their faces matched. Precisely.

Mariette, our attorney, grabbed my elbow. "I see who Sammy Jr.'s father likely is. It *wasn't* Sam." She'd waited at the back of the church for me to come out of the service. I hadn't even recognized her. She pulled me closer. "Come with me."

She grabbed my hand and led me to the back of the banquet hall into the women's restroom. She looked around to see if we were alone.

"I'm *not* okay," I said, wiping my eyes.

"Yes, I can see that." Mariette had been to court with Sam in response to Colette's petitions for increased financial support on the day he killed himself. She had been to court with him many times over the years. Sam trusted her. I trusted her.

That Sammy Jr. wasn't Sam's son wasn't a surprise. It was that Sam was dead. That was why I wasn't okay. The funeral had made it official. I was now a widow.

Mary came to visit from Georgia one weekend in early November. "How are you going to get through the winter?" Seeing my day-to-day existence, she worried.

"I don't want to leave," I said. I couldn't leave. I could still feel him there.

"Well, I'm still your phone-a-friend lifeline," she said.

A bunch of friends and friends-of-friends came out to the farm and harvested everything left in the gardens: a crop-mob. They left me with onions, beets, and potatoes to last me the winter. Sam's cousin and another friend came to check on the power inverters and wiring for the solar panels. They replaced one panel and tested the bank of batteries. I bought a cord of wood.

Sam's sister sold off the livestock. She sold the tractors. His welding equipment. Whatever farm implements and personal effects that didn't have my name stitched on them. If it was Sam's, it needed to be disposed of as part of his estate. She made sure there was nothing left for me to inherit.

Once the estate was settled, it would mean the property would be mine. Free and clear.

The family had more trouble letting go of the land than letting go of Sam. Chuck and Jan had wanted my name on the deed, but they hadn't anticipated the land wouldn't stay in their family.

"I am willing to sell some acres for deer hunting," I offered his sister. I offered the same to her son—Sam's nephew—who had used our land for hunting for years.

"You ought to give the land back to my grandparents," was his reply.

I couldn't do that. I had invested everything I had into the farm.

The tractors, wagons, fencing, tools, and all his guy stuff disappeared before Thanksgiving. Sam's family included me in their invitations to their Christmas Day gift exchange, but it was the loneliest two hours of my life.

This land had called to me. It had owned me. I had been its steward. Now the land set me free. It took me years to appreciate that this might have been Sam's final wish.

CHAPTER 20

It had been a surprise for Don to learn in probate court that Mary Angus had been considered a Red Lake tribal member when she died. In searching through US Indian Census tribal rolls, I found her sons Albert and George listed as "suspended" tribal members. When and how Albert and George Angus were added as tribal members, much less when they were suspended and what for—all that is unclear. I didn't have access to their records.

It is what I find in the public record that continues to perplex me. In a letter dated March 19, 1941, to the commissioner of Indian affairs in Washington, DC, the acting superintendent at Red Lake Indian Agency in Minnesota requested guidance. The Roseau County Welfare Board inquired whether Albert Angus would be eligible for treatment in an Indian Services hospital. In his letter the acting superintendent mentioned that Albert Angus's application for enrollment in the Red Lake Band was disapproved by the General Council on May 23, 1936, by Resolution No. 2, because of Canadian ancestry. "Whereas, the attention of this Council has been called to the enrollment of the following: George and Albert Angus, Robert Gah gay ke shig [Kakaygeesick], Max Jones and Louis Goodin," the letter quotes from the minutes, "Whereas, this Council believes they were trespassers from Canada . . . found to be affiliated with Indians in Canada, and would not be eligible for enrollment in the first place nor their descendants on the Red Lake rolls." Acting Superintendent Brott recommended Mr. Angus apply to the Roseau County Welfare Board for whatever treatment and hospitalization he needed.

Earlier in the 1924 Indian Census rolls, however, I had found Mrs. John Angus and her sons Albert and George with the notation "Enrollment approved: 92786-24." They were assigned annuity numbers. In 1936, Kakaygeesick and Kakakeese (Little Crow) were recorded as full-blooded Red Lake Indians found on Oak Island in Lake of the Woods. John Kakaygeesick and his son Robert were listed the same year, 1936, as 4/4 in Warroad and also assigned annuity numbers 537 and 548 by Red Lake Agency.

When I look further back, I find Kakaygeesick first enrolled at White Earth Reservation, southwest of Warroad about a hundred and forty miles, in July 1891. This was only a few months after his wife Wahsaygeshig died. Then he appears again as full-blood under the Red Lake Indian Agency in 1900. Kakaygeesick appears in the Indian Census for Red Lake in 1919, 1924, 1936.

The legal arguments in the summary judgment against Don's appeal didn't consider the contradictory historical evidence. Instead the arguments raised questions about whether the Kakaygeesick family was American or Canadian, whether they had sufficient blood quantum to be considered members of Red Lake Nation, whether they were Indians at all. It left them no legal ground on which to stand.

Caught between borders, bloodlines, bureaucracies. No-man's-land.

The probate court decision in 2005 left Allotment 3 in the inventory of Mary Angus's estate. Because George Angus had no children, the court divided the estate among Albert's seven heirs. Allotment 3 became the official property of Albert Angus's descendants. I cannot confirm the dates when the Angus heirs of the land were added as tribal members without access to the archives, but Don told me he had read their names in a list of recently enrolled members in *Red Lake Nation Newspaper* after 2002.

While the Kakaygeesicks thought their legal battle was against Red Lake Nation's claim that Mary Angus gifted the land to the tribe, Red Lake Nation effectively divided the descendants of Mary Angus and John Kakaygeesick against each other. They backed the descendants who would sell it to Red Lake Realty for the Seven Clans Casino.

Stunned and hurt by the probate court's decision, Don sought help from Minnesota's congressional delegation. He turned to those elected to represent him as a citizen before the federal government. None of the Angus family members had lived on the land since George, who had died in 1990. Surely possession was nine-tenths of the law. What about squatters' rights? They had stayed put on the property. One family for more than two hundred years. Unlike the tens of millions of acres transferred into white hands during the past two centuries through the sale of allotments, the Kakaygeesicks had been good stewards of this land.

The Bureau of Indian Affairs and the Department of Interior clearly recognized the land on Muskeg Bay as Indian land, but didn't recognize the lifelong residents of that land as Indians. Without Red Lake tribal status, Don was persona non grata and had no legal standing before the court. This meant he and his family were also denied all the rights requiring official tribal status: exercising hunting or fishing rights; harvesting medicinal plants; possessing an eagle feather; access to tribal health care, social services, scholarships, and fellowship opportunities.

Across the Canadian border at Buffalo Point First Nation Reserve, there is the tiniest band in the province of Manitoba. They have a white chief. John Thunder inherited the leadership position from his father, who had been adopted by his Indian stepfather, who was the great-grandson of Chief Ay Ash Wash. Non-Native cottagers spend summers on residential lots leased from Thunder, while the fifty or so tribal band members are segregated to a single dirt road in the southwest corner of the reserve and live in substandard housing. Don's brother Robert Jr. was a longtime resident there. So was his uncle Eddy Cobiness, a world-class artist. None of the band members on Buffalo Point lived above the poverty line in 2007 when Thunder brought in $2 million in gross annual revenue, according to an article in *Macleans Magazine.*

Tribal status in Canada doesn't help Don, John, Karen, or Martha Kakaygeesick or their family or clan members of the Kah-bay-kah-nong band living in Minnesota.

Don could petition the Department of Interior for tribal recognition of the Kah-bay-kah-nong, but it would take twenty or thirty years and hundreds of thousands of dollars in legal fees to wade through the Bureau of Indian Affairs bureaucracy. And BIA has always seemed more interested in eliminating tribes from federal recognition than in adding new ones.

Don garnered considerable media attention in 2005 from Minnesota Public Radio and newspapers around the state but could not find support for any congressional remedy to the situation. So he pursued the matter in court with appeals. On November 13, 2007, the Interior Board of Indian Appeals adopted the decision of the lower court to award Allotment 3 to the seven heirs of Albert Angus. They denied Don's petition because he had failed to file for rehearing within thirty days of the probate court's decision.

After this denial, Don appealed to the federal courts again to reopen the case because, first, he had no actual notice of the original proceedings; second, he was not on Red Lake Reservation, where public notices of the hearing were posted; and third, he filed the petition within three years after the date of the final decision.

On March 26, 2009, a hearing on a motion for summary judgment filed by then Secretary of the Interior Dirk Kempthorne was granted by Raymond L. Erickson, United States chief magistrate judge. Don's final appeal went before Chief Judge James Rosenbaum of the United States District Court in the case of *Kakaygeesick v. Salazar*. The decision, based on a de novo review of the record, did not overturn the summary judgment.

Judge Rosenbaum wrote in his final analysis that Donald Kakaygeesick as petitioner took "a 'shotgun' approach in this appeal, haphazardly firing objections in most any direction in the earnest hope that one may hit a target." The altered will, the fuzzy memory of notary Willard Leaf in his deposition, the lack of notification that Mary Angus's estate had been probated in 1978, the lack of notification of Albert and George Angus's estate sent to probate in 2001, and the loss of George's will—there are so many bullet holes. But Don needed to have argued points of law instead of arguing the facts.

Marianna Schulstad investigated their case but couldn't do much more than file Freedom of Information Act requests. As an attorney, she gathered information the Kakaygeesick family didn't have but did not represent them in probate court, which doesn't require the use of an attorney. But the lack of legal representation and the passage of time clearly hurt their case. There had been no challenge from the descendants of Kakaygeesick after the death of Mary Angus in 1973 or after the death of George Angus in 1990. There was no challenge until 2002—and the court held this gap in time against them.

Under federal and Minnesota statutes, the right to recover improperly distributed property is barred three years after the decedent's death or one year after the distribution of property. So by the end of 2007, the land belonged free and clear to seven members of the Angus family.

Predictably, they turned around and immediately sold it to Red Lake Realty.

They divided the million-dollar proceeds seven ways, minus their substantial attorney fees.

Red Lake Nation claimed ownership and proceeded with their plans to build a new Seven Clans Casino. Removing Robert Kakaygeesick Sr.'s widow, Florence, and her family from the land was a more delicate matter, however, so they waited.

Don and his siblings rarely left their elderly mother alone on the property. Don, Charlene, and Dakota spent as much time there as in their own home.

But Charlene's health continued to deteriorate. The doctors had prescribed her blood vessel dilators that were continuously injected through an intravenous catheter from a small pump she wore in a pack on her shoulder. She taught Don how to help her with the injections and keep the pump working and the IV site clean.

In spring of 2011, Charlene went to the Roseau Hospital because she was having difficulty breathing, and there was something wrong with the pump. Instead of taking her into a sterile examination room, they tried to address her problem in the office. They got the pump going after several hours, but it took only a few weeks for an infection to set in. Eventually Don could see the pus oozing around the injection site. Charlene was mad about it. As someone who had graduated nursing school, she knew the infection had resulted from the hospital's less than sterile procedure. It took weeks for it to clear. By summer she started to feel better.

That fall Don decided Charlene was well enough to stay alone with Dakota while he worked the potato harvest over in East Grand Forks. It was his last day, October 23, and they planned to be done by 6 p.m. and head back to Warroad. He got a call at 5:30 p.m. from Dakota.

"Mom is having difficulty breathing." Dakota explained Charlene did not have the tube in the injection site, and Dakota couldn't figure out how to make the pump work.

"Why didn't she have the pump on?" Don asked.

"She took a shower."

Don learned she had taken it off because the cord got tangled in the tub and then couldn't get it to go back in properly. She'd called Dakota into the bathroom to help her.

Don tried to explain how to connect the tubing and make the pump work, but time was of the essence. "Dakota," he said, "call an ambulance."

The EMTs arrived, but they couldn't make it work either. Charlene lost consciousness. They couldn't resuscitate her. She was dead on arrival at the Roseau County Hospital.

Don deeply mourned her. "D-A-B-D-A. I went through all the stages. D. Denial. Driving home I couldn't believe it was real. Charlene couldn't be gone. A. Anger. I wanted to blame the hospital, the idiots who didn't know how to reinsert the line and make her pump work. B. Bargaining. If only I'd finished the harvest a day earlier, or they'd called me sooner. A half hour before quitting time, end of season. Too late. D for Depression." Don paused. He signed deeply. "Acceptance. A. It took a while to get to acceptance."

When Charlene died, Dakota was seventeen years old. She was deeply depressed by her mother's death and stopped going to school. She took her GED before the end of the school year. Don continued to pay the rent on the house owned by Red Lake Housing Authority where he and Charlene had lived with the children. Don had kept his trailer next to his mother's. He and Dakota split their time between the house in town and the trailer on the bay. He feared Red Lake Realty would make it impossible for him to stay with Dakota in Charlene's house because he was not a tribal member. He moved most of his personal belongings to his trailer and kept the beds and a couch in the house in town. Don made sure Dakota received her mother's Social Security survivor benefits, and within a year his daughter moved to Windigo Island, out on Lake of the Woods, on the Ontario side of the border.

When Dakota left, Don lost the home he'd shared with Charlene. He moved to the trailer on his great-grandfather's allotment even as the courts proceeded to evict them. He helped care for his aging mother. Red Lake Nation threatened to remove the Kakaygeesicks from their land, and now Don lived with that threat daily.

CHAPTER 21

"I need help," I said to Sam's sister when she came in the door. She had walked down the snowy lane to the cabin. As executor of her brother's will, she came with paperwork about his pickup truck.

"His title and registration must be here somewhere." She rifled through a file folder of important papers Sam kept near the phone.

"I can't go on. I'm so sad." I spent the day crying, bringing wood in, and feeding the stove to stay warm. I drowned my sorrows in Sam's brand of Natural Light beer. Pisswater. Slurps of self-loathing. I drank the way he drank. Starting at dusk until I passed out.

"I think we'd all understand if you decided to leave and go home to Minnesota," his sister said. "You should be with *your* family."

She offered me nothing but an exit. That wasn't the kind of help I meant. I relied on the backup generator fueled by propane. I knew the tank would soon be empty. I was empty. I needed help paying for propane. I needed help coping with my grief. She couldn't help me because she was dealing with her own grief.

When my parents had suggested the same thing right after the funeral, it had pissed me off then, too.

"Come back," I called out across the pond as I wandered aimlessly around the farm. "Come back," I cried across the field, the way Rose DeWitt Bukater called out to Jack Dawson in the freezing waters of the Atlantic when the *Titanic* sank in the movie we had watched on video multiple times together.

In so many ways I felt Sam's presence and clung to it. I could still smell Sam in the stack of shirts he wore, in his bed pillow. I saw him in the pencil drawing on the rough-cut lumber walls where he'd connected the knots and wood grain to reveal a picture of a goat. I saw him in the diorama he'd built for his Lionel train set on the three-season porch. In the nuts, bolts, and wrenches on his workbench in the barn. I saw his thinking spot where he'd tug on his beard sitting at the short end of the table on the bench worn shiny from his Carhartts. I didn't want to go anywhere. At any moment, I thought he might walk back in that door.

"I dreamed I was on a reporting assignment in Afghanistan searching for insurgents when I found Sam inside a cave wearing camo and carrying an assault rifle," Adam Ellick told me on the phone late one afternoon in March. "He told me to give you a message."

I knew Adam, a former journalism student at Ithaca College, had actually been on reporting assignments that put him inside some of those caves for the *New York Times*. But I knew the cave was not in Afghanistan. It was from a scene in Sam's favorite movie, *First Blood*, starring Sylvester Stallone as Rambo in the original 1972 release. Sam and I had watched the video hundreds of times and could recite entire scenes from memory.

When the sheriff (played by Brian Dennehy) tries to run Rambo (played by Stallone) out of town as a long-haired vagrant, things escalate quickly. Former Green Beret John Rambo resists, and a manhunt is on. The sheriff and his men blast the entrance to an old mine, where they've captured their fugitive inside a cave. They think he's dead. But in the greatest action-adventure movie of my generation, Rambo survives, escapes out the other side of the mountain, takes his vengeance on the National Guard convoy, diverts dozens of cop cars with sirens screaming and flashing lights, blows up a gas station, shoots out the town's electrical grid, and destroys the gun-and-ammo depot on Main Street. The climax is when Rambo shoots the sheriff from the roof of the county jail, and he crashes through a skylight.

When Adam started telling me about his dream, I got goose bumps. Immediately I felt Sam's rage against this messed-up world.

"Go on," I said to Adam while I stared at the place where Sam sat.

"He told me to write down what he said. And get it to you."

I could totally imagine Sam commanding Adam to take notes. Sam and Adam had established great rapport when Adam visited the farm the previous October for a video news story about living off-the-grid during a recession. "What did he say?"

"That you get back out there and survive."

"What?"

"I don't know. It was a really weird dream. I felt like I needed to tell you. He wants you to survive."

I watched the video story Adam did in the *New York Times* about us. I watched it over and over again. At one point during the interview with Sam, Adam mentioned that we didn't have health insurance and asked Sam what would happen if he got sick or had a heart attack.

"I'll quit," Sam replied.

What he meant was: *quit the game of life.*

How could I not have seen his suicide coming? It was predicted in the *New York Times*. Sheesh.

Kakaygeesick published a letter to the editor, made a will, and told everyone his land would be taken. Why didn't they see it coming?

I replayed the video again. There is one moment when I explain why I left academia to get a real-world education working with Sam to make our farm self-sustaining. Then in the next moment Sam speaks to the camera.

"Because of living with me, she could go back out in the world and survive."

Why Adam had a dream about Sam hiding in a cave in Afghanistan, I'll never know. As for what I thought the dream meant to me then? I thought it sounded like some macho-survivalist bullshit excuse only Sam could have come up with for a message from the beyond. Did he know me better than myself? Could I go back out there in the world and survive? Or was it a mystical sign that somehow Sam made it out alive—he escaped? I never saw the corpse.

Maybe he's in Bolivia. We'd talked about moving to Bolivia after watching *Butch Cassidy and the Sundance Kid* on a cold winter afternoon the previous year. In my magical thinking, I only had to hold on until he came back for me.

In the years since, Sam has come back to me in my dreams. He returns to the farm, where I'm run ragged, things are falling in on themselves, and everything is in need of repair. I'm angry he left me. That he deceived me by faking his own death is too much to bear. Instead of abandoned, I feel betrayed in these dreams, six years after he died. When Trump was elected in 2016, I realized Sam might have voted for him, or not voted at all, and we would have argued about it. If he weren't dead, would we still be together?

Funny how he doesn't visit my dreams much now, after a decade. When he does, the visit is usually triggered by my writing about him and our life together. He still thinks he gets to have the last word.

That second week of February in 2010, the delivery truck showed up to refill the propane tank. I hid inside and didn't answer the door when the delivery man knocked to give me the ticket of charges. He stuck the bill in the door jamb. I knew I didn't have any money to pay for it, but I needed the fuel. That full tank got me through until spring.

Sam's daughter stopped over one Sunday afternoon. I hadn't seen her since the funeral.

"I guess you miss your dad," I said to her when she appeared at the front door. "Come on in." Her shoulders nearly touched her ears, and her straight blond hair, parted in the middle, hung over most of her face. She gave me a half-smile.

"Yeah. I do." She sat down in her father's spot. Closest to the door, next to the phone. She didn't belong there. She didn't say anything more.

"Me, too." I sat there in silence. I had nothing to say to her. Nothing to offer her. Everything that had belonged to Sam had been sold by Sam's sister. What remained in the cabin was mine. I watched her looking around at what few objects remained in the room.

"So, what happens now? Will I get some of Dad's inheritance money?" she asked meekly.

Gut punch. Had no one told her? "There is no inheritance," I said gently. "Your aunt settled his estate. His will would have left whatever he had to me, but there's nothing left. And the land is mine by right of sole survivorship."

She stared at me as though she didn't believe me. She swung her hair and showed more of her face. Deep dark rings around her eyes.

Pale. No makeup. She came by herself, without the older cousin for whom she'd left her husband, Chad.

I thought about her wedding to Chad in that moment of silence. She'd asked her dad to help pay for it.

"You want to get married; why don't you pay for it?" Sam had asked her. Then he'd smiled. "What do you have in mind?"

"We've reserved the church in Watkins Glen, Dad, and we can rent the Clute Park pavilion for the reception and dance." She wanted a traditional ceremony, and she wanted Sam to be part of it. I knew the hardest part would be convincing him to wear a tux and walk her down the aisle.

"Mom said she'd buy my dress," she said coyly.

"Sam," I said, "the bride's family is the one who ponies up for the wedding. You and I will have to help her out here." I wanted him to make his daughter happy.

"I know somebody who has a limo, and maybe I can borrow it and drive you to the chapel." Sam grinned.

True to his word, Sam worked a deal to make that happen. He wore a tux. He drove the limo. And he walked his daughter down the aisle. The reception in the pavilion was simple but elegant. Aunts and great-aunts catered a buffet dinner. The polished hardwood floors inside the pavilion glowed with the golden sun that hot August Saturday afternoon. At the head table sat the bride and groom and their wedding party. After the newlyweds cut the cake, the deejay put the music on. Watching Sam dance with his daughter made me cry.

She and Chad bought a house about ten miles away, and they moved in after the wedding. Sam and I went to see their new place once, but we only stayed a half hour or so. Sam didn't like to be away from home for long. But he liked Chad.

So when Chad drove over on his motorcycle the following year, shortly before his first wedding anniversary on a Saturday afternoon in August, I wasn't surprised that he and Sam spent time alone talking, sitting by the pond. But I was surprised by what Sam had to report when he came in that evening. He told me they wouldn't be coming over for chicken BBQ the next day as we'd planned. Chad had told Sam that his daughter was cheating on him. With a man who was her first cousin. Older by almost twenty years. The son of her mother's eldest sister.

Chad had gone home after talking to Sam and rolled the BBQ grill with its propane tank inside the garage, shut the door, opened the valve, and left his motorcycle running. She found him dead the next morning when she came home.

Sam told his mother there was something wrong with her cousin. There had always been something creepy about the way he liked his little girl. His daughter had told her grandmother she had never been happier, and of course, when his mother delivered that message, Sam fumed. He hadn't talked to his daughter since Chad died.

She had lost her husband, then her father. She took the gold in the grief Olympics, but I didn't intend to compete with her.

We sat in silence for a long time.

The enlarged photograph of her dancing with Sam at her wedding hung on a wall outside the bedroom. I got up and took it off the wall. "Here, you can have this." I handed her the eighteen-inch-by-eleven-inch framed picture. She wanted something of her father. She could have that.

She took it and looked at it a long time. "Well, it's starting to get dark," she said, as the sun crept lower in the sky and hovered over the pond, "so I better get going." She carried the picture with her.

I didn't get up to see her out. It was the last I saw of her. I couldn't help her with her grief, because I couldn't yet deal with my own. Denying Sam's death, bargaining for his return, tasting bitterness and anger, I fell down deep and could not accept Sam was really gone.

"You're crying," Melissa said when I opened the door. She stopped by because she was worried about me. She and her partner, Jimmy, lived on Seneca Lake and had grilled chicken with me and Sam at the pavilion the previous summer.

"C'mon in." I put the hot water on to boil for tea. She let me cry and listened.

"You should call Hospicare," she said.

"Hospicare. Why? Sam is dead. I'm not terminally ill."

"No, but they have grief support groups. Maybe you could go to one if it meets during the day." Melissa knew I couldn't leave the cabin for long without the fire going out.

A four-week sudden-loss grief group met early in the afternoon on Wednesdays at Hospicare. I didn't feel any different, except to know that what I was feeling was grief and not the bottomless pit of depression into which I had thought I was free-falling. After the last session, the group facilitator referred me to Suicide Prevention and Crisis Services.

"Wait. You don't think I'm suicidal, do you?" I'd stopped drinking beer and started cooking meals for myself again. I thought therapy was starting to work. I didn't know if I wanted to live without Sam or how I could go on, but I knew I didn't have it in me to kill myself.

"No, but they offer bereavement counseling to those who have lost someone to suicide." She put me in touch with a therapist, and I joined a support group. I felt seen and heard and wasn't alone. Suddenly my community grew, and tendrils of practical support grew up all around me.

"What am I going to do? The credit card company keeps adding more fees for being over my credit limit," I unloaded on Brendan Wilbur behind the closed doors in his office. "They lowered my credit limit when Sam died. I'm not making enough money to pay the minimum payment each month."

"Well, you're going to stop paying on the credit card. Don't make another payment," Brendan said. Someone in my support group had recommended financial counseling at Alternatives Federal Credit Union in Ithaca. I had shown up at his office on the verge of tears.

"What? I can't do that. It will only get worse. I don't know what to do."

Brendan pushed the box of tissues across his desk toward me and tilted his head sympathetically to one side. "Listen to me," he said. "Stop making payments. Stop."

I hadn't considered refusing to pay. I'd been so desperate to manage my bills that I couldn't see I didn't have any money to manage. Because the estate had not been finalized, I didn't yet have clear title to the deed.

"Stop paying, and then they'll have to negotiate with you," Brendan said. He leaned forward across his desk. "These credit card companies are about to face new regulations. You aren't the only one who can't pay on their cards."

Brendan helped put my situation into a larger context. I wasn't alone. It was the worst of the economic recession. Home foreclosures.

Bankruptcies. "Pay the bills you have with locally owned companies where you have face-to-face accountability. Forget the credit card companies for now."

His advice shocked me at first. But he was right.

You can't get blood from a stone. Sam used to say that about people who owed us money. I felt like a bleeding stone.

"Have you been applying for jobs?" Brendan asked.

"I've been to the offices at the Department of Labor. They had nothing for me." I didn't qualify for food stamps or housing assistance or anything. "I've been cleaning houses for cash. Selling pies."

"Keep doing that," he said. "If you open a savings account and take this class here at the credit union on personal finance, then I will recommend you for our CEO workshop." Brendan told me about a business planning course, to figure out how I might be able to keep the farm and make a go of it.

It would be another decade before I realized how much keeping the land was my wish to keep Sam alive. And for most of a year, it felt like he was there.

I knew every inch of ground after working those forty acres for a decade. I knew what day to pick black raspberries. When to plant a fall crop of arugula. Whether I'd find morel mushrooms down by the creek in back. Under what tree to find the trillium in bloom. Where to step into the deer paths to cut through the hedge rows. When it would be warm enough to swim in the pond. How to harvest the wild Saint-John's-wort, and where the sun would set and when. I did not want to leave this place that was as much a part of me as my flesh.

Cleaning and sorting seeds I saved from my heirloom hollyhocks, variegated sunflowers, calendula, cilantro, pea, bean, poppy, and tobacco plants, I tested out some of my ideas for a new business plan. Spread out on the table in the cabin, I conducted research on germination rates and designed labels. The homework assignments for the CEO class at the credit union gave me a distraction from my grief.

At least until the class assignments turned to spreadsheets of cash projections, price points, and profit margins. I didn't want to sell the land, but the bottom line made me realize it was more realistic than trying to become a seed farmer or keep Sam alive. When I looked at what required the least capital investment, best opportunity for growth, and potential for long-term sustainability, I realized my greatest asset was me and what I still loved: reading, research, writing, editing.

CHAPTER 22

The question of blood quantum was central to the court's determination that Allotment 3 would be awarded to the descendants of Albert Angus, who were now Red Lake tribal members, and not to the Kakaygeesicks, who were not. In the 2002 court decision, the judge wrote the following explanation:

> *It appears that you [Donald Kakaygeesick, plaintiff] and the other appellants are claiming eligibility through a Chief Ay-Ash-A-Wash, and his son, Little Thunder. The records show that Nay-May-Puck, son of Ay-Ash-A-Wash was allotted land on the ceded portion of the Red Lake reservation under the Act of May 27, 1902. The Act permitted the Indians to retain lands on which they resided and improved instead of moving them to the diminished Red Lake Reservation. The Act, however, contains no provisions reserving or extending Red Lake membership rights to these Indians or to their descendants. The documentation furnished does not prove that you or the other appellants possess any Pembina Chippewa blood. As outlined above, an individual must possess at least ¼ degree Pembina Chippewa blood. You and the other appellants may possess Indian blood, however, only Pembina Chippewa blood can be considered for this award.*

The probate court ruling denied the descendants of Robert Kakaygeesick Sr. the claim to eligibility for the inheritance of Allotment 3 because they were not the right kind of Indian as determined by blood quantum registration as a Red Lake Nation tribal member.

The Department of Interior defined the Pembina Band of Ojibway as those people originally living along the Red River of the North, which includes the Red Lake and White Earth Bands in Minnesota, Turtle Mountain Band in North Dakota, the Chippewa Cree Tribe in Montana, and Roseau River Anishinaabe First Nation in Manitoba. The original deed signed by Roosevelt includes the words "Red Lake Indian" in describing Kakaygeesick. His appearance in the first Indian Census at White Earth records him as Pembina. The court decided Don and family did not possess any Pembina Chippewa blood by their lack of official tribal membership. They sure aren't Cree or Navajo or Arapaho or Seneca or Oneida. It's a legal catch-22. Doublethink is needed for it to make sense. Circular reasoning. Bureaucratic absurdity.

They lacked official tribal membership because Red Lake Nation had denied it to them. There had been times—for example, in securing a loan for the trailer homes in the 1970s or when they pursued claims against Canada for flood reparations—their official tribal status had not seemed to matter. But now that Red Lake Nation wanted their land, and the Kakaygeesick family members did not want to relinquish it, the status of the plaintiffs before the court mattered.

The probate court ruling referenced the allotment made in accordance with the Allotment Act of 1902. Except Red Lake Nation was not supposed to have any allotments because land was owned communally by the tribe. Otherwise known as the "Dead Indian

Act," this legislation extended the Dawes Act of 1887, which created the policy of allotments. Indians issued allotments were considered incompetent to handle land affairs, and the US government retained legal title to the land as trustee. Indians could use the land but did not have the legal rights of ownership. The 1902 act stated that twenty-five years after the allotment was issued, if the Indians had lived on the land and made good agricultural use of it, then they could complete a "fee simple patent" and gain clear ownership with a title. It also meant that when an allottee died, the federal government could declare his descendants de facto incompetent and sell the land to non-Natives. As a result of the Dead Indian Act, twenty-seven million acres passed from the hands of Indians to whites by 1928. But Red Lake Nation was not subject to the Dawes Act and had no other allotments except these original three on Lake of the Woods.

Kakaygeesick never sold his allotment. He never completed an application for a "simple fee patent," though he clearly had met the terms for a clear title. There is nothing in the Indian Act of 1902 or other laws related to allotments that I can see that suggests that an allotment nullifies one's tribal lineage and affiliation. What the court decision does not, and cannot, explain is how the deed signed by Roosevelt in 1905 granting Allotment 3 to Kakaygeesick as 4/4 Red Lake Indian negated his blood quantum, his Indian status.

What the court ruling did reveal is how Indian blood quantum remains a flexible tool of domination. In the past, it has been used to position an individual as an Indian ward of the federal government. Similar to the three-fifths rule in the Constitution, which treated slaves as less than a full person, the origins of blood quantum are rooted in unquestioned notions of white supremacy. Blood quantum as federal policy was established by the 1934 Indian Reorganization

Act, and its intent was to destroy the sovereignty of Indian Nations through a form of generational genocide. Senator Burton Wheeler of Montana suggested at the time that defining Indigenous status by blood quantum offered the best method to "get rid of the Indian problem."

Defining tribal membership by blood—not by kinship, nor by language, material culture, customs, beliefs, or practices—is a biological fallacy. Race is not determined by drops of blood. Race is a social construct, rather than a biological one. The idea that blood can determine which tribe one belongs to is even more preposterous.

White Earth Band, another Ojibway tribe in Minnesota, voted to end blood quantum for tribal membership in 2013 when it adopted a new constitution, which defined the membership requirements in terms of kinship. But Red Lake doubled down on blood quantum. In 2019, tribal council affirmed members must have one-quarter Red Lake ancestry to enroll in the tribe. They did, however, alter the terms for determining blood quantum. For anyone who was an enrolled tribal member on or before November 10, 1958, Red Lake Nation redefined their blood quantum as "full-blood," or 4/4 blood degree, effectively turning the biological timer on extermination back three generations for currently enrolled members. But for anyone who has enrolled since that date, Red Lake Nation continues to enforce the pseudoscientific definition of tribal membership in terms of blood quantum.

Don continued to live in his trailer out on Muskeg Bay and care for his mother, Florence, through all the years of court proceedings and after the final summary judgment denying their appeal. Florence had moved her things from the old trailer she'd shared with Robert Sr.

into Don's. Karen and Martha would stay with their mother for a while off and on, and their children and grandchildren would come often to visit. Even though the court decision had been final and binding, things remained the same. Red Lake officials sent letters instructing the Kakaygeesick family to vacate the property. They ignored them.

Month after month, the letters continued to show up in their mailbox. Red Lake told them to leave. But they refused. They did nothing.

Don didn't have any answers for what to do about the land. The appeals process came to an end in August 2010. He'd spent years fighting in court, exhausted every legal possibility, and lost. So he turned to the news media, appealing to the court of public opinion. Minnesota Public Radio aired a story on November 4, 2010, reporting that Red Lake Band of Ojibway had told Don Kakaygeesick and his mother to be off the Lake of the Woods lakeshore property by October 15.

The deadline passed. And nothing happened. Nothing. Doing nothing became Don's way to resist. Winter set in, and things stayed the same. Spring arrived, then summer passed, and still Florence Kakaygeesick lived out on Muskeg Bay.

Sitting with the heaviness of the injustice, Don vowed he and his mother would stay there until physically removed. Red Lake tribal officials bided their time.

As July 2011 came to an end, Don took a trip with his mother to Eagle Lake. Migisi Sahgaigan. Reserve No. 27. First Nation. They call it sunset country. Every year a traditional powwow is held there in the region of freshwater lakes in northern Ontario, bringing together people from hundreds of miles around to the campgrounds and swimming area. A weekend of drums, dancing, and dressing in full regalia.

In Canada, Don's status was undisputed. Great-great-grandfather Chief Ay Ash Wash himself had been at the Northwest Angle in 1873 when he signed Treaty 3.

"It's like, my buddies here recognize me as a Native person, even though Red Lake says, 'Well, you're not a Native, according to our files,'" Don told me. "But I know who I am. I know I'm a Native person. I know our traditions. I know our values. I know all these things. I have ancestors who signed Treaty 3." His frustration over not being acknowledged in the United States subsided during the weekend among friends and relations north of the border.

Don broke camp by 7 a.m. on Monday morning, August 1. He drove with his mother in his 1992 Ford F150 into the Town of Eagle Lake looking to fill up with gas for the drive home. Except the station was out of gas. He would have to drive another twenty-nine miles to Dryden, the nearest town, to find fuel. Around 7:30 a.m., as they headed southeast, he saw something off the road to the left, walking out from the hedgerow, coming from the east.

It looked like a man. Except extraordinarily tall. He had a cone-shaped head that rested on massive shoulders. Light emanated from him. Bright, cold, white light.

Don looked over at his mother in the passenger seat. She looked straight ahead, at the dashboard.

"What the hell is that?" Don pointed his chin left. He took his foot off the gas pedal.

Florence looked in Don's direction but couldn't see past him. Her glaucoma had worsened over the last few years. She shrugged her shoulders and dropped her eyes to the hands in her lap.

Don stopped the truck to look more closely out his window. What he saw was real but appeared like a vision. The tall and muscular form stomped toward them. The sun that had crept up over the horizon backlit him in silhouette. His breath came out a cloudy mist. Surrounded by white radiant light, the giant cast no shadow.

Sabe. Sounds like *Saw-bay*. In southern Minnesota, they call him Mesabe. The one who keeps the land for those who will someday come.

When Sabe noticed Don, he turned at the waist toward him and aligned his head square with his shoulders, as though his neck would not turn. He lumbered through the knee-high grasses, putting all his weight on one large foot while extending the other leg forward, then twisted his torso to the right before hurling his other leg forward. His head tilted right and left like he was trying to focus. Then he stopped and turned his entire body to face Don in the driver's seat of the truck. They locked eyes.

Sunlight hit the hairy arm of the creature; it looked as though it were flames on fire. The luminous glow from the creature grew brighter, whiter, and merged into the sunlight, which suddenly flared into Don's eyes. He had to look away. When he looked back, Sabe was gone.

"I believe Sabe visited me for a reason that day," Don said. "He came to hear what was in my heart and take it to the elders, the Grand Council of Treaty 3."

Don had felt no fear in that moment. He knew Sabe to be a sacred being. Don belongs to the Duck Clan. Zhiishiib (*Szhee-sheeb*). They live by the lake, and no matter how hard Winter Maker tries, ducks do not freeze or starve. Hardships may come, but according to legend, treasures shall be hidden until the winter of no snow.

Another year passed. Red Lake Realty sent an eviction notice to remove their belongings and vacate the property by Saturday, September 15, 2012. The notice included a threat to arrest Don and his elderly mother if they did not comply.

Nothing happened until September 19.

"The day arrived when Red Lake came to throw us off our land," Don told me. "I got a call from the sheriff."

Don had previously spoken to Roseau County Sheriff Steve Gust about the situation. Gust was sympathetic but had no jurisdiction. When the sheriff called Don that morning, his voice carried a sense of urgency.

"Where's your mother?" Gust asked Don that Wednesday morning. "Get her out of that trailer and away from there," the sheriff told him. "They are on their way from Red Lake, and they come armed."

Gust paused. Don didn't respond.

"They aren't fooling, Don. What have you got planned?"

"I'm going to meet them at the property line. I'll be in front of my pickup. Don't worry, I'm not armed." Don didn't even own a gun. "I don't want to be arrested. But I'm not leaving."

Don took a breath. Gust continued to listen.

"I think there's fraud here. There's something really wrong here, and a crime has been committed, but it wasn't by me," Don said.

"I understand your position, Don. I'm calling to give you a heads-up. Get your mother away from there."

Don appreciated Sheriff Gust letting him know they were on their way. Don called Karen and asked her to pick up ninety-one-year-old Florence and take her into town for the day. Then he set up sawhorses and plywood across the road a half mile from the trailer at the curve in the road. He set up his roadblock where the driveway heads east away from Cherne's land onto theirs, and then he waited—leaned back against the grill of his pickup truck, arms crossed.

The days had already grown cooler. The leaves on the birch trees had started to turn yellow. The first tinges of red and orange could be seen in the few maples, and the oak tree leaves looked a shade darker green. The sun felt warm as he leaned against the truck and listened to the birds. He waited.

A dump truck pulling a trailer with an excavator arrived first. Don heard it turn off the highway and rumble down the road toward him. He uncrossed his arms and stood up tall. Red Lake Police arrived right behind in a squad car. Red Lake Law Enforcement Director William Brunelle sat in the vehicle.

The truck driver leaned out his passenger window. "Get out of the way!" he yelled at Don.

Sheriff Gust drove up in a Roseau County squad car. He watched as the driver and another man took the excavator off the trailer. Then one of the men started up its engine, crawled up into the driver's seat, and started forward in the unpaved road toward Don.

Don wouldn't move. "I'm not going anywhere," he shouted. "Don't come any further." The excavator faced Don's pickup truck directly.

"*Move!*" the operator yelled at Don.

Don stood there.

The dump truck driver stomped off toward the Red Lake squad car and vented his frustration through the open passenger window at Brunelle. Brunelle called Chairman Floyd "Buck" Jourdain Jr. back in Red Lake on his cell phone.

Brunelle said Jourdain would give Kakaygeesick two weeks to move his trailer from the property. Don told him he couldn't afford to hire someone to move it. And he had nowhere to move it to. Negotiations continued from Brunelle to the council chairman back in Red Lake over the phone. Buck Jourdain agreed to pay the cost of moving the trailer. Don negotiated for having new skirting put around it after it was relocated. Sheriff Gust witnessed their verbal agreement. As for his parents' old 1970s trailer, Don didn't intend to move it.

Don put the sawhorses and boards in the bed of his pickup and backed his truck up the half mile, closer to his trailer. Don thought about the appliances in that old second trailer. He thought about the pictures on the walls, the old blankets, the things his mother had never moved out of her home into his. He thought about how he was going to have to find a place to move his trailer. And the costs of renting in a trailer park. Where would they go?

The excavator proceeded onto the property. The earth rumbled under the noisy, slow tracks moving steadily toward the bay. The dump truck pulled forward slowly and sat idling its engine outside Don's trailer. Don stood watching in the yard while the excavator approached his parents' trailer. Crows circled overhead, but the loud engines drowned out their squawking. The excavator cab spun around and lifted up its long arm with the claw of a bucket on the end. It swung hard against the old empty trailer and knocked a hole through the middle of it. The arm pulled back. It reached over and grasped the roof, slamming the bucket down hard. With several more swipes, the excavator leveled his parents' home.

The engine idled, and then it took out a few old oak trees. Using the bucket like a plow, it pushed the trunks to the edge of the clearing. Back and forth, the excavator scraped the area level, making room for their big machinery to come in. It was hard for Don to watch the destruction. But he stood there as a witness.

Brunelle informed Don later that afternoon by phone that Jourdain had reduced the time extension to one week. Don called his cousin, Ron Prelvitz, to ask for help. Ron was the brother of Billy, who had died in the car accident with Don's brothers Kenny and Kelly back in 1987. Ron brought a work crew a week later on Wednesday, September 26, to move the trailer to Brewster Trailer Park, about a half mile west on Highway 11. It cost Don seventeen hundred dollars to move the trailer. Red Lake Realty never paid for that new skirting Jourdain had promised. And now Don had to pay rent to Brewsters.

Once his trailer was gone, the excavator began clearing the land for construction of the casino.

CHAPTER 23

What was so complicated about my grief for Mom? That I had always believed Dad would die first. That she would enjoy life after Dad as an independent woman. Despite the evidence of her oxygen tanks and a diagnosis of COPD. Despite the evidence that I didn't like the person she'd become, forwarding my sister and me emails claiming Obama had been born a Muslim in Kenya. That she'd made herself a martyr to my father's ego. Yet if I am honest with myself, I waited on Sam hand and foot in much the same way Mom had Dad. I learned to do things Sam's way. I gave up a job with a lifetime guarantee. Shit, I even drank Natural Light beer. When he felt miserable, he made me miserable. The same way Mom allowed Dad, I let Sam emotionally abuse me because I loved him. I thought loving him would be enough. That my love was plenty reason to live. When he died, I thought he might pull me down with him. But he didn't.

When I think about these years living without Sam, I have to confess I don't miss having to pick up his dirty socks off the floor or wait until he's ready to eat before serving supper. Not having to check in before making a social commitment or making a purchase or a life decision. Not deferring, not waiting. That Sam died set me free. Independence. It's what I always wanted for Mom. I didn't know it was what I wanted for me. That I got for myself what I always wanted for Mom is bittersweet.

I returned almost every summer to Warroad to get grounded in the girl I used to be—curious about the world and my place in it—and remember when I loved Mom most, when she didn't need my sympathy or pity, only love. The Mom who didn't complain how unfair it was that her side of family lived so far away. I couldn't let go of the sense that she got cheated by life.

It felt like the Kakaygeesick family got cheated, too. Yet my first question to Don had been, "How did Red Lake take your land?" As if he let it happen. When I first read the judge's summary judgment denying Don's appeal, I found myself angry at the Kakaygeesicks. Why hadn't they done more to secure the title to their property, or fought sooner, or harder, in the courts? How could they have allowed it to happen? How could Mom not see that she let Dad treat her poorly? Why had I let Reggie give me more than one black eye? How could I have allowed Sam to dominate my every waking moment and not seen his suicide coming? How could I still keep smoking when it eventually killed Mom?

When I found out the Kakaygeesicks had been forced off their land, I got angry because I couldn't be angry at Mom. I couldn't be angry that she couldn't quit smoking. I couldn't be angry that she beat herself up about it. I couldn't be angry that she loved Dad. That she never got to live on her own. That she died.

That Seven Clans Casino now stood on Muskeg Bay made me angry, too. What happened couldn't be undone. But everywhere I pointed, my anger reflected some blame back on me.

I had needed a distraction from the reality of Mom's death, from the denial of my nicotine addiction, from my own twisted dance with mortality.

People were often surprised to learn I smoked cigarettes. Someone once told me it was the single most "off-brand" thing about me. I didn't start until graduate school, old enough to know better. I smoked Reggie's brand: Kool Kings. Menthol. Mom smoked Salems, and so did her mother.

Grandma Kling quit cold turkey in her sixties and took up chewing gum, Juicy Fruit clacking her dentures. It took more than a decade for Mom to stop. She took smoking cessation classes more than once. She read books and listened to audiotapes. Tried hypnosis. When she finally did stop, it wasn't long before she was diagnosed with COPD. Mom was on oxygen tanks by my age.

I'm not my mother. But I am my mother's daughter.

I was angry with myself that I couldn't quit. That I didn't want to quit. So I compartmentalized to avoid beating myself up that I can't quit and still smoke. The rabbit holes of research about this piece of land gave me a place to channel my angry psychic energy.

"That first week was flush," the bank teller told me at the Security State Bank in Warroad. I'd come in to get some cash. I'd asked him if the new casino brought more money into the local economy. "We had a lot of cash deposits come through here that first year. But then it went down, and it hasn't really come back up since," he said. He wouldn't give any figures.

"Did you see Red Lake closed the restaurant on the city beachfront?" the teller asked me. "Guess they want everyone to go to their new one in the casino now."

I'd loved that restaurant. Excellent fresh walleye. Great view of the lakefront. I hadn't yet been to the new casino because I felt it would almost be a betrayal to the Kakaygeesick family. But I knew I needed to see it.

Before I went to the casino, I stopped first at city hall—located in the old railroad station across from the library—in search of answers about how Seven Clans Casino convinced Warroad city government to annex the land in Kakaygeesick's allotment and the Cherne property into the city limits.

"Do you have the minutes from the meeting when they approved annexation of the land for the new casino?" I asked the city clerk. Her office in the restored depot had been the old ticket booth; the upper half of the Dutch door to the office was open.

"No, those would be in storage." She walked over to the city map on the wall. "You're talking about this part," she said, pointing to Kakaygeesick's land.

"I read in the newspaper that city council voted unanimously to annex that property. I'm surprised they agreed to provide city services to a nontaxable entity."

"Well, I guess everyone thought the casino would bring more money into town, and that would be a good thing," the clerk replied.

Downtown Warroad had been struggling to keep shops open since the new Seven Clans Casino was built and they closed the restaurant at the public beach. A second Dollar General store was built, near the edge of town, closer to the casino.

I left the library and drove over to Seven Clans Casino. Turning off the highway, a long boulevard cut through the woods with streetlights and hanging flag banners welcoming guests in the Ojibway language. The freshly paved street with concrete curbs emptied into an enormous parking lot in front of the casino entrance. Midmorning, there were few cars in the freshly paved lot. More cars were parked in the section for employees. A bellhop in uniform stood outside the bank of glass doors to the grand first-floor foyer. To the left and down the hall were the tables and slot machines, the casino. I peeked in; it looked like every other casino I'd ever seen. To the right, a hallway led to the Willow Café. Elegant. White cloth napkins and tablecloths. And yes, they did serve wild-rice-and-cranberry bread.

I ordered toast for a late breakfast and sat there by myself, looking out onto Lake of the Woods. Less than fifty feet from the lake behind a large wall of windows, I watched reeds wave back and forth in the breeze. The vista filled me with a sense of how sacred this place was.

Beyond the swaying grasses, the blue open water flashed shimmering diamonds, refracting the sun from its surface. And above it all, an everlasting sky.

That evening Don sent a message agreeing to meet up the next day in Warroad. I told him I'd made progress in my writing. I'd crafted a biographical profile of his great-grandfather for the annual Chamber of Commerce *Warroad Visitors Guide*. I thought maybe I had more to write about.

"Great. Do you think that will help us get the land back?" Don asked.

Dad had asked me the same thing. He knew about my research, and he had been outraged to hear they had forced Don and his elderly mother from their home. I told Don what I'd told Dad.

"To be honest, no. But I'm not a lawyer."

Having read so much of the legal documentation of this case, and the final court's opinion, I did not think there was anything to be done in the courts. And I knew by then not to think like a white savior. What had once made me think I could identify a legal loophole had been sheer arrogance.

Don and I revisited this discussion of what might come of my writing about what had happened with the land many times.

"I do believe there might be two things that could be achieved," I texted Don. "One, some kind of historical justice. Writing the story of what really happened to Kakaygeesick and his family after all these years would set the record straight. There is some justice in that."

"Hunh. Historical justice. Getting the last word," Don messaged back.

"And two, there's restorative justice," I said. "But that might be even harder to get. And will involve more than me writing a book."

"What do you mean?" he asked.

That things might be made right in ways outside the courtroom. That something good might come from all of this that could tip the unbalanced scales of justice and fairness in their direction for a change. But it wasn't for me to say what reparations might look like for the Kakaygeesick family.

"I don't think you're going to get your land back. The casino is open. How can this wrong be made right?" I asked.

In response, Don sent me a long message in first-person plural, speaking on behalf of his family and the Kah-bay-kah-nong band, which began:

"Have the federal government recognize our plight. We need new land and federal [tribal] recognition. Monetary compensation as my mother wanted. Civil lawsuit? Idk."

Don started with the unfulfilled wishes for legal and economic justice. For him, it clearly had not ended.

Idk either. It's that lens of whiteness I saw through that made me want to come to the rescue. Who was I to think I could make this right? What power and privilege did I have to make the federal government recognize and pay reparations to them?

Also—new land? Whose land? I agreed some kind of monetary compensation seemed reasonable. But who was going to pay for it? Not Red Lake Nation. They had already paid the Angus heirs a million dollars for the property; they owned it free and clear now. Of course, Don didn't say a word in his response to my question about Red Lake Nation. The entity he focused on was the United States. He wanted to be recognized by the federal government. To no longer be made invisible by bureaucracy.

Don and his siblings are not alone in lacking official tribal status in one of the 574 recognized tribes in the United States. By the end of the nineteenth century, the federal government's extermination policy left only a quarter million Indians alive. There are almost ten million people in the United States today who identify as American Indians but only two million enrolled in federally recognized tribes.

John, Karen, Don, and Martha felt a part of this land, but they did not feel as though they belonged to the Red Lake Band. So it was not a surprise that Don did not ask for tribal membership.

"We need a place with land to continue practicing our way of life and culture," he continued.

To hold sweat lodges. To harvest willow to make baskets. Tell stories under the night sky by firelight. Greet the dawn in gratitude.

I knew the kind of deep spiritual attachment Don had to that special place on the lakefront. Such a place *would* be restorative. He and his family didn't need me to save them; they needed to be seen and heard.

"Land and water" were what Don wanted.

"We are lake people here," he said.

But as for where along the shores there might be real estate, I couldn't begin to imagine. And the price for such land might be well more than a million bucks. In recent years, this pristine wilderness environment had seen its share of new McMansions. Private islands with modern amenities go for skyrocketing prices. For many wealthy owners, a place at the lake was a second seasonal home. For long-timers, a cabin on Lake of the Woods was an inherited family heirloom, a rustic wilderness cabin.

Even in this extremely remote location, land was precious.

Lake of the Woods sits in the center of the North American continent, on the humped back of Turtle Island. As global temperatures rise, one might think this enormous body of fresh water would be the perfect spot to ride out climate change. But the lake *is* warming up. There are still the occasional extreme freezing temperatures in Warroad, but now there are more record-breaking highs in summer than lows in winter. And the lake *is* rising. More than a century ago, the lake rose almost three feet when they flooded Lake of the Woods for a hydroelectric plant in Kenora. Now the waters in all the oceans rise, and the ice caps melt. Kakaygeesick once worried about the flooding and destruction of wild rice habitat, fearing his family would have no place to call home, no clean water, no fresh air, no fish, no manoomin—and now we all find ourselves worrying about the future of Mother Earth.

From the European settlements until the Clean Water Act passed in 1972, whites dumped raw sewage and then industrial waste from timber mills from International Falls along the Rainy River into Lake of the Woods. In the past fifty years, the contamination has mostly stopped, but the blue-green algae is a perennial problem and getting worse. A century's worth of pollution remains beneath the surface of the water.

Most lakes have shorelines and bottoms that slant toward depths in the center. Because Lake of the Woods is shaped more like a soup plate than a funnel, the sedimentation and natural healing processes one might expect of a freshwater lake have not happened. Core samples show the phosphorus hasn't settled. Instead, it feeds the cyanobacteria on the shallow bottom, which creates toxins. In most lakes, the phosphorus gets buried in sediment over time, and the lake can heal. Not here.

The effects of climate change exacerbate this situation. Average water temperatures continue to rise, and the lake is less windy. Less wind means the top and bottom waters don't mix together as much. Colder water settles on the bottom, where cyanobacteria absorb phosphorus. This creates a situation research biologists Mark Edlund and Adam Heathcote call "internal loading," where the pollution from the past creates new pollution. The toxic algae blooms are one way the lake attempts to heal itself.

For the past decade, Edlund and Heathcote have gathered data from Lake of the Woods as part of the St. Croix Watershed Research Station, which is associated with the Science Museum of Minnesota. Toxic algae covers the lake every year, and the blooms are especially severe on the southern end near Warroad. On the north end of Lake of the Woods, there are twenty-eight more days of open water per year than there were thirty years ago, which gives the lake another month of blooming algae. When the algae dies off, it falls to the shallow bottom, where it stirs up the phosphorus and starts the cycle again.

The legacy of the past is still with us in the water of Lake of the Woods.

While there is some good news—pelicans have returned, no more DDT, and the walleye are back—there will be no more caviar, and the sturgeon will never swim in these waters.

Lake people need a lake.

"Fish and wild rice. Hunting on land." These were the answers Don texted in response to my asking what would make this right. But for Don to exercise his fishing and hunting rights would require tribal membership. Minnesota DNR officers abide by these treaty rights, but only for those who can provide official tribal status identification.

As for wild rice, there is no more local habitat on Lake of the Woods near Warroad. The word "manoomin" is related to Manitou, which means Creator or Great Spirit. Loosely translated, "manoomin" means good berries. The first prophecy of the seven fires to the Ojibway people foretold they would travel west until they found their new homeland, "where food grows on water." When the Ojibway tribes found upper Lake Superior, the Rainy River, and Lake of the Woods, they found wild rice and settled there. Without official tribal membership, harvesting wild rice in Minnesota requires a license and is permitted only in restricted areas.

Wild rice is not really rice, but a grass that grows in water. One person uses a push pole to guide the canoe through the standing rice. The second person uses two sticks, called knockers, to bend the grasses over the canoe, where some of the seed heads fall. Some rice falls into the water. This seeds next year's crop. Some rice is left in place to share with others. Of the rice that falls into the canoe, some will be shared, some will be stored, and some will be eaten. A spiritual practice of reciprocity, generosity, and balance is built into the relationship to this sacred plant.

"Land and water," Don texted. A place where they belong and

an acknowledgment of their dispossession—not only of land but of their heritage, their identity, their history, their language, their wisdom. This was about more than real estate.

"If only they could see," Don texted me. "By recognizing us, they could bring us out of poverty and darkness."

Financial reparations and property would go a long way with disenfranchised and dispossessed Lake of the Woods Indians, who could benefit from a place, land and water, to call home.

"What a great future we could have," he wrote.

CHAPTER 24

Maybe I should thank Donald Trump for resolving most of my daddy issues. When Trump won the nomination in 2015, Dad stopped supporting the Republican Party. When Trump won the 2016 election, he was furious.

"If his brains were dynamite, Trump couldn't blow his nose," Dad yelled at me over the phone. "A complete ignoramus!"

"Did you see he wants to ban all Muslims from entering the United States?" I had called him from my house in Appleton, where I had moved nine months after Mom died. He had helped me with the down payment and coached me through my first home purchase. We talked regularly on the phone to review the latest outrageous behavior of the president. We were mad about the same things and shared a common enemy. And Dad wasn't mad at me anymore.

Father's Day coincided with Dad's eighty-sixth birthday on June 20. I spent the weekend with him at the senior housing facility, where there was a guest room for out-of-town visitors.

"I want to be *early* to church tomorrow morning," Dad said after he'd taken me out to Red Lobster for Saturday night supper. He enjoyed socializing with his friends before as well as after the service. "Be ready in the morning."

Sunday morning I knocked on his apartment door to find him on his motorized scooter ready to go. We made our way to the bank of elevators, where he stopped to push the button with the butt end of his cane. When the doors opened, he swung his scooter into the elevator, and we went down to the basement garage, Dad raced to the end stall against the back wall. By the time I walked there, he had gotten off his scooter, unlocked the door, and slid into the front seat.

"You're going to have to back out for me to get in," I said, as he started the engine. The car was parked too close to the bright yellow wall to open the passenger side door. It took him two or three times of backing up and moving forward before he maneuvered the vehicle between the wall and a concrete divider so I could get in and put my seat belt on.

Dad headed south toward Afton Memorial Lutheran Church; the highway ran parallel to the St. Croix River, the natural border with Wisconsin. I noticed him using the cruise control instead of the gas pedal. There were a series of three roundabouts, and he took all three without tapping the brakes once to disengage the cruise control.

"Slow down!" I said, thrust against the passenger door on the third roundabout.

"Knock it off!" he yelled. "Don't tell me what to do, young lady."

I prayed during that church service. Coming home, he used his cane to push down on the brake pedal to stop. He used his cane. To brake. His cane.

Barb took him to the doctor. She'd called in advance and asked for the physician's help in taking away his driver's license. The doctor did not get the message. Then someone told Barb about making an anonymous tip, which would require Dad to take an in-person driving and vision test to retain his license.

"Somebody turned me in," Dad told me on the phone.

"What do you mean?" I asked.

"I got something in the mail. They're trying to take my driver's license from me. And now I can't find my car keys."

"Well, I've done that before. Set them down someplace and can't find them when I'm ready to go."

"You were here a couple weeks ago. That's the last time I saw my keys. Go through your purse and see if you didn't pick them up by mistake."

I knew he suspected me. He'd lost his patience with me in the car when I caught him using the cane to brake. His anger still scared me. He had every right to suspect me. But it would be Barb who picked up his keys when he was in the bathroom after church, and it would be Barb who made the call to the tip line. Mom left Barb in charge as Dad's health care proxy, holder of his power of attorney, executor of his will, and the primary contact for the prepaid funeral, and I was incredibly grateful for her foresight. Barb would remain the anonymous tipster.

Dad didn't need to drive. Barb arranged church members to pick him up for Sunday services. Barb did his grocery shopping and brought him meals. She'd even found a home health aide who came in every midmorning to give him a foot massage, made sure he took his medications, and visited with him for a while. Barb told him she was an old friend of hers from work. He didn't question it. But he did question me taking away his independence, his mobility, his car keys.

"I don't have your car keys, Dad," I replied. "Where do you need to go today?"

"I don't need to go anywhere at the moment, Jill."

"Well, how about I come over this weekend? We can go to church and out for Sunday brunch, if you'll let me drive."

I should have known he'd never let me drive. The ride to church on Sunday was a replay of my June visit, but afterward he wanted to go to Not Just a Café. An old-fashioned diner in downtown Bayport, the mom-and-pop operation had an off-street parking lot Dad pulled into. He got his walker out of the backseat and headed toward the front entrance. It wasn't until I got out and walked around the car that I noticed the bright yellow streaks of paint down the entire length of the vehicle on the driver's side.

"What is *that*?" I pointed at the paint and dragged my right index finger along the dent in the sidewall.

Dad stopped in his tracks. He shuffled his left foot around and picked the walker up and dropped it about six inches to his left. Wearing his favorite Scottish tam, he dipped his head and squinted back in my direction. "What?"

"What's with the yellow paint, Dad? Where's that from?"

"Never mind. C'mon. Let's eat." He picked his walker up, moved it to the right, and reoriented himself to move toward the front door of the café.

"I want to know. Dad, you scraped the side of your car more than once? Did you file an insurance report? Are you taking that in for bodywork?"

He had had enough of me. He bent over the walker further, scrunching his shoulders. Dad couldn't move fast enough. I'd made him angry. I opened the front door of the diner for him.

"I don't want to talk about it. Let's have a nice breakfast. I'm getting eggs Benedict," he said. Then he smiled at the waitress who seated us. He struggled to get situated in the booth comfortably. The noisy din of a cramped full diner on a Sunday morning drowned out my chance of having any further conversation on the matter, because I knew he would only yell at me and embarrass me in public. Delighted to be out at a restaurant, he read the entire menu, absorbed by the descriptions covering four pages of offerings. The waitress brought us cups of coffee. Dad ordered eggs Benedict. Then he pointed to all the funny sayings decoupaged on the walls.

"Your mother used to think they were funny." He wanted to talk about Mom more than the damage to the car. I let him talk while I finished breakfast. He gave the waitress his credit card.

I left the tip and asked for his car keys.

"No." And no meant no.

He pulled into the underground parking lot in his building and let me out at the elevator doors. Then he pulled up to the last spot at the end of the row and turned in. I heard the driver's side scrape along the yellow concrete divider. He got out of the car, left the walker in the back seat, grabbed his cane, and got on his scooter. When he got inside, he left his car keys on the table and went to the bathroom.

Barb was waiting inside his apartment for us. When he came out of the bathroom, Dad sat down at the dining room table with us. We raised the issue of giving up his driver's license.

"We don't want you killing someone," I said. "You can't properly use the foot pedals. Your feet don't react. Your cane is not the solution."

"Don't tell me what I can and can't do."

"Dad, you could run over a child," Barb pleaded.

"And if you kill somebody, who do you think they'll hold liable? I couldn't live with myself if you died and killed someone in a car accident," I said.

"What would people say? That if I were a good daughter, then I should have taken your keys away." Barb paused, staring at him, her eyes welling up with tears. "Please don't do this to us."

He never asked about his car keys again.

Dad had sold their Afton townhouse after Mom died and moved into a senior apartment with the same high white ceilings and walls, nearly the same layout, and all the same furnishings, originally from Pearson & Swenson Furniture. The place felt so familiar it had made his transition easier.

"I still hear her in the other room sometimes," Dad told me on the phone. "I think she's out in the kitchen mumbling, and I'll ask her to speak up so I can hear her."

I imagined him sitting at his computer screen in his office chair and forgetting that she was dead, that she hadn't ever lived there. But he is certain he hears her start to prepare his lunch because time collapses and his body knows it's hungry. Like hearing his father come up those back steps from the dock every morning at the furniture store to begin his day. Dad lived with ghosts.

And regrets. After Mom died, he softened. I heard him say "thank you." Every time I said goodbye, he said "I love you." I hadn't heard those words from him in more than forty years. He now needed other people, and not in the ways he had before. He didn't need people to wait on him or serve him but simply to be with him and his losses.

I let him talk on the phone for hours. Telling me stories of growing up and his version of my childhood, and of course, stories about Mom.

"Your mother complained about you girls not taking care of Rocky," Dad said. Rocky was our miniature dachshund, who looked like the flying squirrel in the Bullwinkle cartoon. "She was mad because it had been my idea to get a dog, but she got stuck doing all the work."

Rocky used to be tied to the crabapple tree off the back patio in Robbinsdale. Barb and I hated the chore of picking up dog poop—rotting crabapples looked a lot like dog poop.

"I came home from the furniture store one day. Your mother put Rocky in my arms and shoved me back out the door." Mom told him we'd been told to pick up the poop, we'd disobeyed, so it was time to get rid of the dog. I have no doubt Mom did this and still remember feeling traumatized, hiding in the basement awaiting Rocky's final departure when my father got home.

Dad didn't get rid of Rocky. The dog stayed in the garage that night. But I do remember Dad coming back into the house without the dog and how mad and sad it made me feel. That my own father could be so cruel as to take our dog away from us, I had never forgotten. And I had blamed him, not Mom. After all these years, Dad wanted me to know he had not taken away my childhood pet because I had disobeyed my mother, but because he would not disobey her.

Dad told me the story again about how every week Mom made her grocery list. She had her own method of planning the week's meals and listing the ingredients she'd need based on the aisles of the grocery. With both of them working full-time, there were times when Mom sent Dad with her list to do the shopping. He found himself at the butcher's counter one day trying to read her handwriting.

He stared at the word next to Tuesday dinner. He couldn't make it out. When he got home, he asked her what the word was. She stared at the grocery list on a scrap of paper. "Something," she said softly. "I asked you to pick up *something* to make for Tuesday night."

"Something?" Dad couldn't stop giggling. "Something. She wants me to buy something. What aisle is that in? Does it come in a can?" He thought it was hilarious. He took her grocery list with the word "something" on it, put it in a picture frame, and hung it on the wall. I knew exactly where on the wall it hung in that moment, within his view from his chair in his home where Mom had never lived.

When Dad started slurring his words and talking gibberish on long phone calls in late July, I wasn't entirely sure what to make of it. His doctor had made him test his blood sugar for two years claiming he was prediabetic, but nobody cared if he had another Klondike ice cream bar at his age. At least he wasn't driving to Marine on St. Croix to get ice cream cones anymore. But these new symptoms worried me.

And they worried him, too, because when he started to feel poorly one afternoon in August, and he didn't know what was going on, he called an ambulance and ended up in the emergency room.

"Dad is at the hospital," Barb called to tell me.

"I'm on my way."

There had been a do-not-resuscitate order on file. Once he signed his name for consent to be treated, however, the DNR no longer applied. The ER physicians stabilized him, but it became clear within twenty-four hours that keeping his oxygen levels up would be a challenge. At age eighty-seven, he would die the way his mother had, living at home until his final days, when simply everything started to wear out at once. Barb and I met with a hospital staff member to proceed with releasing him to home hospice. We both knew he likely wouldn't make it back to his apartment, but the switch to palliative care made an immediate difference. The orders to release him would take a couple days to complete. His last meal was sweet fruity yogurt, which he thought was ice cream.

When he lost consciousness, Barb encouraged me to head home quick and drive right back prepared to stay for the funeral. When I arrived in Appleton, I called Barb. Dad had died before I even got home.

Home. He'd been so happy I'd bought a house here. Barb had brought him for a day trip to see my house that spring. It was the last road trip he took. He had fond memories of Appleton and who I was becoming then. And now he was gone. And so was Mom.

Given the financial insecurities my parents faced when I was a child, I had feared one day I would have to support them in their old age. That did not come to pass. I didn't get to inherit my childhood palace of dreams, Pearson & Swenson Furniture Store, but I am lucky my father left me a little money to support me during my retirement years. Like my parents, grandparents, and great-grandparents, I became a homeowner because I had help from family and the trust of a mortgage company. And like my father and grandfather, I became a small business owner. I'm grateful in the end for my modest good fortune.

CHAPTER 25

The same year I bought a house in Appleton, 2015, Don sold his trailer and moved into a two-bedroom low-income apartment in Warroad, caring for his mother, Florence, full-time. Martha often came to visit her mother. Robert, too, visited frequently from Canada. John worked in food service at Concordia College in Moorhead and would drive over to see her. Karen and her husband, Dan, also visited regularly to give Don some respite. They all gathered for the holidays and birthdays. Her grandchildren and great-grandchildren called her Kookum, the Ojibway word for grandmother.

Family had begun to observe Florence's symptoms of dementia. Don made sure she was never left alone. In 2017, Florence's health began to deteriorate further, and she was admitted to full-time care for the final months of her life. She died in the nursing home on November 6, and the family held a traditional service on Saturday, November 11, 2017.

Don mourned his mother's loss, but her passing also liberated him in some ways. He did not have to worry about finding respite care to attend Treaty 3 Council meetings in Manitoba, where he was a ceremonial pipe carrier. Having been the primary caregiver to his mother for so long, he enjoyed spending more time with his grandchildren. When his stepdaughter got into trouble with Red Lake police over drugs, he took custody of his granddaughter, Bug, and brought her from the reservation to Warroad. Her Kookum's bedroom did not stay empty for long.

I had sent Bug postcards when she lived on Red Lake Reservation. Sometimes notecards. A board game. YA novels. She had reminded me of a younger version of myself. The version of me who couldn't wait to get away from the tensions at home and spend time in Warroad with my mother's relatives. Under Grandpa Don's supervision, she created a profile on Facebook, and after that she and I were able to message back and forth freely. She told me how much she hated going to school in Warroad, how the other kids called her fat and stupid, how she missed her friends in Red Lake but liked living with her grandpa. When I returned to Warroad the next June, Bug wanted to attend the powwow and watch the dance competitions with me. I picked her up at Don's apartment.

"Do you like to swim?" I asked Bug as we were crossing the bridge over the Warroad River.

"Yeah." Bug sat in the front seat of my car and helped me navigate the way to the powwow grounds to watch the dance competitions. "I used to go swimming in Red Lake. The Seven Clans Casino there has a pool."

"I like to swim, too," I said. I turned onto First Avenue and then pulled onto the fairgrounds, where hundreds of cars were parked in rows across a field.

"I was waiting for my ride in the lobby there after swimming one day when I was twelve," she began while getting out of the car. "This young woman, who I didn't know, sat down next to me on the bench. I didn't see her shoot up. Just nod off and die." Bug kept walking and did not look at me.

I kept a steady pace beside her. "Whoa, that's heavy," I said, after a long pause. We walked across the fairground parking lot following the crowds of people in the sunshine.

"It wasn't my first experience with death." She said it so matter-of-factly. I listened. She didn't say more, but I knew from Don how much she still missed her grandmother, Charlene.

We walked past vendors selling snow cones, T-shirts, jewelry, leather goods, and dream catchers. We stopped and stood behind the drumming circle. The slow and steady rhythm and the drummers' voices were loud and filled my body with their beat. Bug was quiet and still.

"Do you want an Indian taco?" I asked Bug.

"Okay."

Fry bread with ground beef and other toppings required both hands to eat. We moved under the yellow-and-white-striped canvas tent and sat on wooden benches in the shade to eat and watch the dancers.

Bug sat down and looked around at the others sitting near us, including people who had brought their own lawn chairs. Then her eyes focused ahead across the dance circle, as a cool breeze came off the lake.

My eyes took in the magnificent regalia all around us. Dazzled by the vibrant fabrics, ornate beadwork, jingles, feathers, and leatherwork, I noticed three brothers grooming themselves for a dance. Their mother stood over her smallest son's head, brushing his hair and setting his headpiece on for him. He couldn't have been more than five or six years old and, with his two brothers, a couple years apart, wore elegant matching custom regalia with beaded piecework on green velvet.

Bug wore blue jeans and a T-shirt that day. She folded her arms high across her breasts and hid her fingertips in her armpits. Did she feel as uncomfortable as she looked? Swollen, like someone had beaten her up on the inside. Sad. Mad.

A young girl walked under the canopy of the tent to our right. I watched her face light up with recognition when she looked in our direction. Bug smiled, stood up, and raised her chin. The girl had arrived with two others about the same age. All in blue jeans and T-shirts.

"Go hang with them," I said with a smile. "I'll meet you here in an hour."

Bug came back without her friends but wearing a shy smile and a more relaxed countenance.

Bug and I never discussed how many young Indian women had gone missing or murdered along the Canadian border. I had no firsthand knowledge about the sex trafficking and drug smuggling among some in the sports-fishing tourist industry on Lake of the Woods. What little snooping I had done made me realize the danger of asking questions in these extremely remote locations. I didn't need to know. Or maybe I knew, but didn't want to think Bug knew. Because she was so young, I guess I wanted to believe she was innocent and didn't know that these things happened.

I certainly knew about the numbers of disappeared women along the North Dakota border, where transient male laborers mine the sand used in hydro-fracking, from the western plains of Minnesota farther west, with remote man camps along the Canadian border. Some of the cases I'd followed in the news were of First Nation women who simply disappeared, never to be found. This area is so remote and sparsely populated. There are simply too many miles of open water, open fields, and forested land. A fluid and easily permeable border. A line across a map. Like a knife ripping through the flesh of a family whose screams are not heard.

Bug had shown me her tween drawings in Messenger. Cartoon-like figures with big faces, big eyes, big eyelashes. Almost anime style. She didn't draw from what she saw around her. She drew an imaginary world with imaginary characters. Big heads. Small bodies. Or maybe that was exactly the way she saw the world.

I didn't want to think about how many struggles she would face in her future or how much loss she had already experienced. I believed Don when he told me Bug's mother loved her, but she couldn't take care of her right now.

After the powwow, we drove back to Don's apartment. Bug brought me upstairs to show me her bedroom. I saw a small closet bursting with clothes and toys. And a birdcage on the top of the dresser. She closed the door and opened the cage to let her yellow canary out, and it flew around the room. She showed me the quilt her mother made for her. She handed it to me, folded so neatly. What she couldn't say was that she needed her mother, but the pipe needed her mother more.

Bug was thirteen when her new best friend in Warroad, her only friend at school, a seventeen-year-old Ojibway youth, lay down on the railroad tracks waiting for the 1:30 a.m. Canadian National freight train. The fatal accident took place on August 19, 2019, near the crossing at South Washington Street. That's not far from the powwow grounds on the south bank of the river where we watched the dance competitions. When I was on Facebook I saw a link to the news report of the accident and read the comments. Bug had left the first one: "he was my best friend. he was the happiest, most loving person ever. he was bullied for being gay and dressing like a girl. he was so nice, and everyone tore him down. we miss him dearly. his name was marcus johnson, 17 years old."

She told me in a series of text messages that Marcus had retrieved his bike earlier that evening. She saw Marcus and talked to him that night on the patio at Grandpa Don's apartment where he had left the bike the day before. She hadn't said goodbye.

I sat with her heaviness. I didn't know what to say.

The bouncing three dots showed her typing. I waited. Then she stopped. Silence.

She never came back to the conversation.

It was months before I noticed she wasn't on Facebook anymore at all. Or at least not using that old profile. Don messaged me she didn't want to go to school anymore.

Don and Bug met me for a snack and cold drink in the restaurant at the new Hampton Inn in Warroad one afternoon in September 2021. It had been two years since I had seen Bug and she'd become a young woman; she had just turned fifteen in June. The last thing I'd heard from Don about Bug was that for her birthday, she had planned to spend a week with her parents, who were trying to regain custody.

"I'm going to homecoming on Friday," Bug said.

"That's cool," I said.

"I ordered a dress on Amazon. It's supposed to arrive today. I got a new pair of black pumps to wear with it," Bug said. She pulled out her phone to show me.

"The screen is cracked," I said, when I looked.

"You can still see it." She pulled it back and touched the screen. "I can't take photos, but I can still make calls."

"How did that happen?" I asked.

"I threw it at my mother, I was so disgusted with her and my dad. It hit the pavement," Bug spit out the words, the smile erased from her face. "I went back to my parents in Red Lake for my birthday. It didn't last even a day before they both used meth. I called Grandpa Don to come get me."

I looked at Don. He raised his eyebrows slightly and nodded once.

"I'm not going back. I'm staying with Grandpa."

On Thursday afternoon, Bug texted me. "Will you come and take my picture before I leave for the homecoming dance tomorrow?"

"Yes," I texted back. "What time?"

"I don't know what I am going to wear. That dress didn't fit." I read her disappointment and frustration between the lines. There were no local or regional retail stores for formal wear. There was no time to order something else.

She reminded me of myself at fifteen in a large body trying on clothes in dressing rooms. The emotional pain and shame. My heart ached for her.

"Be here at seven to take pictures," she texted back.

Bug and her girlfriend were putting on makeup when I stopped by Don's apartment after supper on Friday. They both looked glamorous and happy. Bug wore a black sweater dress she had found in the back of her closet.

"No one is going to pay any attention to anything except my new heels," Bug said. The slit up the side of her sweater dress parted from her ankle to her knee as she lifted and pointed her right foot.

I snapped a photo.

CHAPTER 26

The postcard of Kakaygeesick hung on my fridge. After years of searching online, I confirmed the original portrait had been taken by Walter Wettschreck, who served as chief photographer for the Minnesota Conservation Department for decades.

Born in 1916, Wettschreck lost his hearing at age ten due to spinal meningitis. A naturalist and avid fisherman, he was the first deaf person in Minnesota to receive his private pilot's license in 1950. He flew a seaplane. I imagine that's how he arrived on Lake of the Woods. I wondered if he might have known Don Hanson or Cal Marvin.

Wettschreck's portrait of Kakaygeesick was used on the cover of *Minnesota Conservation* magazine in 1961. Only weeks after Kakaygeesick was admitted to the Warroad Hospital, the image also appeared on the front of *Picture Magazine*, included with the February 10, 1963, Sunday edition of the *Minneapolis Star.* Charles B. McFadden, the editor of the magazine, acknowledged all the white dignitaries who had visited Warroad to meet the 124-year-old medicine man himself. How long he had lived proved more newsworthy than how he had lived.

The *Warroad Pioneer* printed and distributed the postcards for decades. The weekly newspaper had been in print for 121 years when it issued its final edition in May 2019. The Warroad Heritage

Center still has an inventory of the vintage postcards for sale as souvenirs, though Beth Marvin is no longer there; I heard she died at the age of ninety-four on Christmas Eve 2019, peacefully at home, surrounded by her family. The first print run of those postcards was done in 1964; I bought my Kakaygeesick postcard in the summer of 1968 at the trading post.

In the photo, tufts of white hair are visible near Kakaygeesick's ears, and his eyebrows are white. A beaded headband lies across his forehead. Bright orange beaded medallions with olive green, harvest gold, and orange leather strips hang from his ears to shoulders. Above the headband stand bright orange plumes over black feathers, and the longest tips are white and fluffy.

When I studied the headdress more closely, I became convinced that the orange feathers were fake. No bird in the northern hemisphere has feathers like that. And leather dyed the colors of mid-century-modern kitchen appliances? The thing on his head didn't resemble the designs of other ceremonial headpieces I'd seen.

I started looking for photographs I'd amassed in my research of Kakaygeesick in his regalia. I found no such headdress in any other photos.

I returned again to the portrait on the postcard. In it, he stands in front of a blurred background of open fields with partly cloudy blue sky. Draped over his shoulders is a green felted wool blanket. It's not an Indian blanket. Nor is it from Hudson Bay Company. There was an identical one in my linen closet. Mom let me have hers. I'd had this postcard for more than a half century as a memento of when I met Kakaygeesick. How could I not have noticed this before?

In the photo, Kakaygeesick wears a blue suit with a bleached white button-down oxford shirt. In Gerald Vizenor's *The Everlasting Sky: Voices of the Anishinabe People*, his last chapter describes the funeral of Kakaygeesick and how the whites of Warroad buried him in a blue suit. I took another look at the postcard in my own possession, then messaged Don on Facebook.

He confirmed it was the same blue suit they'd dressed him in to place him in his casket, and he told me he thought Maggie Aas made the headdress and bought the orange dyed feathers and mixed them in with the black turkey feathers. "Ojibway never used headdresses like that in ceremony," he said. "It was used for tourists."

Maggie had given Wettschreck what she thought he wanted to see and kept their actual sacred objects out of this game of iconography.

Maggie Lightning Aas had been one of the first Ojibway children removed from Warroad and sent to Indian boarding school. And it was Maggie at Kakaygeesick's bedside in 1968 who translated for Willard Leaf at the signing of the will. Her baskets, beadwork, and jingle dresses were on display in the Warroad Heritage Center's collection.

The beaded headband Kakaygeesick wore in the photo was likely Maggie's work; it bore the floral patterns typical of this geographic region of bead workers. Or it could have been the handiwork of Verna or Florence Kakaygeesick—Don's mother or grandmother. Don wasn't sure. They had all passed on, so we couldn't ask them.

In the postcard image, Kakaygeesick looks away from the lens of the camera and off to the distant horizon. It's such a cliché of the white gaze. The pose reflects the tourist's expectations of how an Indian should look.

This image could not capture the way he'd held my head in his hands. It wasn't the way he looked when I first met him in the nursing home, in a wheelchair, wearing blue slacks and ordinary white tube socks. The depth of his eyes, the curve to his smile, his gnarly hands—they were not in the picture. I almost didn't recognize him in the photograph. Yet only now, after all these years, could I see clearly through the artifice and recognize the use of costume, perspective, and framing.

The postcard told a story about a soon-to-be-extinct Indian. But it wasn't the story Kakaygeesick told. The story he told, to everyone, was that they would come for his land. That he prophesied this was no secret to members of his family, clan, or Red Lake Nation, or to the white people of Warroad. Everyone knew.

Everyone knew what would happen if they kept dumping raw sewage and timber waste into the lake, too, yet they kept doing it until it became illegal. By that point, of course, banning that kind of pollution was not enough for the lake to heal itself. The Supreme Court overruled the 1972 Clean Water Act fifty years later, and still Congress fails to act.

Everyone knew smoking was hazardous to your health when the federal government mandated every cigarette package contain a warning in 1965 when I was in second grade. I was old enough to know better than to start, and yet I did—and never quit.

Everyone knew the exponential rise in population, production, consumption, and waste would deplete the planet's resources. Everyone knows we're running out of fossil fuels, yet I'm still putting gasoline in the tank of my car. Everyone knows we are dangerously close to beyond the tipping point for sustaining life on earth. Yet, here we are.

No happy ending. No easy solutions. Mad. Sad.

Inheritance is about more than land as property. It is a spiritual matter.

Kakaygeesick was a Grand Midewin. From what I have learned, the Ojibway spiritual belief system is based on nature and a series of seven prophecies, seven fires, which define epochs in their history. Kakaygeesick lived during the time of the fifth fire, when waves of light-skinned people killed or forced Indians onto reservations. During the sixth fire, children were taken from their parents and grandparents and stripped of their language and cultural practices, forced to assimilate. Now is the time of the seventh prophecy, which addresses a world out of balance. When the cup of life becomes the cup of grief.

According to Ojibway spiritual teachings, it is prophesied that a time will come when the waters become so poisoned that the plants, animals, fish, and birds will fall sick and die. The forests will disappear, and air will lose the power of life. From the clouds of illusion, people will retrace the past to find the treasures left by the trail. The lost stories will be found when the search takes them to the elders and they ask for guidance. Some elders walk the path, but others will have forgotten. Some point in the wrong direction. Others remain silent because of fear. But according to the prophecy, the light-skinned people will be given a choice between two paths. If they find trust in the circle, in the way of things, they can let go of ego and trust their inner voice to act. If they choose the wrong path, the destruction they brought with them will destroy them. The people of the earth will suffer and die. If they choose the right road, the seventh fire will light the eighth and eternal fire of family, love, and peace.

In searching for a better understanding of the Ojibway Midewin, it surprised me to learn the choice between materialism and spiritualism is on light-skinned people.

I'm not off the hook. I know there is truth to this prophecy.

The destruction whites brought with them to Turtle Nation includes what was done to the Lake of the Woods. The biological phenomenon of "internal loading" is a metaphor for helping me understand how the past shaped my life and holds the future. Genocide, slavery, misogyny, and the toxic legacy of white colonialism are like the lingering phosphorus that feeds the blue-green algae in the shallow beds on Lake of the Woods. The shameful past is not buried under sediment; there has been little healing. Instead, the past gets stirred up with the winds of change and cultural currents, feeding on racism and sexism to yield economic inequality, inadequate health care, addiction, homelessness, illness, violence, child abuse, depression, and suicide. Unless we deal with the past and clean up the mess, it will destroy any future.

Loons are water birds. The only time they go ashore is to mate or incubate. They carry their babies on their back. Loons return to the same lake year after year. They hoot, yodel, wail, and tremolo. Their populations continue to dwindle due to pollution, human disturbances, and climate change.

Loons fell from the sky around midnight on Sunday, April 25, 2021, in northern Wisconsin. Hundreds of birds. Due to icing conditions that coated the migrating birds' feathers, they literally fell from the air and crashed. Loons, like many birds, migrate at night. They can fly at several thousand feet above ground. A sudden shift in atmospheric conditions and the freezing rain can compromise basic aerodynamics.

Loons can't walk on their webbed feet. They're made for

swimming. They have to "wing walk." Their body shape and the anatomical angle of their legs make it extremely difficult for loons to move across land. If they're caught on the ground too far from water, survival becomes a struggle.

Wildlife rehabilitators from across the state arrived Monday morning to respond to more than thirty-five calls about stranded loons. Farmers checked their fields, ponds, and ditches. Some birds found water, but those big feet needed bigger runways for liftoff. Small ponds meant they remained captive and couldn't migrate further.

Mother Nature doesn't often make mistakes like that. Was it a freak event? Or an instance of an extreme weather condition resulting from climate change? Scientists don't know everything, but they know a lot, and from diverse scientific specialties and disciplines a clear consensus has emerged. There is no disputing the rising global temperatures, the growing carbon load, the poisons that have contaminated our environment. Freak weather events are symptoms of climate change.

Sightings of species out of their usual range are also harbingers of its impact. An arctic loon was spotted for the first time ever in Wisconsin at the start of June 2021. I first heard the news on Wisconsin Public Radio.

"It was in beautiful breeding plumage, silvery gray crown on the head and down the back of the neck, with white checkering and white on the flanks above the water line," said Brady, an expert birder who works as a conservation biologist for the Wisconsin Department of Natural Resources. Brady and a group of friends who spent part of Memorial Day birding on the Bayfield Peninsula spotted the lone arctic loon swimming on the surface about five hundred yards from shore.

What was the arctic loon doing in the waters of Lake Superior? A bird found outside its normal range is called a vagrant or accidental in wildlife terms. In other words, it's not supposed to happen, but it does.

There weren't supposed to be any allotments to Red Lake Reservation either.

I had given some early pages I'd drafted about the history of Kakaygeesick and Allotment 3 to my writing buddy, Jordan. He asked me to meet him for coffee to discuss it.

"There's nothing wrong with the writing. I mean there are a lot of facts and figures and dates and stuff, but tell me why I should care?" Jordan said to me.

It wasn't feedback I was prepared to hear. "What do you mean?" I thought the injustice to the Kakaygeesick family an obvious cause for concern.

"Why do *you* care so much, Jill?"

When I started to research the dispossession of the Kakaygeesick family, I had immersed myself in the routine tasks of a journalist and tried to keep myself out of it as an objective reporter when I was writing up what I had learned.

"If I know why you care, then maybe I have a reason to learn all this history."

I spent a lot of time thinking about the answer to that question. I kept coming back to that memory of when I met Kakaygeesick and he held my head in his hands. He had made me part of the story. He connected me spiritually to this place. Every step I took to find the answers to my questions about how Red Lake Nation acquired Kakaygeesick's Allotment 3 took me back to the ways white settlers had defined the terms and conditions, and established the bureaucratic structures and systems, which had largely been invisible to me before I returned to Warroad after Mom died.

The group of ten writers gathered in the glass-enclosed conference room between the library and the local history museum on a Friday afternoon, the first of October 2021. The last workshop session of the weeklong retreat featured the art of Don Kakaygeesick and his brother, John, and sister, Karen. Karen displayed her photographs, which captured images of nature, many taken along her great-grandfather's trapline along the shores of Lake of the Woods. Her brothers exhibited a few of their paintings.

"Let me tell you the story of the moong," John said, wrapping up their hour-long presentation. He stood next to one of his watercolor paintings, a loon with its black-and-white checks reflected on the smooth surface of blue water.

"'Moong' means loon in Ojibway," John continued. His painting reflected the Woodland School of Art, a style recognized by art historians and museum curators as distinctive to First Nations and American Indian artists from Ontario, Manitoba, and northern Minnesota. On the internet, I had found the artwork of the Kakaygeesicks of great interest to art collectors. The use of symbols found in nature and stylized imagery convey a story that brings the past into the present.

"The legend is about a man and a loon stranded on an island," John continued. "The man was hungry, so he said he would give the loon a gift if he would catch him a fish."

This was the first time I heard John tell the story. I straightened up in my chair to listen closely.

"Back then, you know, the loon was sleek black and had a white chest. This was a long time ago, back when loons could talk." John paused to smile. "The loon could speak with other animals—including man."

Listening to John Kakaygeesick tell this legend made me reflect on how painting contained spiritual lessons. John and Don both painted in the same style as their eldest brother, Robert, illustrating stories they learned as the great-grandsons of Kakaygeesick. Sadly, the previous October, their brother Robert had died of complications from COVID at Buffalo Point First Nation.

"The loon caught a fish. They had a big feast that night," John continued. "But the man asked the loon to wait for his gift until morning."

I took a glimpse around the room. All eyes were on John.

"When morning came, the loon asked for his gift. The man reached around the back of his neck to untie the shell necklace he wore. Then he tied the choker around the loon's neck. It was so tight, the loon couldn't speak. It could only make the sound *moong*." John put his hands around his throat and made the sound of a strangled and muffled cry again: *mooooong*. "The shell necklace became *so* tight it broke. And the shells fell onto the bird's back. Which is why we see the loon as it is today—little white shells scattered across its back and wings."

John looked toward his painting and took two steps back.

The room full of writers sat silent for several moments. I contemplated the spiritual lessons on voice.

Earlier that year the Northwest Minnesota Arts Council had awarded Don Kakaygeesick the 2021 Northwest Star, a lifetime achievement award for his artistic contributions. Don told me he first started drawing in 1971 when he came home from foster care and reenrolled in the Warroad Public School in seventh grade.

"I saw the Warroad Warrior logo, and I wanted to draw something better," Don told me. The cartoonish feathered bonnet and war signs painted on the face of the Indian head logo in the gymnasium bothered him. "Mine had a couple feathers hanging down from his hair and no war paint on his face." The public school athletic teams had been known as the Warroad Warriors since the end of World War II.

"How did your drawing end up becoming the logo the school uses today?" I asked.

"Funny question, because I don't really know the answer," Don said. "I must have left it behind at school. When I moved back to Warroad in the early 1980s, it was all over town."

No one had asked his permission nor acknowledged him as the logo designer in forty years. The artist-of-the-year award from the arts council recognized his contributions, which went far beyond his seventh-grade sketch, but I find myself mad and sad that the high school from which he did not graduate took his artwork as though it belonged to them.

My mother's death brought me back to Warroad and gave me a deeper connection to this place and the past. I better understand how I am implicated in the dispossession of the Kakaygeesicks, racial inequities, the destruction of the planet, even my own death. I've learned so many things from knowing Don and the Kakaygeesick family.

How to quit smoking is not yet one of them. But I'm entirely to blame for that.

While I know I'm not to blame for the hundred years of dumping timber waste into Lake of the Woods, I also know my great-grandfather Charlie Kling was one of many white men who came to Minnesota and cleared land for the timber industry. There are photographs of my grandfather as a boy sitting with his siblings on top of a wagonload of enormous logs. My blood and bones carry the legacy of their homestead. Even though I didn't pollute the lake, if I care about drinking clean water, eating fresh fish, swimming in clean lakes and rivers, enjoying the land's culinary bounty, and hearing the call of the loon, then the pollution in the lake—both past and present—*is* my responsibility.

While I know I didn't have anything to do with the federal policy of removing Indians from their homelands, I also know my great-grandfather homesteaded on Indian land. Without the Homestead Act there would have been no allotments. I had nothing to do with the historical practices of my country's government, but it was too easy for me to blame Red Lake Nation for the dispossession and disenfranchisement involved in the case of Kakaygeesick. Listening to Don tell his family history and reading a fuller account of the historical record, I am reminded of the discomfort I felt the first time I visited Dachau, thinking everyone knew about the genocide when it was happening and how those who survived had to live with the horror of what they had let happen. I wished to be dispossessed of this nation's shameful legacy of genocide. As though I could rid myself of responsibility for the privileges that legacy affords someone like me.

"Let me grab the door for you," Karen said to Don, who carried two oversize painted canvases in the side entrance to the exhibition space. An overcast day, it had started to drizzle.

"Thanks," Don said. "I'm not sure the paint is even dry."

I carried the third canvas in behind Karen. The gallery director appeared before us and showed Don the three easels where he could set up his triptych. When he set them side by side, the image of a turtle in brilliant hues of blues and green spread across the three panels.

RiverPlace—the new arts, culture, and events center in Warroad—held its grand opening on Saturday, October 5, 2024, with an exhibit of the work of area artists, including Don. The Smokey Hill Drum Group performed during the opening ceremony. The modern twenty-thousand-square-foot structure was built on land in Warroad that had once been part of the allotment issued to Kakaygeesick's brother, Naymaypoke.

After the grand opening of RiverPlace, I drove east from Warroad and took County Road 12 north to Rocky Point Road. On the curve in the road at the northern edge of the old Kling farm, I pulled over onto the shoulder. Across the road was a large rock outcropping in a cypress grove. I got out of my car, crossed the road, and climbed up onto the flat stone surface under the big sky.

It was here on this spot where my mother played as a child to the music of birdsong, the peeps of tree frogs, and the chattering of squirrels and chipmunks. Here were her toys of pine cones, feathers, spiders, lichen, and moss. I wept, not because my mother was gone, but because I felt her presence here. The stone outcropping connected me to my ancestors, and to those who had been here long before my great-grandparents arrived. I inherited the history of this place. It is a gift, if I claim ownership of the past.

Land doesn't belong to me. I belong to the land.

ACKNOWLEDGMENTS

This book would not be possible without the permission and involvement of Don Kakaygeesick and his siblings. I regret I did not complete this in time for their mother, Florence Cobiness Kakaygeesick, his older brothers—Robert Jr. and John—and their younger sister, Martha Kakaygeesick Johnson, to see this published. Karen Kakaygeesick-Dethmers, especially, helped me with spellings and terminology. Delainey May kept me grounded in the present and oriented toward the future. Their trust in me to write this story is an honor.

My gratitude to the late Henry Boucha, his daughter, Tara Boucha, and granddaughters, Sky and Shalese; and to Hugh Ringling and Jamie Snowden for answering questions and sharing memories and family history.

The staff, volunteers, and board members of the Warroad Heritage Center, the Warroad Public Library, and the Roseau County Museum deserve an acknowledgment for opening their collections and helping me with research. The Gale Family Library in the Minnesota History Center and the Minnesota Genealogical Society offered expertise and access to archival materials. I am especially grateful for the Artist in the Pines writing residency in Marine on St. Croix in 2021 at the St. Croix Watershed Research Station, part of the Minnesota Museum of Science.

I am grateful for the opportunities to learn more about the craft of writing from David McGlynn, Pam Houston, Eleanor Henderson, and Staci Lola Drouillard. My deepest appreciation to Anton Treuer, whose expertise and knowledge of Red Lake Nation history are unparalleled.

Christine Barone, Jonathan Winslow, Deb Sinness, and Karen Fehringer of the Wild Rice Write Club held me accountable to show up to write the past five years. And to my Ithaca writing buddies—Alison Fromme, Rachel Lampert, and Maria DiFrancesco—thanks for the encouragement.

First readers of early drafts—Jenna Goodman, Laura Jean Baker, Carolyn Porter, Jordan Brown, Kathy Anderson, Jessica Gigot, and Nicolas Tseffos—generously gave feedback and provided me with insights.

A special note of appreciation to Kim Hruba, who welcomed me to Warroad with her warm heart and open mind more than a decade ago. And to Brenda Yanok, Gretchen Mehmel, Leanne Fournier, Karyn Santl, and Kathy Magnussen for your friendship.

Thanks to Cathryn Prince, Elizabeth Rynecki, Chris LaTray, Nickolas Butler, Doualy Xaykaothao, Staci Lola Drouillard, and Rebecca Clarren, who agreed to read an advance review copy.

In Appleton, thanks to members of my poetry group, especially Linda Nett-Duesterhoeft, Connie Morgenstern, and Peter Sherill; to Kalan Bavinck at The Book Store; to Katie Stilp, local history librarian at the Appleton Public Library.

Thanks to Stephanie Hueseman and Audrey Arnold, who saved me from embarrassing typos and misplaced commas.

I'm grateful to Brooke Warner and Megan Milton at She Writes Press for all the support and guidance through the publishing process. A special note of appreciation to my editor, Krissa Lagos, and to Leah Paulos of Press Shop PR.

Finally, thanks to my best friend, Mary Whitehead, for listening. And to my sister, Barb, whose memory is even better than mine.

ABOUT THE AUTHOR

photo credit: Sara Stathas

Jill D. Swenson grew up in the Twin Cities and moved to Wisconsin in high school. She graduated from Lawrence University and earned an MA and PhD from The University of Chicago before going on to teach journalism and media studies at the University of Georgia-Athens and earn tenure at Ithaca College. For a decade she lived off the grid on a small-scale sustainable farm in upstate New York; now she lives in Appleton, Wisconsin, where she works as an editor and literary consultant, belongs to a curling club and a poetry group, and enjoys walking her dog.

Looking for your next great read?

We can help!

Visit www.shewritespress.com/next-read
or scan the QR code below for a list
of our recommended titles.

She Writes Press is an award-winning
independent publishing company founded to
serve women writers everywhere.